A Bone in my Flute

A BONE IN MY FLUTE

Holly Johnson

Century · London

For the purposes of anonymity, some names have been changed throughout this book.

First published 1994

1 3 5 7 9 10 8 6 4 2

First published in the United Kingdom in 1994 by
Century Limited
Random House, 20 Vauxhall Bridge Road,
London SW1V 2SA

Random House Australia (Pty) Limited
20 Alfred Street, Milsons Point, Sydney,
New South Wales 2061, Australia

Random House New Zealand Limited
18 Poland Road, Glenfield
Auckland 10, New Zealand

Random House South Africa (Pty) Limited
PO Box 337, Bergvlei, South Africa

Random House UK Limited Reg. No. 954009

A CIP catalogue record for this book is
available from the British Library

ISBN 0 7126 6145 X

Typeset in Times by
SX Composing Ltd, Rayleigh, Essex
Printed in Great Britain by
Clays Ltd, St Ives plc

Contents

This book is dedicated to
Wolfgang Kuhle
who has put up with me
for all these years.

'Dreams are like angels
They keep bad at bay
And love is the light
Scaring darkness away'

Holly Johnson
Courtesy of Perfect Songs

'Rage, rage against the dying of the light'

Dylan Thomas
'Do not go gentle into
that good night'

Foreword

I started to write this book a few weeks after I was diagnosed with an AIDS-related illness. In my state of panic I thought that I had perhaps six months to live. A matter of days after my diagnosis I saw an international rock star who had died of an AIDS-related illness pilloried and patronised in the gutter press. It seemed that one tabloid journalist had already prepared a cash-in biography for this very event. The book hit the streets almost immediately.

With friends like mine, I thought, I'd better write my own story and quick. Before they get the chance to rewrite it. Before those little anecdotes from people claiming they knew me intimately ('A close friend disclosed last night') become legends written in stone. They can say whatever they like about me when I am gone, of course, and I'm sure they will. I had read some of these stories which over the years had cropped up in the press. Exaggerated, sensationalised and highly-coloured versions of the truth given to eager journalists desperate to uncover some embarrassing titbit from the past, some sordid skeleton in my cupboard. 'As a teenager he used to dress up as Judy Garland', said one so-called friend to a yellow-press hack on condition that their name would not be divulged. And of course, this 'friend's' name *was* divulged by the two-headed snake of a scandalmonger. At least the 'friend' had the nerve to tell me the story as I had not even read this particular article. At that time there were too many to read.

Of course, everyone's perception of any event is slightly different, and perhaps my views are as distorted by my own agenda as the next person's, but at least it is my view that is related here and not that of some pretend friend. I'd always known that how others perceive us is not necessarily what we are, long before fame hit me. Around 1976 a distraught woman wrote to the *Liverpool Echo*, claiming to have seen an alien get on the 86 bus to town: 'He had a bald head painted green, even his lips were green. I do not drink but perhaps I should give up my wine gums.' At the time I had no desire to appear like a space alien. I believed I was making a unique Pop Art statement.

To tell the truth, as I saw it, was not my only motivation. I had a desperate need to focus on something creative. Creating songs, poems, paintings, anything, had always been my *raison d'être*: the underlying reason, I believe, for my presence on this planet. A book would be a fresh challenge. A real chance for me to exorcise the past, come to terms with my relationships, release old resentments. In my worst moments of self-inflicted alienation and loneliness, the book would be my personal psychiatrist's couch. I could be bitchy, condemning, and vent my spleen on a world where fascism, homophobia and betrayal are still rife. I could get it all off my chest so I could carry on living (I hoped) with a lighter load.

While writing this book I read several autobiographies and biographies of well-known homosexual artists and writers: Duncan Grant, Tom Driberg, Derek Jarman, Keith Vaughan, Truman Capote and Andy Warhol. These books were all highly inspirational. I hope my book is in turn an education to some teenager going through the throes of sexual awakening, someone who is unsure of their identity, someone who has been brought up in a hostile heterosexual environment, someone who feels they are alone. Anyone who believes in truth, honesty and fairies wearing sequinned slingbacks.

Holly Johnson
June 1993

A Bone in my Flute

I remember what I think was my fourth birthday, the 9th of February 1964, how the Christmas decorations had been left up on the ceiling, the twisted, crepe paper chains. Chiming music floated in from the ice cream van. I had been given one of those silver plastic guns that fired black darts with red rubber suckers on the end. When I fired one into the air towards the ceiling, it tangled with the decorations, and disappeared.

We lived at 206, Rathbone Road, Liverpool 13, the end house of a long terrace that was truncated by Pighue Lane (pronounced 'piggy'), and a railway line that was the site of the maiden voyage of Stephenson's Rocket, the first steam train. Directly opposite was a pub called The Rathbone, and next to it a disused Territorial Army barracks painted sky blue. Only once can I remember seeing any military activity there. A jeep with handsome soldiers dressed in khaki stood around it as if they were posing for a photograph, waving and smiling in the sunshine.

Christened William Johnson – Billy for short – I was the third child of four, born to Eric and Pat Johnson. Pat had been a Mcglouchlin before they married. My mother's father, Patrick, or 'Cocker' as he was known, was three quarters Indian – though I can't remember him looking particularly Asian. His father was Irish, hence the name Patrick.

The house we lived in was very small, three up and three down, none of the rooms bigger than eight foot in any direction. When I visited it years later, just before it was replaced by Barratt housing, it was in a derelict state and I was shocked by its matchbox proportions. The front door opened into a square room, with a doorway in each wall, one leading to a small triangular living room to the right, one to the stairs on the left and one to a tiny kitchen to the rear of the house. Upstairs was a similar layout

1

with a narrow corridor linking the triangular parents' bedroom, square boys' bedroom and the small back bedroom belonging to my sister Clare. Out of her window was the flat roof of a square brick shed that reduced our backyard to a concrete pathway at the end of which was the outside lavatory.

My parents washed in the kitchen sink and the kids were washed in a plastic baby bath or bowl in the living room. I was always embarrassed by this public display, especially on one occasion when I had an involuntary erection. The euphemism used in our house for a penis was 'a flute'. Years later, at bath time, one of my nephews said, 'Look Mum! I've got a bone in my flute'.

I have very few early memories of my parents. Eric I remember as a sort of Liverpuddlian Sid James, a poor man's Spencer Tracey with tightly curled red hair fading to sand. I remember also not being allowed to kiss him any more after a certain age. My mother, Pat, always seemed to be in bed in the morning. She would surface eventually, wearing a pale blue quilted dressing gown printed with red rosebuds. Her jet-black hair was tied up in a turban of her own invention. She was dark and exotic, runner-up in a Miss Liverpool beauty contest. My father, when at sea, was told by a fortune-teller that he would marry an Indian princess, and she certainly behaved like one. At sixteen she had been the owner of a forty-inch bust, which grew and grew, as she did, with the birth of each child. And she didn't give a toss about the housework. It was left to my father to get us ready for school. He would comb our hair, or try to. My brother John and I both had red curly hair, John's being more of the ginger variety, mine a darker auburn. Clare's was sleek and dark and straight, short with a fringe.

Pat was brought up Roman Catholic and Eric was Church of England. Apparently this had caused a scandal in my mother's family. They wanted a Catholic church wedding, whilst my father wanted a C of E registry office one. My mother's family did not go to the wedding, I believe. There was bad blood between the clans from day one. 'My fuckin' kids are being brought up Protestant,' said Eric. And that was that.

My father's parents ran a sweet shop in a neighbourhood that no longer exists, somewhere near Edge Hill. Edge Hill train station was one stop before Liverpool's Lime Street station, hence the local slang expression, 'We got off at Edge Hill', which means, 'We used the withdrawal-before-ejaculation method of contraception.'

Grandie and Nanny Johnson, as they were known, provided a fairly regular Saturday dumping-ground for Pat and Eric's kids. I remember the jars of sweets that were out of bounds and the ticking of a clock in the dark back room. The oriental buddha on the sideboard, the statue of a turbanned Moor holding a torch that lit up, were souvenirs from my father's seafaring. And, I remember too, the smell of old people and roast dinners. Nanny Johnson was the daughter of Irish parents.

These were the round, plump grandparents, as opposed to the long, skinny ones, Cocker and Granny, who lived about a mile away. They had a dog called Racky Roo that was skinny too, and not what you could describe as cute – some kind of whippet blended with greyhound. I preferred visiting the skinny ones because Granny had dyed red hair and blue and white striped crockery. Cocker made the best egg and chips in the whole wide world.

And then there was Auntie Kath.

'Cha cha cha!'.

Cha was a childhood nickname given to me by my auntie Kath who was Pat's younger sister by ten years. You'd never have known they were sisters. As far as I know she slept in the same room as her mother – Granny – until she was at least twenty years old, while Cocker slept downstairs on the couch. She was Twiggy-thin in her late teens, and this was the Swinging Sixties. She would close her eyes when she drank Pepsi Cola out of a glass bottle while she ironed clothes in the front room dreaming of Gene Pitney. For some reason she moved in with us for a spell while I was quite young. The house was spotless while Kath was living with us, obsessed as she was with housework. She had friends that came to visit, bright young things, one a girl called Val whose long, sleek, red Mary Quant hairdo I fell in love with. I wouldn't believe it was a wig.

3

A medical mishap occurred when I was about five years old. My sister claims that while in her care I had a terrible fall in a back entry, as a result of which my right eye developed an astigmatism and an extreme blurring of vision known as amblyopia. Although I can't remember the fall, I've still got a bump on my forehead. I recall endless visits to opticians and eye specialists and being told to wear spectacles – 'Four Eyes', freckly and five years old. I was also made to wear an Elastoplast eyepatch over my good left eye every day to school, which in effect blinded me. Heaven only knows how I learned to read and write. The skin around my eye was always inflamed from the Zinc oxide plaster.

My sister Clare would take me along Rathbone Road, past St Mary's Church of England primary school, up by the Old Swan pub, and across a busy dual carriageway to the Allenby Square Children's Nursery. Nowadays mothers would be shot for allowing an eight year old the responsibility of seeing a four year old through rush-hour traffic.

At school I was allotted the clothes peg shaped like a watering can to hang my coat on, which my mother said was appropriate because of my bed-wetting problem. This habit drove my mother to distraction, as sheets had to be washed by hand daily and hung on the line to dry. I could have done without the constant nagging, which from a very early age made me feel there was something wrong with me, some kind of weird deficiency.

I must have been about eight or nine when I was admitted to Alder Hey children's hospital in West Derby, where my hospital bed was fitted with a kind of metal undersheet that set off an alarm when it detected excess moisture, or if I moved too much in my sleep. I was also given some kind of drug that made me sleep lighter – apparently – as bed-wetting is more common in heavy sleepers. I hated being in hospital, especially for something as embarrassing as peeing the bed, and had to suffer this for about two weeks. It didn't alter anything except my relationship with my mother, whose judgement I never quite trusted again.

So I learned to put on my own nappy before I went to bed. I must have been four or five years old. 'Nappy On!' I would repeat in frustration when the grown-ups were too busy gabbing to take me up to bed.

From quite an early age my sister Clare was expected to do housework while our brother John, two years older than she, was not. Looking back she took on the role of an indentured slave. At eight years old she was sent to the launderette – a two-mile walk away – with all the family's dirty washing in a pram, and in charge of me, an awkward four year old, with at least one busy main road to navigate. This delegation of responsibility increased with the birth of our younger brother James.

Clare and I clung together, being the two unfavourites, as opposed to John, the first born, and James, the baby. My parents had difficulty in treating Clare as equal to any of the boys. In fact, my mother's relationships with other women were marred. According to family legend, her own mother gave up the responsibility of bringing her up, leaving it to Cocker's mother Great Gran, a deeply religious Indian woman. The other version of the legend paints Great Gran as a domineering matriarch who, after losing one of her own children, took custody of my mother, spoiling her with private schools and the best of everything. The truth is probably something in between. Anyway, my mother's feeling of rejection was accentuated by the fact that Cocker and Granny, when they left Great Gran's house to move into their own in Gladstone Road, left her behind, taking their new baby with them. My mother never learned to deal openly with and discuss these kinds of family problems.

Great Gran shared a house with her daughter (our great aunt), Auntie Pat in Wavertree, just round the corner from the not-yet-famous Penny Lane. Auntie Pat was the Greta Garbo of the family, a one-time circus performer and Bluebell Girl, who gave up showbusiness, and ran the house as a children's nursery for a time. There was always something strange and distant about Auntie Pat who, now blind, lives in a convent, and has given orders that she should not be visited.

Most of the time my father Eric was out at work: selling insurance, a Credit Draper selling clothes door to door on a weekly payment basis, driving a van, working on a building site, often juggling two jobs at once to feed and clothe four kids and a wife. After working as a ship's steward for the early part of his working life, Eric's subsequent jobs were of the self-employed variety. This meant meticulous bookkeeping, the accounts prepared at a mahogany desk in the front room. Pat later took conveyor belt jobs in the local Meccano and Plessey factories to supplement the family income.

The desk was out of bounds, strictly my father's domain, and therefore most interesting: a source of manilla envelopes, sharp pencils and paper glue. This was the brown, clear, liquid variety unfortunately, not the white rubber solution glue that they used on 'Blue Peter', the childrens' programme that showed how to make gifts for parents out of Fairy Liquid bottles, sticky-backed plastic (or 'fablon') and other objects that could (never) be found around the house. On Mother's Day Clare and I decided to present Pat with a gift of bath crystals made from washing soda and food colouring, scented with eau de cologne. It never occurred to us that we didn't have a bath in which she could use them. Anyway, it served our purpose, which was to put her in a good mood for a while. There were always large cardboard egg-boxes with my father's samples in around the house. Clare even remembers him putting clothes in the window of the front room for display – there was, for example, a summer frock at 19/11d. Because of Eric's job, it was very rare for us ever to wear clothes that were bought in normal shops. My mother used to take us on trips to the backstreets of the city centre, to strange warehouses with names like Sorenson's or Erskine's where she shopped without money on my father's account.

On these trips Pat paid particular attention to her make-up as one of the warehouse assistants had sworn blind that she was the spitting image of Joan Crawford. The main difference between Pat and Mommy Dearest was that Pat's preferred weapon of punishment was the wooden hairbrush rather than the metal coat-hanger. 'Be sure your sins will find you out!' was one of her catch-phrases as she doled out smacks on our behinds for some misdemeanour or other.

When Jamie was born, the responsibility for looking after me as a child was swiftly handed over to Clare. Jamie was a particularly beautiful child with huge blue eyes, and Pat doted on him. So, wherever Clare wanted to go, Billy had to go too, and I was dragged along to Silver Blades Ice Skating Rink a three-mile walk away. Being too young at about four years old to wear skates with blades I was bought Bob skates that were like mini sleds tied on with red leather straps. Wearing these, I was deposited on the ice by Clare, who sped off round the rink in her royal blue Lurex skating outfit with matching knickers, perhaps a bid for a childhood that was being cut short by the responsibility of a child of four.

I was the type who would much rather stay indoors with a drawing pad, a record player or my sister's taboo *Bunty* comics to read. On the occasions when my mother couldn't stand this 'antisocial' behaviour I was ordered to go and play. Instead of football, I'd find Pauline Pigfat, the childhood friend who gave me my first kiss. Or I would play around the now derelict barracks building opposite and the huge bomb site next to it, obscured from the road by massive advertising billboards which extolled the virtues of smoking menthol cigarettes, 'COOL AS A MOUNTAIN STREAM'. There was an old unshaven man smelling of drink, who claimed to be the caretaker (or Cocky Watchman) of the barracks, and who would pick the kids up in his arms and put his hands up the back of their short trousers while rubbing the kids up against him. Most kids didn't think anything of this friendly old man, but I remember saying to my mother, 'That man picks you up funny.' She became strangely interested in my conversation all of a sudden, and asked me to describe in detail exactly what he had done. This sudden panic of probing immediately set off alarm bells, and I somehow persuaded her that nothing strange went on. I must have been only five or six years old, but had already learned that to avoid trouble it was sometimes necessary to lie. In retrospect, I think that if I had gone through with my mother's questioning and possible further involvement from the police, it would have been much more damaging than the Cocky Watchman's mild molestations. In fact, I remember being quite keen on receiving his attention, something I missed out on at home.

Rhythm and Elegance

On summer Sundays we would pack everything, including knives and tin openers, into the back of Eric's blue Ford transit van, then drive to Southport beach. Here the contents would be unpacked and Pat would start to make the sandwiches al fresco. On one of these trips, I quickly changed into my turquoise swimming costume and headed for the sea. I was warned that it would be too cold for swimming, but I wanted to be first in, so off I went. It was quite a way for a four year old with dodgy eyesight, and by the time I'd reached the sea I could hardly make out the transit van in the distance, and yes, the water was too cold, so I started back. By this time the beach had filled up with cars and people. I made my way back to the van in the distance. When I arrived however, it was not the familiar blue van, but a green one, surrounded by complete strangers. I panicked and went off in search of our van. Soon I was crying my eyes out and confused at the direction I was going in. I started to write my name in the sand in big letters with arrows pointing in the direction of where I had gone, hoping that my parents would see the signs. They didn't. After an hour or so of this searching I was in quite a mess. A kindly lady eventually collared me and sat me in her car with a jam butty, while she went to the lost children depot in Southport's fairground. I had somehow walked along the beach all the way to Ainsdale, which was the neighbouring resort.

My friends and interests were girls and girls' things. I was eventually banned from ever playing with them. To my father's annoyance, I was not interested in football at all. In 1966, the year England won the World Cup, one of the qualifying matches was to be played at Liverpool's sacred Anfield football ground and tickets for this match were like gold dust. I was taken along to this hallowed occasion by my father, where I promptly fell asleep ten or twenty minutes into the game. People looked on in disgust, apparently. I was never again invited to The Match, as it was called. World Cup Willie, a cartoon lion, emblem and mascot of the games, failed to work his magic on me.

My elder brother John on the other hand had all the hallmarks of a macho young Scouse, adept at football and hanging around street corners with The Ozzie Gang (short for hospital). He was the cock of the school: St Mary's Primary School, Rathbone Road, just two hundred yards up the road from where we lived. If anyone bullied me in the area, I was told to quote his name and I would be left alone. And I did need some kind of protection, as a spectacle-wearing, ginger-haired boy who played with girls, especially one who answered back in an annoyingly eloquent way. After my first year at St Mary's, John passed the eleven plus examination and started to attend grammar school, St Margaret Aigburth – SMA as it was called. So again, it was left to Clare to be my protector, which she did well, not even being afraid of the Headmaster's secretary Mrs Morissey (previously the chief dinner lady), who liked to pick on me. Clare screamed at her to leave me alone one afternoon in the playground. No one messed with our Clare.

One hot summer, during my eye-patch wearing days, a school sports day was organised at Sandown playing fields, as the school itself only had two concrete playgrounds edging on to a busy main road. Clare, in one of her acts of protection, negotiated for me a head start in most of the races: wheelbarrow race, egg and spoon race, three-legged race and sack race, all of which still I failed to win. That day I wore my favourite Spiderman logo T-shirt – free with a brand new comic, the logo was a transfer that had to be ironed on. I was so proud.

On the occasions that John was ordered to look after me at home, he usually ended up torturing me, hanging me upside down from the top bunk bed, or sitting on my chest pinning my arms under his knees and hitting me in the face. Once he was torturing both Clare and me while my mother was out getting her hair done in someone's front-room-cum-hairdressing-salon. Somehow I managed to escape through a loose panel in the back door, Clare screaming, 'Get me mother. It's the house with a yellow door and a pixie door knob!'

I wandered up and down the Binns Road for an hour or so, unable to find the house. When I gave up and went home, Pat had already returned, hair high and wide with loads of lacquer, to restore order. When Eric came home, John ran up the back yard to hide behind the shed, which is where Eric found him and gave him what for! This, I suppose, was our revenge but it was not a joyful one. John was once caned by the headmaster in front of the whole school, much to Clare's embarrassment, as he stood there with his 'skinhead' hairdo, yellow teeth and terminal acne.

I suppose it was a kind of playground gangsterism that allowed John to beat us up, yet which would not allow any other kid in the area to bully us.

John who had once been quite a promising student and football player (according to Eric) now started to smoke and play truant. Of both these things I was sworn to secrecy, but they did come in handy occasionally as blackmail threats: 'I'll tell me dad you smoke if you don't . . .'

* * *

I liked going round to Cathy Clarke's in Pighue Lane. Cathy was five or six years older than me, and had long black hair that her mother braided into thick plaits. She was a Monkees fan, and a bit on the big-boned side. Her mother was from St Helens and spoke with a fruity accent, calling the kitchen 'the scullery', which she kept spotless. Even her back yard was whitewash immaculate. This was a peaceful haven from the constant fights and screaming of kids in our house, where standards of housework left much to be desired.

Being houseproud was something of which you could never accuse my parents; they preferred to spend every penny of income on food. Pat would send me out for seven pints of 'sterrie' (sterilised milk), which came in glass bottles that were too heavy for me to carry – bringing it back, I had to drag the shopping bag along the ground behind me. This milk, a disgusting yellow colour, was specified by Eric for some reason to do with hygiene. Everyone else we knew drank fresh milk that was delivered by a milkman. On Sundays he would cook the breakfast, endless rounds of toasted omelette sandwiches. Delicious.

Cathy Clarke took me to the ABC Picture House in Old Swan on Saturday mornings – mostly Elvis movies in vibrant Technicolor. On the way she would take me into a Catholic church (St Oswald's) so she could go to confession. Holy water (rumoured to be nun's-piss) and the low-light ambience I found rather mysterious and alien compared to the clean and bright, red-carpeted St Mary's Church of England where John was a choirboy.

The vibro-colour visions of Elvis and his navy-blue comic book hair were a strange contrast to the black and white of The Beatles, who were launching themselves from our very doorstep. The house became invaded by Beatles records, Beatles caps, plastic Beatles wigs, and in my sister's bedroom, Beatles wallpaper. John, George, Paul and Ringo's autographs and portraits stared down at you in an orgy of black, white and flesh-tone multiple repetition. Once, when I was quarantined in Clare's bedroom for some childhood illness, I sent myself dizzy by reading every autograph off the wallpaper like a litany. John, Paul, George and Ringo; John, Paul, George and Ringo. I believe I was born in that room.

My mother would tell us that she knew Paul McCartney and George Harrison when she lived in Kenyan Road as a child – it was just around the corner from Penny Lane. Auntie Kath would join in with, 'I saw them at the passport office in town as I was waiting for my passport, so me and Margie Massie could go and work in Jersey.' This was a town firmly in the grip of Beatlemania. I was not of the generation who could truly appreciate The Beatles as a musical and cultural phenomenon, although the sound of the 'Sergeant Pepper' album was extremely familiar, and I read the lyric sheet religiously, trying to sing along. I didn't fully appreciate their achievements until much later.

In fact my first act of pop culture consumption, with seven and six burning a hole in my pocket, was to ask for 'Daydream Believer' by The Monkees in a local record shop – a choice influenced by Cathy Clarke. Unfortunately they didn't have it in stock so, determined to come away with something, I settled for 'Blackberry Way' by The Move. Walking home down Pighue Lane I wondered if I had done the right thing. Still, 'Goodbye Blackberry Way . . .' was a good example of Sixties English Pop. Around this time, Tamla Motown was creeping into the house via John, the skinhead in his two-tone Trevira parallel pants, the latest thing, petrol blue and red being the favourite colour combination. And he had a Crombie coat with the breast pocket turned inside out to look like a red silk handkerchief.

My first fashion statement was a Ben Sherman button down shirt, worn under a blue denim Wrangler jacket with Wrangler jeans. Pocket money saved for years in the school savings bank was raided for these grown-up clothes. Clare was sent with me one weekend to the Old Swan shopping centre to buy these items, but we came back with the wrong size trousers. Somehow they had sold us a men's size instead of a child's size. To disguise the fact Clare shortened the trousers to fit me in the leg, so I ended up modelling these very wide yet short-legged jeans. Eric hit the roof.

So there I was in my Wrangler suit and checked Ben Sherman: hair shorn skinhead fashion like my big brother's, eight years old and ready to terrorise the neighbourhood. Well not exactly. The next thing on my agenda was ballroom dancing. Every Saturday morning I would walk up to Old Swan on my own and attend Billy Martin's School of Ballroom Dancing. I don't know where I got the idea from, maybe from watching 'Come Dancing' on the TV. I learned a kind of homogenous waltz, cha cha and rumba, somehow getting promoted to the Rhythm and Elegance class. This was not a popular pastime from Eric's point of view, who tried to discourage all such 'cissy' activity.

In order to finance this I inherited my sister's morning paper round at a shop called Rainey's, further down Rathbone Road towards Picton Road, where I wasn't familiar with the streets of larger and slightly posher houses. I had to get up early and carry a heavy bag of papers through the rain and snow, most of the time daydreaming and only half awake. I think I delivered the wrong paper to the wrong house just once too often, as one day I turned up for work and the shopkeeper gave me a week's wages (£1) and said don't come back. I got another paper round in a local shop a year or so later which I also messed up. Obviously work just didn't agree with me.

*   *   *

Sometime earlier I was encouraged to join the Wolf Cubs (a junior scout troop) which met once a week in the Church hall. I pestered my parents for the uniform, which in fact was all I was interested in, especially the red and yellow neckerchief that was tied at the neck with a leather toggle printed with a gold wolf's head. The only badge of merit I managed to get was the Troubadour's Badge. It had the symbol of the theatre on it, the masks of comedy and tragedy, in red and gold. I had asked what I had to do to get it and was told, 'you have to tell a joke and sing a song in front of an audience'. I can't remember what I sang or what the joke was, but I managed to pass the test at a weekend camp that was set up for Cubs of the North West. The major worry was whether I would wet the bed in the camp dormitory and get laughed at by the others. Somehow I managed to refuse all offers of drinks after about four o'clock and so managed to stay dry.

Bed-wetting was also a problem on school trips and when staying at friends' houses, so I avoided both – especially after one school trip to Penmaenmawr on the North Wales coast, where I managed to wet the bed every night.

Colomendy was another place in Wales I remember. This was a set of wooden dormitories and classrooms in the Welsh countryside that schools in the north could use for nature study. It was very near Moel Fammau, a mountain in the Clwyd Valley not far from Denbigh which we were obliged to climb. These trips had me in fits of terror. On one such occasion a printed note was sent out to parents telling them of a forthcoming trip, the cost and destination etc. But at the bottom of the notice it said in block capitals 'BEDWETTERS CANNOT BE CATERED FOR'. My mother took this as victimisation on the part of the headmaster and was up at the school like a shot, complaining: 'Why didn't you just write "Billy Johnson cannot be catered for on this trip" and have done with it!' This just caused me further embarrassment and I begged for the subject to be dropped. I hated out-of-school activities anyway.

Seen with Coons

When I was about eight years old I joined the church choir of St Mary's. The choir was run by a Mr Soul, the organist. I loved dressing up in a cassock, surplice and ruff that my mother used to get starched at a local laundry. We got about threepence a service paid at the end of each quarter, I think. If there was a wedding on a Saturday we would get half a crown on the day, so weddings were always well attended. There would be choir practice every Wednesday and even choir outings. One choir outing was a trip to the Abbey Cinerama, the biggest screen in Liverpool, to see *2001: A Space Odyssey*. This was a great visual experience, if a little confusing for boys between eight and twelve years old. Mr Soul had to go out and buy the book of the film and then explain to us what had actually happened. One Christmas I pestered Mr Soul to let me do a solo at the Christmas service: 'Once in Royal David's City'. I still feel embarrassed at the confusion I suffered during Mr Soul's florid musical introduction, not knowing exactly when I was supposed to come in.

Mr May the headmaster was not my favourite person, but one thing he did realise was that I had some kind of theatrical ability, giving me the main parts in the school Christmas plays – once as Good King Wenceslas who, stabbed and killed at the end of the production, miraculously came back to life to make an appeal for contributions for a Christmas dinner for the elderly. I was somehow so moved by this speech that tears rolled down my face.

The following year I played a TV news reporter covering the discovery of an alien who had arrived in the area by space ship. I wanted to play the alien but this role was given to Joe Harrison, a nice-looking dark-haired boy, the kind the girls went for. He wore a cut-down and painted rubber ball on his head which gave him a kind of bald, alien appearance. The idea was that this alien was a Jesus figure whom the human race treated badly. I was given the job of writing my own dialogue, which resulted in my having rather more to say than the alien.

Such was my desire to perform on a stage that I organised a Magic Show armed with a Magic Set and a book on conjuring. My attempt at disappearing fooled no one, as my feet were clearly visible under the curtain I was concealed behind. But the cutting-a-child-in-three trick got a big laugh as it involved some other child's humiliation. I rigged his shirt under his pullover so that if I pulled on the back of his collar his shirt would come off his back through the neck hole in his sweater, giving the illusion that the shirt had been drawn through his arms. So, after assisting me with a card trick, the boy jumped off the stage leaving his shirt behind, which I held up to the laughing audience. Realising this was the only round of applause I was going to get, I quickly terminated the act.

During this part of my life, when people asked me what I wanted to be when I grew up, the answer varied from week to week. Archaeologist, magician or ventriloquist were three favourites. At other times I'd want to be an artist, a poet or a dancer. What I really wanted was to live a life like Gene Kelly and Judy Garland in their Vaudeville days, as depicted in those Saturday afternoon re-runs of their old movies.

My father decided to take us all on holiday to Butlins Holiday Camp in Pwllheli (pronounced 'pathelli'). This was a wonderful place where everything was free, or so it seemed to us. There was a fabulous outdoor rollerskating rink with pink flagstones that you could skate on as long as you liked, if you had a chalet key to exchange for roller skates. Fairground rides were free, as was the swimming pool that had a cafe below it with an underwater window, so diners could watch the swimmers' submerged bits.

Here in Butlins I had my first crush on an adult. Both my sister and I fell in love with a handsome Redcoat. I think there's still a black-and-white faded photograph of him hanging round, in a blazer, shorts and plimsolls with a Fifties hairstyle. I remember going painfully pink and shy whenever he was around.

16

The chalets were wooden slat huts painted in pastel colours, arranged in terraces that were patrolled by nursery nurses in the evening so parents could go out to the site's bars and dancehalls. There were huge communal dining halls where you could eat as much as you liked. If ever the working class of England had halcyon days then these Sixties summers were they.

*   *   *

During my time at St Mary's I got a yearning to play the recorder. I gained a rudimentary knowledge of musical notation through this, but the recorder didn't hold much glamour and I started to look around for another instrument. The piano was out of the question as we neither had one nor could afford one, nor could our house accommodate one. So it had to be the concertina. I heard from a boy in a neighbouring street that if you joined the Orange Lodge (an organisation popular in Liverpool due to the high Irish Protestant population) you could borrow a concertina and be taught to play it, as well as dressing up and participating in annual parades that got you a day off school; all too good to be true. So off I went with this boy from Handkinson Street (whose mother *my* mother thought was common) to a meeting of the local chapter of the Lodge. Here I was told that I would have to make certain oaths, never play with Catholic children and never enter a Catholic church. I was then sent out of the room while, I was told, secret rites would be performed, designed to strike fear into the hearts of our enemies. I stood outside the room petrified and confused, thinking, 'I'll never be able to play with Cathy Clarke again'. I then heard fearful stamping and chanting getting louder and louder, grown men with whisky breaths in an orgy of hate. I never went back, King Billy's Parade would have to pass by without me.

I was sometimes sent to the Edge Hill Boys' Club on Saturday mornings. I remember winning sixpence in a miming competition. I had to mime to 'Bits and Pieces' by The Dave Clarke Five. Nowadays, watching re-runs of 'Ready Steady Go', I realise that miming competitions were a particularly Sixties thing.

17

I remember, too, sitting for hours with a record-player trying to learn the lyrics of 'Bonny and Clyde' by Georgie Fame, 'Everlasting Love' by Love Affair and 'Daydream Believer' by The Monkees. I drew the needle back and forth over the record, which infuriated my brother. He told me to give up as my voice would never be good enough, which of course only made me more determined.

I only got half a crown for pocket money, which wasn't enough to go out and buy records. I was pretty ungrateful and resented my elder brother and sister getting five bob. I used to get lost in a fantasy that I was not really a part of the family and had somehow been abandoned by my real parents, who of course were rich, genteel and lived in a palace. 'One day . . .' I dreamt that I would return to my true station in life.

Because playing with girls had been banned I would escape to school friends' houses – Gary or David in Cheers Street and Rodney in Handkinson Street. These were the back-to-back streets behind us, parallel to Rathbone Road. My mother didn't like Rodney, whom she used to call 'Little Hitler'. She had special names for different people in the neighbourhood. One woman who lived round the corner she called 'Bomber Command'; I can't remember why, although I remember her real name was Alma. Pat would have liked Rodney even less if she had known what we got up to in his backyard shed or in the disused railway buildings up on the embankment along the lane. These, I suppose, were my first sexual experiences, apart from Pauline Pigfat pulling the crotch of her knickers to one side, revealing something I didn't quite understand or like.

All I can remember of this sexual apprenticeship was that we would pull our pants down and rub our pre-pubescent willies together: no illusions of romantic love or anything like that. I did this with some other boys, too. I have memories of playing in a similar manner with Roger who lived in a big house up the other end of Rathbone Road. This was the day that I think I experienced a kind of orgasm. Roger got a bit keener on doing this than I, which rather put me off him. I do think, though, that my sexuality was formed to a large degree at this early age, from the way I was attracted to my sister's increasingly older boyfriends (usually friends of our John's) that she would let into the house when everyone was out and she was supposed to be babysitting me. One particularly, with whom we were both in love, was Billy Roddaway, a footballer, who later played for Burnley. Billy was an attractive, strapping lad, whilst Roger was just a skinny, spotty kid.

By this time Clare was in secondary school – St Hilda's Church of England School in Ullet Road. She wore a bright purple blazer and her skirt, as she got older and bolder, would slyly get shorter and shorter.

The fashion for soul music started in the late Sixties and was associated with skinhead style. There were clubs in town, of course, such as the Victoriana, where people like Johnny Johnson and the Bandwagon would come and play. Freda Payne's 'Band of Gold' was a big hit of the time. This was the music my elder brother and sister would go out and dance to.

A love of black music didn't seem to stretch as far as black people, who were referred to by my parents and John as 'Coons'. I was told that black people lived in Upper Parliament Street in Liverpool 8. There were rumours of gang fights between skinheads (of which my elder brother John was one) and black people. It was in this climate that a teenage girl we knew became pregnant, after an affair with a coloured boy who was in a then unheard of Liverpool vocal group. The racist image of black boys was that they got white girls pregnant and then buggered off. This probably happened on more than one occasion but I'm pretty sure it happened with white boys too.

A school friend of John's had seen fourteen-year-old Clare talking to a black boy called Ivor in the vicinity of St Hilda's, not too far from Liverpool 8. All hell broke loose when Clare came in on that dark winter's night. I watched in tears as my mother and brother John baited her. Later, when Eric came in they were still at it, taunting and berating her. He watched while they did it, then gave me a slap and pushed me into the other room, and called me a 'Drama Student!' when I begged them to stop.

'Is yer aarse sore?' someone screamed as they hit Clare again. 'You were seen with Coons!'

19

This wasn't the only violent incident in the house, but it is certainly the one I remember most graphically. It led to Clare running away from home: she didn't know where she was going, she just ran. She put on her best clothes, stole my mother's purse and climbed out of her bedroom window.

Eric and John went in the transit van to find her. Spotting her on the back seat of a single decker bus, John mouthed 'You just wait 'til we get you home' at her. Then, when the bus stopped at a bus stop he jumped out of the van and boarded the bus. Luckily Clare had the presence of mind to jump off from the exit at the middle of the bus. She ran like hell in her high-heeled shoes pursued by my father who was now out of the van. In the grounds of a convent called The Cenacle she hid behind a tree, panting and out of breath. Eric followed but couldn't find her.

When a day or so later Clare returned home, she was confined to her room for what seemed like weeks. Her best clothes were ripped up and there they hung in tatters in the wardrobe. For the next six months she had very little freedom to go out on her own.

As Clare got older I began to see less of her. She was becoming a rebel at school, and needed her freedom.

On one occasion, my mother took Clare, Jamie as a baby and me into town to a professional photographer. What seemed like hundreds of cute baby photos were taken of Jamie with his big blue eyes while I sat in a corner, sulking at not being asked to have my photo taken. After about an hour of moaning 'When's it my turn?', I was eventually sat next to Jamie and a Bugs Bunny doll for one photograph. I couldn't take my glasses off as they had made red marks on either side of my nose.

One day Eric took me aside and said, 'I don't like the way you talk. Only girls use names like "Jamie". You've got to learn to talk like a man.' This piece of advice was given in the normal threatening way, forefinger pointing into my face with a 'Do you hear me?' which had to be answered with a 'Yes' or something terrible might happen.

Eric's code was very much, 'If you live in my house you do what I say', even down to eating tomatoes, which I hated. On one occasion he force fed them to me until I gagged. Food – always in abundance – was a kind of love replacement in our house. The family credo seemed to be 'stuff your face until you can't take any more', but I was a fussy eater.

Pat's childhood was very strange. Born just before the war she was evacuated to Wales. She told me the people who took her in didn't feed her properly, and kept the money the government gave them. To top it all she was of Indian descent and suffered racial abuse. Eric was working at sea by the age of fifteen, sending money home. They were doing the best they could with their lack of education, and the cold and affectionless upbringing that, I suspect, they both suffered.

Silver Blades and Blue Choppers

Some time between the age of eight and ten I started to go regularly to Silver Blades Ice Rink again. At first I would use hired skates until, when I could skate a little, I pestered my father to buy me my own, a new brand with plated blades that were about seven pounds, a lot cheaper than the professional-type skates with Coronation Ace blades. I started to make friends with some of the regular serious skaters, who wondered who this unaccompanied child was. Most of the middle-class boys and girls were accompanied by their doting mothers, who made a social event of the Sunday morning sessions.

Boys were rather thin on the ground, as free skating was considered a bit on the effete side. So girls who were interested in pairs skating or Ice Dance were a bit stuck for partners. One of these girls, Ellen, a tall, pretty, Princess Diana of a girl, with short blonde hair, asked me to share a lesson with her once a week so she could do some pairs skating. Her mother would pay for the lesson as I couldn't afford them. Unfortunately Ellen was a bit older and a bit taller than me, which made it difficult for me to lift her in the way that was expected, so after several lessons the idea had to be dropped, and she went back to her solo skating. This attention did encourage me, though, and skating soon became an obsession. I would find myself rehearsing steps whenever I was alone at home or in school. Once, one of my school teachers caught me doing what he thought were peculiar dance movements in the classroom during playtime.

Of course I should have been out in the playground. I hated the playground, where football was God.

So the ice rink was a kind of refuge, where the odd sequin wasn't frowned upon too much, even on boys. I loved the smell and the stars that shone on to the ice from the huge mirror ball above. 'Telstar' was the ultimate skating rink record, although 'Chirpy Chirpy Cheep Cheep' came a close second. Upstairs was the 'Bumble Bee Disco' (closed during the day) where I used to sneak in to admire the psychedelic lighting and decor.

I persuaded my mother to buy me a couple of yards of chocolate brown bri-nylon so a friend's mother could make me a catsuit with a square neckline, under which I wore a beige button down Ben Sherman shirt, *de rigeur* for the serious Seventies skater. My father scoffed: 'You'll look ridiculous if some rag-arsed kid turns up that can skate rings round you.'

Auntie Kath heard about my new obsession. In her youth she had also been a skating fanatic and still had a few pairs of good quality skates with Coronation Ace blades. She kindly gave them to me saying, 'Dye them black before your father sees them or there'll be murder.' (Girls wore white skates, boys wore black.) So there I was, all dolled up in my new boots that I had to keep re-dyeing every couple of weeks when the white showed through.

Going to W.H. Smith's, buying notepads and pencils (sometimes shoplifting them), writing poetry and drawing pictures were my only other pastimes. Often I would sit down with the new blank paper and be at a loss at what to do on it. Writer's block at eight years old. One of the first poems I wrote, all of two verses, drew a rave review from my English teacher at that time. I can remember the second verse.

Waiting to burst into life,
The bud has waited too long,
Life! I want Life! shouts the bud,
In the dark Before Life.

This poem, which I was particularly proud of, drew taunts from my elder brother John, who jealously swore that I had copied it from some obscure source.

Whenever I was alone in the house I would rummage around in cupboards and drawers or anywhere else I was not supposed to look. Somewhere I found a hoard of old 78's, heavy discs that broke if you dropped them. They were strange and exotic with

23

titles like 'She Wore Red Feathers And A Hula Hula Skirt'. Some were by the Peruvian princess Yma Sumac, the girl with the four-octave voice. In one of the drawers there was also a black and gold kimono elaborately embroidered with dragons, that my father had brought back for my mother from some port of call, and lots of Tretchikoff prints of oriental green ladies, rolled up unframed.

Sometime around the end of 1970 and the beginning of 1971 my father started to decorate the house. This was a previously unheard of activity apart from my mother painting the bare concrete floor of the front room Doorstep Red. We were about to move house. I was not supposed to know. My father busily carpeted the stairs in a peculiar red plastic padding. His choice of wallpaper was large, repetitive 'Wonderloaf' emblems, like the inside of Dr Who's Tardis.

At this time the actual eleven plus exam was abolished and some other sort of assessment was brought in. A form was sent out to parents asking them to make three choices of the secondary schools their child would like to attend. Eric took charge of this and of course took no notice of my opinion. My main fear was that I wouldn't get into a grammar school and would end up in a local comprehensive like The Holt, which was considered very rough then. The mixed sex aspect of a comprehensive school did appeal to me though, girls being my preferred company. Eric chose The Bluecoat and Hillfoot Hey, both grammar schools very near the house we were about to move to, and Liverpool Collegiate, a school near the town centre that Eric's father had attended, as a third choice. Eric even took me in his van to show me the first two, which were admittedly in pleasant locations. However, The Bluecoat, being a bit on the snooty side, required a special recommendation from the headmaster of the primary school you were attending. Mr May, who didn't like me for leaving the church choir and other minor misdemeanours, and who suspected me of writing SEX and SHIT on Mrs Briscis's blackboard (guilty), was not about to give that. So effectively the first choice on the form was completely wasted.

Around April, the official announcement was made that we were to move, a week beforehand. We were going to move into the house where the mysterious Great Auntie Pat now lived alone, as our great grandmother had passed away. Auntie Pat would be moving into our house and, under a private loan scheme, Eric would make up the difference in the value of the houses. Auntie Pat's house was much bigger and in a better location. It even had a bathroom.

We had definitely come up in the world. The thought of having a bathroom, however small, that could be locked on the inside, was quite a thrill. The only other time I had experienced a bath was in Picton Road Public Baths where my mother sent me once. It was next door to the swimming baths and you paid to have a bath in a cream and green tiled room. There were small holes in the walls of these cubicles that had been blocked up with pieces of soap, to my disappointment. The atmosphere was a bit like a Victorian hospital and I hated it. I made the mistake of leaving my father's pink plastic comb at the baths and was sent back on the two mile walk to get it. It was a fruitless journey, so a new comb had to be bought.

I really can't think why Auntie Pat would want to come and live in a house without a bathroom on a busy main road. Maybe she was being kind as she knew that we needed a bigger house. The move was fairly painless, and as we sat in the living room of our new house, we could hear birds singing instead of cars and trains going by. It felt like we had moved to the country. And just round the corner there was Penny Lane, with a barber shop showing photographs, just like in the song.

Then the results of the school selection came through. I was to go to the Liverpool Collegiate Grammar School For Boys, a huge sandstone Gothic structure near the town centre. No one else from my year at St Mary's managed to get into a grammar school. But then, no other parent would have their child journey the three or four miles into town.

I had secured a promise from Eric that if I managed to get into a grammar school he would buy me a Raleigh Chopper – a strange kind of bicycle vaguely based on the design of a motorbike – but I was a bit peeved when he bought Jimmy one as well. Anyway, it was a nice bike, painted blue and white which my father thought was masculine – I'd asked for a green or an orange chopper. Anyway, I still thought I was the bee's knees cycling around our new area. One little accident occurred. When I was struggling with it to get it in the hallway, I put the front wheel through the glass front door. I went out to play for a long time, too petrified to come home. For some reason I didn't get punished for this particular incident as I thought I would.

The Freemans Catalogue

During this first spring in our new house, Clare dragged me into the backyard one day and whispered to me the following story. She had pestered our parents for weeks to buy her a pair of moccasins, which must have been in fashion at the time. While she was playing truant in Greenbank Park, hanging out with boys, the kind she was not supposed to, she got thrown into the lake where her new moccasins sank deeper and deeper into the mud. She knew that I had a TSB savings account. I had about ten pounds in it. She wanted me to buy her a new pair of moccasins without our parents finding out, as she was sure to be punished and grounded for another six months. Reluctantly I agreed, though I was not normally the kind of person who parted easily with money saved over a long time.

I was still skating up a storm at the Silver Blades. I now lived very near to Lawrence, a friend from the ice rink who I started to see more of, and my skating obsession deepened. I had entered into the Skating Association's yearly junior competition and I was busy trying to put a thirty second programme together, including the music. I had found a record of war movie themes and was trying to skate to the 'Dambusters' although it was a bit fast, as I discovered after I had persuaded the DJ at the ice rink to play it for me. So someone gave me a Mantovani and his muzak of the mountains LP, with 'Lawrence of Arabia' and 'A Stranger in Paradise' on it, which I ended up using.

I came third or fourth in my skating class out of about six, which was quite good considering I'd never had a lesson. I remember the excitement of having the whole of the ice to myself, although a thirty second programme was over in a moment. I felt a bit disappointed that neither of my parents came to see me compete, especially as most of the other kids' mothers had turned up, but that was just the way it was.

Vivat haec sodolitas, Decus Esmaduna
Vivat haec sodolitas, Decus Esmaduna
Nulli usquam posthabenda, Semper in caelum tolenda
Magnae verum cunae

The Liverpool Collegiate Grammar School For Boys song (approximate spelling).

One cold and damp September morning I took the 46 bus from the Penny Lane terminus into town to the grammar school. It went through the dreaded Liverpool 8, past Paddington comprehensive school where all the black kids went. I showed my education authority bus pass to the conductor on the green and cream, one-man bus. Then past the huge building site which was later to become The Liverpool Royal Hospital. Over the next five years this mammoth construction would take shape slowly and awkwardly through strikes and setbacks, just as my awkward personality would form itself through teenage trauma and sexual awakening.

I walked in circles around the massive playground behind the school, a playground skirted on each side by wasteland and council tower blocks. The school was situated on the edge of the town centre near the terrible housing estates of Everton Valley. The famous housing scheme disaster 'The Piggeries' was nearby. Directly opposite was the Roman Catholic school Saint Francis Xavier; there was a tangible tension between the two schools.

The school building was a dreadful, drafty old place with a ridiculous sense of its own importance. There was a house system for which boys were picked at random. A rugby shirt of your particular house colour had to be purchased from the school office: mine was a vile maroon. An exeat had to be granted if time off were needed for a doctor's appointment, and some of the so-called masters wore black academic robes. Pupils had to stand when teachers entered the room. It was a strange aping of the public school system. The study of Art was restricted to boys who were in the lower achieving streams C, D and E. I was put into the B stream, which put a stop to any artistic leanings I had at this stage.

My first form teacher was a Mrs Muir, a nice old dame near to retirement age who also taught us mathematics. 'Johnson! What is the coefficient of X?' was her cry. She wore loose-fitting dresses, open-toed sandals and a slash of red lipstick across her mouth. Her grey hair was piled up like Vanessa Bell's.

Unfortunately in my first year I decided to act the class clown, asking stupid questions and playing for laughs, probably to disguise some fundamental differences in my personality. Games, which lasted the whole of Thursday afternoons, was agonising. The whole concept of having to play football or go cross country running was hideous to me. We had a twat of a Welsh games master, nicknamed Taffy (of course), who used to threaten boys with the slipper. All that changing-room business and communal showers were fearful experiences.

In the first year I made a few friends, one called Derek who lived near the town centre. His father worked for the university and had a pass for the university baths. He took me one weekend to the Olympic-sized swimming pool. I was visibly shocked when I realised that the changing rooms were communal. There were grown men walking round with no clothes on. My eyes were on stalks at these fit, tanned bodies, covered with pubic hair and wet from the showers.

'What's wrong with you?' said Derek. 'Are you a Queer or something?' This sounded strange coming from him as he was quite camp, often lapsing into nasal Kenneth Williams impressions – 'Niice'. Nudity was something that was hidden in our family, and I had previously only ever been to the old-style swimming baths with separate changing rooms. I asked to go to the university baths with Derek quite often after that, but I think he got a bit suspicious.

Derek's question reverberated in my brain, and started the 'fear of being Queer' syndrome that I was to suffer over the next few years. 'Please God don't make me . . . One of Them,' I prayed. I read problem pages in magazines which always said that this attraction was probably just a phase that teenage boys went through. I hoped this was true.

Towards the end of this school year I got a not-so-glowing

school report sent home to my parents. 'Must try harder' and that sort of thing. My father took offence at this and decided to ban me from ice skating forever. It was the whole basis of my social life and something I felt I was good at, the only physical exercise that I enjoyed. When you're twelve years old and something like that is taken away, you think the whole world has come to an end. There was no use trying to defy Eric as all financial assistance would be removed. And possibly worse.

* * *

Sometime during that year of 1971, Clare was given T Rex's 'Electric Warrior' by an admirer. She wasn't overly interested in the record but it changed my life. T Rex were the perfect pop group for the time, coming out of the hippie, psychedelic Sixties and into the glam rock tastelessness of the Seventies. Marc Bolan was the only charismatic figure around, as far as I was concerned.

Every Saturday my mother used to send me to a butcher's shop in Lodge Lane, probably for some reason of economy as our family's intake of meat was quite phenomenal. A couple of doors down was a record shop which had a club that you could pay into weekly and this enabled me to eventually buy the record of my choice. I can't remember the exact arrangements, but this was how I managed to get records, by paying into the club most of my pocket money, which by this time must have been about five shillings. An LP was about two pounds, maybe less, and a single about fifty pence.

Music replaced my ice skating obsession. A girl called Susan who lived down the road had a piano and attended piano lessons, which impressed me. She taught me to play the first few bars of the 'Moonlight Sonata'. I pestered my father to buy me a secondhand upright piano – at this time pianos were going very cheaply – and when he'd agreed I would bash out endlessly the bits that Susan taught me. Eric, however, refused to pay for piano lessons, saying that if I had any aptitude it would reveal itself. I bought a 'How To Play Piano' manual and endeavoured to learn to play the thing, without much success. One day I returned home from school to find the piano removed from its place in the front room. They had got rid of it while I was out.

By this time I think, Eric had become a private hire taxi driver. He had an aquamarine Ford Zephyr that I had to wash every Saturday morning and deck out with plastic wedding decorations, white plastic roses and lampshade trimmings that fastened to the inside of the car windows with transparent rubber suckers. I discovered I had a flair for arranging fake foliage. I also had to vacuum the inside of the car with a hoover and a very long extension cord. This task ensured that I got a raise in my pocket money.

It was the fact that Jimmy and John were not expected to do any sort of manual work about the house, while Clare and I were, that annoyed me. They were never required to wash the dishes or peel the potatoes. I used to take it out a bit on my little brother, as John had abused me, though I never went quite as far.

By this time I had started to grow my hair and refused to wear the spectacles I had been forced to use from such an early age. I would spend hours locked in the bathroom, experimenting with makeup and wanking over the underwear section of my mother's Freemans catalogues.

A Pfuckking Taart

In my second year at the Collegiate a new boy, due to an alphabetical accident, sat in the desk next to mine. His name was Heath, and he was also a Marc Bolan fan, which gave us plenty to talk about when we should have been paying attention in class 2B. He had been in the C stream the year before and we had not met.

Heath was tall and thin with a fey manner that made the other boys regard him with sexual suspicion. We became inseparable: two avid pop music fans who both hated football, and who tried to stay in class through the compulsory playground breaks in the morning school session. Often we were discovered by prefects patrolling the corridors, and turfed out into the violent schoolyard.

As soon as we became friends the problems really started: we were tagged Honey Heath and Joyful Johnson. In the playground it was not unusual for us to be surrounded by thirty boys who would kick, spit and scream in our direction. 'You fuckin' Queer bastards!' or 'You fucking arse-bandits, I bet you wank each other off!' And other similar displays of intelligence and refinement.

Whenever either of us had to take the stairs for another class we would be hailed with a rain of sputum and phlegm from the stair landings above, which of course we had to clean off before we reached the next lesson. We learned to carry quite a bit of 'Kleenex' in our pockets (the definite sign of homosexuality according to Heath). Sly kicks and punches somehow always came our way and each journey through the corridors was like running the gauntlet. Some of our tormentors were more aggressive than others. One in particular was a fifth former who, whenever he saw me in the school building, would kick me up the arse or punch me in the face, once chipping the corners off two of my bottom teeth. He was the meanest human being I've ever come across.

My red hair would easily identify me in a crowd of mousy brown, but Honey Heath's treatment was just as bad as he was tall and stood out too. Once, on his way home for lunch in nearby Kensington he was pelted with house bricks as he crossed a piece of wasteland. Despite this, our hair colours became progressively more vibrant. We were determined NOT TO BE LIKE THEM.

Somehow our friendship survived this persecution. As I lived so far away from school I was expected to stay for dinner at the school canteen, but this just exposed me to more abuse from the other boys, so I started going home with Honey Heath, or sometimes we would both go into town and spend our dinner money on records.

This was the year we discovered David Bowie, whom Honey Heath slightly resembled. By this time I had grown my hair fairly long in a loose approximation of Marc Bolan's corkscrew coiffeur, which suited my unruly, auburn, curly hair. It looked a bit like a loose afro which became fashionable a bit later as 'the curly perm' sported by footballers and cartoon scousers. I would go through a hair-teasing ritual every morning: this consisted of me with my head upside down in front of the gas fire in the front room, for about twenty minutes, much to my father's dismay.

'You look like a pfuckking Taart.' For some reason he put an almost silent 'p' in front of his 'f' words.

Clare left St Hilda's around this time. She had blossomed into a full-grown rebel, tormenting the other girls in school and disobeying the nuns who tried to teach her. In this she was similar to my elder brother John, who, as I say, had started to smoke and play truant. This put a stop to his footballer aspirations, and Eric could no longer officially be proud of him and say, 'The best out of all you shower of shite!' as he had often done. There must have been some reason why we all went off the rails as soon as we hit our teens.

Pat had started to work in geriatric nursing at a hospice in Old Swan, presumably to help Eric with the bills. In fact, initially, she had to make over her entire salary every month to Eric who doled out to her day-to-day expenses and food shopping money. Eric was extremely tight and dictatorial where money was concerned. To give him his due, he was a hard worker and knew how difficult money was to come by. Money worries were always uppermost in his mind to the point of obsession.

As we grew older and became teenagers, family rows, fights and disagreements increased. John was temporarily at a technical school learning bricklaying – Eric's golden rule was, 'Learn a trade'. John would come home drunk some nights, sometimes accompanied by the police in the early hours of the morning, much to my mother's embarrassment. At other times she would open the front door in the morning to find him asleep on the doorstep.

'Stinkin' of ale, you drunken bastard!' she would scream. Yet this was, in a way, accepted masculine behaviour. Boys will be boys. Not 'sick' and 'perverted' like 'Our Billy' who had taken to experimenting with make-up and hair dye at an alarmingly early age.

My David Bowie obsession had reached fever pitch. It was not enough to play 'Ziggy Stardust and the Spiders from Mars' full blast on the teak radiogram. Honey Heath and I had to embrace the lifestyle of the then 'openly bisexual' pop star. I bought the 'Ziggy' album from the record club and along with Honey Heath would scour the *NME* or the *Melody Maker*, which I had delivered every week, for interviews and pictures of our new hero. This record had a huge effect on kids of my generation, not just the homosexual ones. Bisexuality became a fashionable pose, along with the idea of androgyny in fashion. Small pockets of girls and boys (especially of the apprentice hairdresser variety) all over the country, started to experiment with their appearance as a direct result of the current fashions in Pop music. Bowie, Roxy Music, Alice Cooper *et al*.

Clare was now at Colquitt Street College, learning ladies hairdressing, a very fashionable Seventies occupation. I would raid her supplies of peroxide or hair colouring and burn my scalp with peroxide until my hair was ten different shades of screaming orange. I even made Clare straighten my hair and would use her curling irons every day to straighten out my natural waves, often burning large tell-tale tong-shaped chunks of skin out of my neck with the overheated implement.

Eric was incensed. A studious, spectacle-wearing child who had been nicknamed 'The Professor' by his grandfather was now turning into a fully-fledged Poof.

'What have I done to deserve a walking freakshow for a son?' said Eric, in despair. 'It looks like that pfuckkin' lunatic woman from Old Swan.' The lunatic in question was an old lady who overdid the henna, which I had not yet discovered as a hair-enhancing substance.

Of course peroxide didn't go down too well either with the boys at school, who were now fully convinced that there were real live 'Queers' in their midst. The abuse had got to such a level that we genuinely feared for our lives. We started 'sagging' school in earnest, beginning with games. I became adept at forging my mother's handwriting which was very simple to copy.

We would hang around Newsham Park near Honey Heath's home or go into town and hang out at St John's precinct, the then-new shopping mall. The option of going into town was a bit more dangerous as we ran the risk of being spotted by my father working as a taxi driver, or even by one of the school teachers.

When we hung round the park we would scour the back alleys for piles of magazines that people would throw out in bundles. These we went through for pictures of 'David', in his various outfits and 'personas'. This photo obsession became quite a thing. I had a couple of rare photos and interviews that Honey Heath wanted. I remember swapping my whole Bowie picture collection with him for a thousand cigarette coupons. His grandmother smoked very heavily, luckily for me.

With these coupons I managed to obtain my first acoustic guitar from the John Player's catalogue. In the first few weeks, after learning the chords of C and G, I wrote my first song, 'The Gremlin' – a T Rex-inspired ditty which fortunately I have no memory of. I must have been thirteen and had already started to commandeer the front room in our terraced house. The room that I would carry around with me for the rest of my life. That feeling of isolation, and that strange desire to be creative. Playing records and writing poetry, and trying desperately to learn more chords than Honey Heath, whose dad had bought him a fabulous twelve-string guitar, just like the one 'David' used. He was an only child and got most things that he wanted. I was jealous, especially of his not having to share a bedroom.

Honey Heath's father played in a cabaret band on Sunday nights in a basement drinking club in Prescott Road. We would sneak up there sometimes and watch him through the window as he belted out songs like 'My Way' and 'These Boots Are Made For Walking'.

Honey Heath's dad had a PA and microphones, and also a reel-to-reel tape recorder. Every week Honey Heath would record the soundtrack of 'Top Of The Pops' from the TV which we would listen to on Sunday nights, when his mum and dad were out. We would have dancing competitions in his front room. We would arrange little set pieces to the hits of the day and give each other marks out of ten. These Sunday nights were our chance to wear make-up like 'David's' or 'Marc's'. We created costumes out of old things that aped Kansai Yamamoto's Kabuki inspired designs for David Bowie's current tour. Pierre Laroche, who designed Bowie's make up for the 'Aladdin Sane' record sleeve, has a lot to answer for.

Honey Heath had a real talent for working out chords and guitar parts from the record collections we had. We would hold concerts for each other. I would bring along my latest 'song' that I'd written, and he would perform selections from Bowie's back catalogue, which he played and sang incredibly well.

To keep up with him and his record collection I began pinching money from my father's change tin that he used as a cab driver. I went through my elder brother's pockets while he lay in bed drunk. Eric started to lock up his tin in the desk in the front room, but I would take out the unlocked drawer above the one the tin was in and raid it. So next day I would rush down to Rumbellow's or NEM's, my pockets weighed down with ten pence pieces to buy the latest Bowie album. The release of

'Aladdin Sane' was a much-awaited day. The reviews in the music press of this record had been works of art in themselves – it was a good period in music journalism, inspiring rather than just critical. Charles Shaar Murray and Nick Kent created star-like personas for themselves.

While my sister and brother were going out to discos and dancing to soul music by the Stylistics and others, I was listening to white art school rock music. Roxy Music burst on to the scene with the fabulously feathered Brian Eno and the posturing Brian Ferry.

Honey Heath and I would look down our noses at schoolgirls in their Bay City Rollers outfits. I used to talk to a hippie in my class who was 'into' Genesis and Zeppelin, but apart from the theatrics of Peter Gabriel this didn't really count. It was this hippie who sold us our first two quid deal of marijuana, which I'm sure was just mixed herbs. We didn't even know how to smoke cigarettes, and when we tried to smoke this green stuff wrapped up in silver paper, I vomited violently.

Appearance was something that suddenly became very important in our lives. I remember Clare's boyfriend Lenny buying a pair of metallic leather two-tone (beige and brown) platform boots from a boutique called 'Cape', a Mecca for the patchouli oil and love-bead wearing, fashion-conscious Liverpuddlians.

'It smells like a Chinese whooer 'ouse in 'ere', Eric remarked at my first joss-stick burning experiment.

I was embarrassed by the bottle-green high waistband Oxford bags that I was made to wear with my school uniform. 'Just wait', I would think. 'One day I'll buy my own clothes,' I vowed, as I salivated over a pair of two-tone split-knee Loons, advertised in the *NME*.

David Bowie was always painfully thin. Most of my immediate family were a bit on the chubby side, from eating a typically Northern working-class diet – chips with everything. I was determined not to be like them, so I started to make myself vomit in the lavatory – nowadays they call this bulimia, and even princesses suffer from it. I would rush to Boots the Chemist in town at lunch time to weigh myself and see what my furtive starvation had achieved. Eating lunch was now a thing of the past as the money allotted to it had to be used for other things. Suddenly I had a visible jaw line where once had been those loathed chubby cheeks.

Multi-Coloured Patchwork Clogs

The poetry I was now writing in copious amounts was heavily influenced by Marc Bolan's elfin style. That is to say it was complete nonsense:

Aznigirdan
Wrought lordlett dipped like a seagull midshift
Frowns to the isle King, Aznigirdan
Who fails to scan my horned forest window
Like a tail tied gutterdog, whimper tired and evergreen.
Sway, Sway said he
And the earth swayed beneath our toadstool footsteps

English was the only subject for which I could summon up any interest. My enthusiasm for French subsided when I was allotted a teacher who was an ex-army type. His favourite mode of addressing me was, 'Are you free Johnson?' in a bad imitation of John Inman's Queer character in the sitcom 'Are you Being Served?' There was also a rash of 'Shut that door', which was the catchphrase of another Queer comedian, Larry Grayson. These stereotypical characters were the Seventies' idea of Queer. Painfully embarrassing for the young who felt that they might be 'One of Them', and who were hoping desperately that they wouldn't end up like one of these caricatures. Or worse, sometimes giving in to, and acting out the stereotype to amuse any possibly hostile hetero and survive unscathed.

In the third year Honey Heath slid to the C stream again while I managed by desperate revision at the end of term to remain in the B stream. We had been allotted a nice female form mistress in the second year, who also took us for English. She at least encouraged my literary extravagance to a certain degree.

39

In the third year my form teacher was a blonde rugby player, and I would sit and fantasise over him during the lesson. He shared a flat with another teacher who was also a blonde rugby player. They were a couple of overtly masculine heterosexual men, which was somehow an increased thrill – their 'straightness' was a definite part of the attraction. I would deny vehemently to Honey Heath that I fancied them – I was still going through a long period of denial – but in my fantasies I would discover these two athletic blonde men fucking each other stupid in their bachelor flat. My attempts at visualising women in my fantasies would come to nothing, so a quick change of gender would be needed to bring myself to orgasm.

On one of these occasions, I was in the outside lavatory, which we had as well as the indoor one. Pat decided to brush the backyard and must have spied me through a crack in the door, as she started to scream something about 'filth' and how she didn't want any filth in this house. But it was much too late for Pat's objections. I was here, filth incarnate, 'a dirty fucking Queer'.

'Why don't you knock the Ciss Lad out of him, Eric?' Pat would scream. As if, in a 'Tom and Jerry' cartoon, after having been beaten unmercifully, the spectre of a Ciss Lad, with handbag, high heels and horns would rise and separate away from my body and ascend to heaven, or maybe descend to hell.

During my first summer holidays near Penny Lane, I started to discover the Bible-bashers' viewpoint of homosexuality. 'Divinity' had always been a strong subject of mine, as Bible stories had been told endlessly at St Mary's. I even learned by rote the sixty or so books of the Bible in order of appearance, with the help of a song at a local Sunday school. I also attended Tent Crusades in the Park in a huge marquee set up in 'The Mystery', a large park a few streets away from where we lived. The Tent Crusades were evangelical meetings for children where more Bible stories were told. If a child answered a question correctly, they would win a ticket. Tickets could be saved up and redeemed for gifts at the end of the evangelical visitation. I collected over a hundred and twenty tickets, being 'too clever for yer own good', as Pat would say.

A great emphasis would be put on letting Jesus into your heart. I asked him several times, but I think he refused to enter. He must have refused because life didn't all of a sudden sort itself out, and become wonderful and easy. Soon, however, I was to read in the 'holy text' that homosexuality or 'a man laying with another man is an abomination worthy of death'. I found this dubious wisdom in the Bible for which I had redeemed my tickets at the end of the summer of 1971. So by the time I was twelve, I knew that the pearly gates of heaven were going to be difficult to climb over.

* * *

Sometime in the early Seventies, a lot of publicity in the tabloid newspapers was given to a documentary on Andy Warhol. Warhol was already interesting to Honey Heath and me, as Bowie had written a song about him and had cited Warhol and the Velvet Underground as an influence. During this heated debate about whether or not the documentary should be shown, cinemas cashed in on the publicity by showing the Warhol movie *Trash*, starring Holly Woodlawn and Joe Dallesandro. One Sunday night Honey Heath and I dressed up to the nines, wearing 'subtle' make-up (or so we thought), to make us look older, then went along to see this controversial movie. It was in a small, seedy, adult cinema down a side street off London Road.

At fourteen years old the sight of a naked Joe Dallesandro was just too much for me. I had an erection (which I might have encouraged) throughout the movie. The transsexual Holly Woodlawn stole the show, though, scouring for items in the trash and in one particular scene pretending to be pregnant for a welfare worker who comes to assess their need. The welfare man takes a liking to a pair of silver slingbacks that Holly has found in the trash and tries to buy them. There was no doubt after that movie that I wanted to become a member of the drug-oriented, Art Underground of New York, where the boundaries of sex and sexuality were blurred.

Another trip to the movies was to see Derek Jarman's

41

Sebastiane, a revelation. The slow-motion love scene in a pool of water was both thrilling and an affirmation that homosexuality could be beautiful, shameless and out in the open. This particular scene was, I think, scored by Brian Eno who we already admired. This was a very exciting period of sexual and cultural discovery.

The opening scene of *Sebastiane* was also our first glimpse of Lyndsey Kemp, a legend amongst Bowie fans as the man who taught Bowie the art of mime. This virility dance, with Kemp surrounded by men in huge, highly coloured pantomime penis masks, while not being sexually exciting (in fact repulsive) was a landmark in Queer Cinema. It was in this climate that we went in search of an underground with which we could identify. We thought: there must be other people like us, mustn't there?

One place where we didn't find any kindred spirits was at a David Bowie concert. It was a day that Honey Heath and I had long waited for. As soon as ticket sales were announced we were there at nine o'clock in the morning, standing in a line outside the Liverpool Empire, the largest venue in town. The concert was, I think, June 8th 1973.

I hassled my father for money for a new pair of shoes to wear for the concert. I managed to get six pounds out of him and rushed into town to that den of chic 'Cape', where I bought a pair of multi-coloured patchwork clogs with a platform sole and a wooden heel that measured six inches. When I presented them to Eric at the kitchen table he was incredulous.

'You're not going to wear them are yer?'

I assured him that with the trousers I was wearing, these monstrosities would not be seen. It was true that I had acquired a pair of extremely wide trousers that were worn long, giving the impression that the platforms were not so high. I had more sprained ankles that year than any footballer.

The day of the concert came. I wore a women's wartime swingback jacket that belonged to Honey Heath's grandmother Evelyn, the dreaded clogs and the concealing trousers. I felt that I hadn't overdone the make-up. As we waited outside the venue before the doors opened we saw very few kindred spirits. There were one or two other boys in make-up but it was of the flash of lightning variety that was more the equivalent of the football supporter daubing his face with the British flag. Honey Heath and I towered above people, him by nature and me by virtue of those clogs. Somehow we got in alive and bought our programmes and posters.

We were completely absorbed. We stood on our third row seats (me precariously in those clogs) in order to get a better view. Short of wetting ourselves with excitement we did everything that teenage girls do when confronted with their idols. The lighting and production of the show would now be considered very crude, but then the costume changes, the mirror ball, the strobe and the aloof pose – no talking to the audience – were amazing to us.

Towards the end of the concert however, we were knocked off our seats, punched and kicked, and our precious posters and programmes were stolen by some older ruffians. Dejectedly we hid at the back of the theatre and watched the final numbers, leaving before the end to get the last bus home. We were quite upset at our night being ruined, but still, we had seen 'David' in his prime, and in the flesh.

A Cut Above the Rest

Embryo in a tin can
The product of man
Since the ages began
A muscular spasm . . .
An orgasm.

This is how I began a short story that I wrote in 1974, set in St John's precinct. It was about a pair of lesbians, one called Karl and the other Veronica, who met in the lavatory of the precinct. Embryos could now be bought, pre-fertilised by men with various physical attributes and colouring; Tall Blonde, Dark Endomorph, etc. This was supposedly implied by the opening lines which, I felt, spoke volumes about the modern world and the human condition. Poor deluded child.

In the shopping precinct itself piped muzak was played in the airless air-conditioned atmosphere. There was a branch of 'Habitat' in all of its bean-bag glory, Indian matting a go-go: a Mecca for the unfurnished-flat-Bohemians-with-an-income, who drank cheap red wine in bistros. Honey Heath and I would hang around here sometimes looking at the latest fashions in household goods, and dream. How wonderful it would be if our parents had taste and shopped here. One day as we walked round 'Habitat' a rather diminutive girl and what looked like a rather tall girl ran in after us. The small one was shaved bald and wore too much make-up. One of her eyes always seemed to be looking in the opposite direction to the other. She spoke from behind two rather large front teeth in a kind of half Liverpool, half Manchester accent. She told Honey Heath how beautiful she thought he was, and then lisped at me, 'Look at you, you're so camp.'

44

I was wearing mascara I suppose, which was then quite unusual for a boy of fourteen. I had never thought of Honey Heath as beautiful and her comments rather surprised me – there's no accounting for taste I thought, probably a bit miffed. Her name was 'Jayne', she said. She had a kind of compelling confidence or largeness of personality. Her tall friend turned out to be a boy. He wore a white T-shirt, black drainpipe trousers, a red and black checked shirt open to the waist and girls' ankle boots with a stiletto heel. His hair was dyed jet black and teased out into a huge curly quiff that defied gravity. He wore a black pullover hung loosely around his shoulders. He looked like a lesbian Teddy boy. Very stylish – to me anyway. Through Ken Dodd teeth he said his name was Pete, and that he'd seen us in the Lisbon (a gay pub) last Saturday. 'Who does your hair?' he asked me.

'Me sister,' I replied. 'She works in Prides.'

My particular hairdo at that time was a hennaed Duck's Arse, brushed up from the sides into the middle all along my head and finished in a point at the front. It also looked a bit like a lesbian Teddy boy hairdo, but one with a Judy Garland fixation.

'Prides' had once been the best hairdressers in Liverpool, when the Shampoo and Set had reigned supreme, but had long been upstaged by the Cut and Blow. The word unisex was on everyone's lips, a style to be had in a rash of trendy new salons, with not a single curler or hood hairdryer in sight. The smell was still the same, mind you.

Anyway, these two exotic creatures worked in a salon called 'A Cut Above The Rest', Jayne as a receptionist on the front desk in the window, and Pete as an apprentice hairdresser. Provincial salon names like this were *de rigeur* in the Seventies – another favourite was 'Curl Up And Dye'.

Jayne had shaved her head and posed for the *Liverpool Echo* in order to get publicity for the salon. Denny the owner had stuck a butterfly on the side of her head as decoration. It was considered rather outrageous at that time, a female skinhead. She would even paint her head different colours to match her make-up or outfit. On this particular occasion I think it was silver.

45

Those two, Jayne and Pete, were to inspire my next round of
hairdo disasters and I fell in love with both of them immediately,
in my own way, though I tried my best not to let them know.

Pete *had* seen us in the Lisbon last Saturday and we had seen
them. My sister Clare had told me about the Lisbon, a pub where
Queers went. She would tell me stories about the Queers she
worked with in the hairdressing salon, their love lives and
terminology. 'An affair', I learned, was a boyfriend, used like
this: 'My affair said this but then my affair did the other.' 'Nafs'
were normals or heterosexuals.

I listened to my sister with disguised yet avid interest and made
notes. I heard about the Bear's Paw and Sadie's, nightclubs,
where Long John Baldry once played, with Elton John as his
keyboard player.

'He's a Queer y'know.'

'Elton John! are you sure?'

'Noooow, whatsisname. I don't think Elton John's a Queer,
no, can't be.' So went the hearsay.

The excuse we made to ourselves was 'At least we'll be left
alone and not get beaten up in a gay bar, the way we dress. After
all, we do think that we're bisexual, don't we?' Just like 'David'.

The fact was, I was dying to get inside the place. My curiosity
had to be satisfied. I think we had been a few times by now, with
what I thought was subtle MU on (MU, short for make-up, had
become a code word and we would use it, for example, in front of
Honey Heath's bemused parents: 'Have you bought your MU
with you?' he would ask, and I'd always say, 'Yes, I have') and
Honey Heath with his hair dyed peroxide blonde. I also wore one
red glove with tiny white stars printed on it that Honey Heath
had purloined from his grandmother's wardrobe. It became my
trademark conversation starter.

'Why do you wear only one glove?' asked a nice middle-aged
man.

'It's my *image*.'

This was on one of our first trips to the Lisbon bar. We would
order a drink, orange juice or something, and quickly sit behind
the stairs out of sight – we were only fourteen and should not

have been served. The nice middle-aged man later befriended us. His younger boyfriend had a St Helens accent. They both lived outside Liverpool and commuted into town on Sunday nights to meet for a drink. They both had moustaches and you would never have thought that they were 'Queer', we both agreed. They never tried to pick us up or anything like that. They told us that anyone that we might meet after 10.30pm when the pubs closed in Liverpool were 'Rubbish' and should be avoided. They also taught us some gay slang or Palare. 'Vada the riah on that bona homie!' meant, 'Look at the hair on that gorgeous man.' They both still lived with their mothers I think; one owned a launderette. They would go on holidays together to Malta every year. Their families were completely ignorant of their relationship even though one of them was in his forties. They made us feel welcome and comfortable.

One of their friends, a dwarfish man in his late sixties who wore a rather obvious toupee, told me that he lived in Childwall (a posh part of Liverpool) and asked me if I would go out to the cinema with him one night. He said there would be no strings attached and he assured me of a good time. I didn't really want to meet him unaccompanied. I never fully exploited my chicken status, which a more street-wise kid might have done.

There was a lack of openness between Honey Heath and me about our true sexual desires. I should repeat that in the early Seventies bisexuality was fashionable – it meant being like 'David' – whereas homosexuality had only ridiculous, stereotyped associations, like John Inman or Larry Grayson.

So neither of us was there for sex. We were still quite naïve, and were looking for something more glittering and glam. The apprentices from 'A Cut Above The Rest' turned up at the Lisbon one Sunday. They were all decked out in various styles, some with a thrift shop Fifties look, all with dyed hair and too much make-up. One of them was an oriental girl with a short blonde afro who looked particularly striking. Another girl called Jackie had a shiny black bob with bright red lipstick and wore a petrol blue boiler suit. In the pre-punk early Seventies it was all very new. They were checking us out just as much as we were

47

checking them out through the crowded pub. We were younger than they were and although we didn't have such good clothes, we looked more outrageous. Which was all that mattered.

* * *

One Christmas about this time I risked my life by asking Eric for a drink whose main marketing motif was a Bambi-like creature. I was about fourteen.

'Watcha 'aving then, our Bill?' Eric had said, in a cheery, Christmassy sort of way. The first alcoholic drink that a father offers his son. 'I think I'll have a Babycham,' I said. Eric's face turned puce. Was he going to have a coronary? 'That's a pfuckking taart's drink! No pfuckking son of mine's gonna have a pfuckking Babycham! If yer ordered that in an alehouse, every fucker'd laugh at yer!'

His little alehouse audience all grinned – Pat, Clare's boyfriend, perhaps John, too. I felt like shit at first, but it turned to disdain.

I was one Christmas fairy without a reindeer.

* * *

I discovered telescopic cigarette holders in gold plastic, which became another of my attention-seeking style statements. If Eric could have seen me, he would have killed me. Which he very nearly did.

My sister Clare snitched on me. She had seen me all dolled up to go out to the Lisbon. She claimed, years later, that she was worried about me going into town looking the way I did. Anyway, she told Eric that I was frequenting the Lisbon. According to Clare, he got into his cab and drove into town, storming into the Lisbon to find me. Fortunately I had left the pub either to get the bus home, or go back to Honey Heath's to stay the night, as I sometimes did. When I got home there was 'murder'.

'Queer baars! What do ye think yer doin' goin to pfuckkin

Queer baars, y'll get yer fuckin' 'ead kicked in going t' Queer baars!' he screamed. I said we only went there because we wanted to dress up. He pushed me into the front room. 'Get up to yer fuckin' room and stay there. You're not going out of that fuckin door again.' He clipped me around the ear, using backhanders to punctuate his words. Then he followed me up the stairs to backhand me some more, screaming, 'I'll teach ye t' go t' fuckin' Queer baars!' He made sure that any unusual items of clothing that I had collected were destroyed and thrown into the bin. Eric said Queers were beaten up in toilets and things, so I should make sure that I did not choose to become one. I believe he had this idea that being Queer was a 'choice', a cop-out from normal society. Men who were too lazy to support a wife and kids became Queers.

I think a meeting with Honey Heath's father was arranged, where it was decided that our friendship was to be banned. All financial assistance was removed and my fourteen-year-old life became a living hell.

But his punishment only heightened my feelings of injustice and persecution. Instead of just going out nights wearing make-up, I started to wear it in the daytime. I would turn up in school wearing Mary Quant kohl eyeliner, and complain when it attracted more mistreatment from both teachers and boys. I was *asking for it*.

I even decided to commit suicide. I persuaded our family doctor, Dr Belin, that I was having trouble sleeping. He prescribed something called Weldorm. After taking six or seven of these tablets one evening, I laid myself out on the couch in the front room, clutching a ring-binder full of my adolescent poetry. Death is sure to come, I thought, as I drifted off into a deep sleep. The empty packet of pills was placed nearby so everyone would know.

Apparently, I was discovered and my stomach nearly pumped, but when my parents rang the doctor he said that it was impossible to overdose on those particular tablets. I only remember the next morning being dragged out of bed and being forced to attend school in a somnambulist daze.

A Glory Hole

Meanwhile my sister Clare was being courted by a blonde boy called Lenny, who was always as white as a sheet. He was a soul music fan and brought some great records into the house. The Jackson Five, The Four Tops, Temptations, Isaac Hayes, Diana Ross, along with some other mainstream music like Elton John. Lenny had moved into a bedsit in Dovedale Road where Clare would go and visit him. Sometimes I would go round there and disturb them. After ten minutes or so of my ringing the bell, one of them, scantily clad, would open the door and let me in to the room where I could smell that unmistakeable smell of sex.

'I was just blow dryin' Lenny's hair, and didn't hear the bell. D'y'wanna cup o' tea?'

I knew that they were already 'doing it' as I had found Clare's contraceptive pills and condoms hidden in her room – probably in the same place where a few years before she had hidden her copy of *Skinhead*, the cultish Seventies trash novel. Teenagers of that time mostly read certain pages of this and other similar books – *Suedehead* was another. *Skinhead* had one well-thumbed passage, where the hero is let into the house and fucks his girlfriend as only a skinhead can ('ramming his pulsating shaft into her', if I remember rightly) only to be discovered by the girlfriend's mother who returns home early.

Lenny asked Clare to marry him and she said yes, at the age of sixteen. Nowadays she thinks she married the first person who asked her, just to have a good reason to leave home. The Johnson household *was* becoming increasingly tense. I was mooning about, commandeering the front room and blasting out whatever record I was absorbed in at the time: Bowie's 'Diamond Dogs' or Judy Garland's Greatest Hits. I had also started caterwauling into a cassette player, recording my 'performances' of Jacque Brel's 'Amsterdam' which I'd heard on the B side of a Bowie single. Or my own songs, dreadful dirges with titles like 'Troubador Mantra' or 'Voidsville'.

When my voice broke I had to relearn how to sing, trying to imitate Marc Bolan or David Bowie. I tried to develop my own style, which consisted of torturing strangulated sounds from my throat rather than natural tones.

Still being grounded after the Lisbon incident I'd often have hour-long phone conversations with Honey Heath. He wasn't on the phone and would ring me from a local phone box, posing in the dark like the back cover of 'Ziggy Stardust'. Sometimes we would meet in Newsham Park near his house instead of going to school as we had often done in the past, and sometimes, if Honey Heath had gone into school, I would end up hanging round there alone. A couple of times I was approached by men in the park. One, a bearded man of about thirty, approached me while I was huddled in a covered seating area.

'Do you want me to, y'know?'

'What d'ye mean?' I replied.

'Ye know,' he said with a wink.

I ran like hell, half wanting to stay and discover what he meant. But I had just read *Beyond Belief* about the Moors Murders, a paperback copy of which I'd found lying around the house.

On another occasion I was followed into the public toilet in Newsham Park by a man who, I'd noticed, would park his car outside the convenience and sit in wait. He was tall and quite attractive. He followed me and my heart started to beat faster. I went into one of the cubicles. He went into the other. A brick had been taken out at waist level (A Glory Hole). He whispered through the hole, 'Turn round and show us yer arse.' I froze. But he put his arm through the stall and gave me a wank. I was petrified and sexually excited at the same time. He said, 'I've got a car outside – do you wanna come?' This was too much, the prospect of actual face to face human contact, so I bolted out of the cubicle. He followed and smiled, motioning for me to get into his convertible. But again I ran like hell, not stopping till I got half a mile out of the park. I often regret not getting in that car and discovering my sexuality then, at fourteen. Other gay men that I know who had early experiences are often more comfortable with their sexuality and themselves.

* * *

Paco's bar was three steps away from the Lisbon. Honey Heath and I began to go there when Eric started to let me out again in the evenings. It was painted very red, covered in Art Nouveau-style mirrors with Mucha women printed on them. It was in a basement – dark and intimate. Boys got away with going to the girls' toilets, to fix their make-up or just to gossip, without too much hassle from the management. Older queens would scream and cackle with laughter when they saw Honey Heath and me. One queen, a chi chi 'Crossroads' queen, said: 'My God, I've never seen anything so camp in all my life.'

I was dumbstruck. I was under the illusion that I looked 'interesting' or 'individual' in my Forties swingback jacket, one glove and gold cigarette holder. Not, horror of horrors, 'camp', which to me then just meant outrageously effeminate.

'And what are you going to be when you leave school?' the poison queen continued, peering over her 'Noelle Gordon' tinted spectacles.

'An actress,' I replied.

In fits of laughter, off she minced into the night.

Another occasion in an upstairs cafe in the town centre one lunch hour, Honey Heath and I were assembled with a couple of the hairdressers from 'A Cut Above The Rest': Pete Burns and his new shadow, Lyn, who had straight red curtains of hennaed hair and was a bit plump, but hysterically funny in a sarcastic way. She was besotted, it seemed to me. A famous hairdresser, called Herbert, approached our table in a mink coat, to tell us how 'Fantastic' we looked, asking us our ages and gagging at our youth. He was famous in Liverpool and his business was, and probably still is, very successful. Liverpool's very own Liberace, he wore a full length fur coat, had as many rings as he had fingers, and lived in a pink house.

One night in the Lisbon, which I'd also begun to return to, Barry the DJ invited us to another club, the Bear's Paw. We told him that we had been once before and the doorman 'Jimmy' would not let us in, as we were too young. 'Just tell him Barry sent you,' which we did. Jimmy the doorman was young, blonde, and handsome, 'A *très butch* little number'.

The 'Cut Above' set were there and a couple of other 'dressers' we had not seen before. There was also a young barman called Pigg, who was later to become the sycophantic confidant of more than one northern Closet-Queen pop star. That night, though, I was overwhelmed by a very attractive twenty-two-year-old girl who said that she liked me because I looked like Angie Bowie.

Anastasia was rather beautiful with dark plum-coloured hair and a perfect white complexion. I told her I was bisexual, which was a mistake. She was all over me on the dance floor.

She asked me my name and 'Holly' came out of my mouth. I think we were dancing to 'Walk On The Wildside' by Lou Reed.

Honey Heath and I both hated our names. Billy Johnson just didn't sound glamorous to me. We would fantasise about exotic stage names we would use when we were famous – which we believed was inevitable. 'Holly', after Holly Woodlawn, the Warhol superstar, or perhaps Holly Golightly, was one of my favourites. On that night, the name just stuck. The androgyny of it suited me and the Zeitgeist perfectly.

Anastasia drank pineapple juice which she would sip and then transfer to my mouth in a French kiss. I was extremely flattered by her attention and did nothing to stop her advances. I arranged to meet her in town one lunch time. I explained that I was still at school and would be in my school uniform. She didn't mind. She took me back to her flat in Aigburth which she shared with a small-time drug dealer called Ricardo, who I thought was her boyfriend. He left to deliver some dope to which he had added mixed herbs, to make up the weight.

Anastasia pounced. She told me she was related to Russian royalty and that her name was Anastasia Petrouchka. I believed her. She climbed on top of me on the couch and we started necking. After about ten minutes I realised that I was supposed to go further. She had hitched her skirt up round her waist to reveal stockings, suspenders and no knickers. She was every (straight) young man's dream. Every time I put my hand on her quim she would give out a gasp. I realised that this was the desired effect. I don't know if I even managed to get it in, but I remember coming quite quickly, and then being extremely embarrassed as we sat smoking in front of the gas fire. I put on a record – a bad choice – a Cockney Rebel song about a sexually aggressive woman who would overpower her male victims. Like many people's first sexual experiences, it was a disaster.

We met once or twice again as 'girlfriend and boyfriend', the last time in the Bear's Paw. I burst into tears when I realised that I didn't want to go out with a girl any more. Anastasia was so embarrassed, as it looked as though she had done something terrible to me, which she hadn't. I'd done it to myself.

She didn't waste much time in transferring her affections to Honey Heath. The exact sequence of all these events is rather muddled in my memory, but I do remember staying over at Honey Heath's house. When it was time to go home, I pretended to leave to get the last bus home. Honey Heath then sneaked me upstairs to his room. I hid, doubled up inside a tea chest in the corner for over an hour. When the coast was clear I got out and into bed with him.

We had perfected this routine during our days playing truant. We would go to Honey Heath's house for lunch. Honey Heath's mum would give us lunch and then return to work. We would hide out in his bedroom, me in the box and him under the bed, so that we could stay in his house for the afternoon session instead of hanging out in the park. Sometimes Honey Heath's grandmother would come and check on the house and we would quickly retreat to our hiding places. She would search his room, breathing heavily after climbing the stairs as she was a heavy smoker. She was unable to bend over to check under the bed, but if somehow she did discover Honey Heath she would throw him out of the house. I would let him in a few minutes later, as she never would have thought to look in the tea chest. We later told people that I lived in a box in Honey Heath's bedroom and that he fed me by tube through a hole. I wrote a poem about it, something which I could always be depended on to do, about almost anything. *Crouched here in the dark, spine bent in my box, white holes in the wood and the smell of China tea across the sea . . .* It continued, making further references to a phallus trapped in vaginal walls and a foetus in a '*womb box*', as my adolescent, sex-obsessed poetry was inclined to do.

Honey Heath and I were never 'bum chums' however, which was the common, schoolyard way of describing our suspected activities. Along with BROWN HATTER, TURD BURGLAR, ARSE BANDIT, SHIRT LIFTER, PUFF, PANSY, QUEER, BODGER and QUEG. Sex involving anal penetration didn't really interest either of us. That was added to my sexual repertoire much later, when I was about twenty, by a headmaster of a primary school in Manchester. But, as they say, more of that to come.

It's Only Life

By November 1974 my sister Clare had escaped the Johnson household by moving into a flat in Old Swan, in a private block called Poulvara House. I would go and visit her and Lenny there in order to escape my parents. They had very little furniture apart from a huge spongy sofa-bed in brown swirling paisley material.

Eric paid for a full church wedding at St Mary's Church with a reception at a local hotel. Clare looked lovely with a plunging Empire neckline and 'leg of mutton' sleeves. I wore a casual tweed suit with extremely wide Oxford bags, and brown platform brogues. I remember dancing at the reception with a school friend of Clare's to 'Jean Genie' by David Bowie.

My elder brother John was moved into my sister's bedroom, leaving just Jimmy and me to share a room. I'd hated sharing a bedroom. At nineteen, John had a habit of coming in drunk late at night and waking me up. Sometimes he fell asleep with his trousers round his ankles and the light still on.

Sometime around then I was forced to go on a family holiday to a place called Gronant in North Wales. We were going to stay in a caravan on a caravan site. For weeks in advance I was dreading being cooped up in a caravan with Pat, Eric, Clare and Jimmy. I wrote a prose poem called 'The Last Resort' about an artificial Holiday Paradise.

The Last Resort was crammed with Zombies of every description. Hot from the production line these plastic people lie on the glass grains of sand. Their winter white bodies toasting under the Ultra Violate light of the giant sun ray lamps which hung from the azure ceiling of the Holiday Camp. Taped sea side sounds drift from the loudspeakers discreetly placed among the polystyrene rockery. Females, young and old, fresh from the factory floor, flock to The Last Resort in search of their male counterparts. A holiday romance, sex among the sand dunes, the last week in June.

After about two days of this holiday I moaned and 'created' so much that I managed to get myself sent home to Liverpool, where John had stayed put. This was a bad idea as he immediately beat me up. There had been an argument, probably my resisting him exerting his authority over me in some way. As he left the room I think I clicked my fingers at his back, which resulted in him turning round and belting me. From that moment on and for about two and half years afterwards I didn't speak to him, even though he was living in the same house. He would make many attempts to goad me into speaking to him but I ignored him with incredible diligence. I despised him, in a way only a bullied younger brother can despise. If anyone ever asked me about him I would reply, 'My brother is an alcoholic, I never speak to him, he is the scum of the Earth.' This exaggeration of the facts I would deliver with the most serious tone I could manage.

*　　*　　*

I had somehow heard of William Burroughs's *The Wild Boys* and also Jean Genet's *Our Lady Of The Flowers*. They weren't readily available, so I would go to Phillips Son and Nephew (the largest bookshop in Liverpool) in my lunch hour and order them. I bought *The Wild Boys* in paperback for twenty five pence, the best five bob I ever spent. This vision of a tribe of multi-racial, shaven-headed, homosexual Wild Boys really fired my imagination. The strange style, half prose, half poetry: I didn't quite understand it, but I knew I loved it. I wanted to shave my head immediately, like the boys on the cover.

Jean Genet's style in *Flowers*, *Funeral Rights* and *Querelle Of Brest* was amazingly beautiful. Often the meaning escaped me, but I didn't care – I had found the 'Wild Side' I had been looking for. These books, along with the records I would listen to over and over again, were my refuge from a world where I felt I had no control, no power to do as I pleased – although, like most teenagers, I think in the end I did what I wanted to do anyway.

I hope this never sounds self-pitying or whining. Most of the problems I faced at home and at school would have been avoided if I had been prepared to conform. I could have taken on the trappings of male heterosexuality – lager, football and girlfriends – and entered the dark closet, as some gay men do. But I never could resist my heart's desire.

'It's only life' was a phrase that Honey Heath and I would use when we talked over our problems. As if we would have our revenge in another state of being. I said this after I had scratched a love-heart pierced with a dagger insignia, copied from the cover of Alice Cooper's 'Killer' album, on to my desk in the physics lab. As we sat at the same bench every time we used this room my handiwork was attributed to me, so I was sent to the lower school headmaster's office. He was a rugby player with a ruddy complexion and blunt, broken-nosed features. A Tom of Finland illustration without the sense of humour. He made me sign my name in a punishment book and then told me to bend over, giving me six sharp whacks on the backside with a bamboo cane that left imprints on my arse for days. Afterwards he just stood there in his black robes with disdain in his eyes. I thought he was a vile man. Years later, when I had left school for good, I saw him again while I was browsing in a bookshop. The look he gave me was meant to wither, but I just smiled back sweetly with the confidence and the knowledge that I was no longer under his jurisdiction.

In a way I should thank all these oppressors: the teachers, the schoolboys who baited me relentlessly, my parents who didn't understand me. It was because of these experiences that I became more determined to travel my own course in life to avoid being like them. I was fuelled by strange desires, revenge being only one of them.

Johnny Go Home

In my third and fourth years at the Collegiate I had as a form master the blonde rugby-playing teacher that I have described earlier as featuring in my sexual fantasies, Mr Jones. Not only was he physically attractive to me – his English lessons, when I attended them, were extremely interesting. The required reading in the curriculum consisted of Charles Dickens's *Great Expectations* and Shakespeare's *Merchant of Venice*, neither of which I particularly enjoyed, but works by the war poets fired my interest – Wilfred Owen and Siegfried Sassoon – as did 'Fern Hill' and 'Do not go gentle into that good night' by Dylan Thomas, and a number of poems by Gerard Manley Hopkins – *'and (ah) bright wings'*.

At home I read George Orwell's *Nineteen Eighty Four* in a paperback edition whose cover had a detail of a William Roberts painting, 'The War Room'. I loved this picture and dreamed of one day owning one by this wonderful artist. My interest in Orwell was in response to the David Bowie songs '1984' and 'We are the dead' from the 'Diamond Dogs' album that I was still playing over and over. The album depicted an apocalyptic future horror show. Reports from America of David Bowie's promotional tour for this album were tantalising: his use of surreal theatrical devices, sets and costumes set a precedent for rock music performance. I was also discovering the Velvet Underground's music and Andy Warhol's 'Exploding Plastic Inevitable', a multi-media art and music performance. This was an exciting period of discovery for me. I wanted to be a 'Multi-Media Artist'.

* * *

One day in a fit of rage – a response to a noisy and inattentive

59

class – Mr Jones demanded from us all a two-page essay on the subject of 'Life'. Everybody groaned, especially as it had to be in the next day. For my 'essay' I cobbled together a rather long poem of my feelings at the time, and snatches of things from the past. I was watching TV and a politician was denouncing 'bastard children' or something. All of this went into the 'work' which I handed in the next day and promptly forgot about for a couple of weeks. As they were written as a punishment, we didn't expect our essays to be returned or a grade given. A few weeks later Mr Jones told me that he had submitted my poem to be published in the school magazine and 'did I mind?' As I had little memory of the contents of the poem and because I was flattered by his attention I said that it was all right by me. As a result of this I was summoned to the head of the English department's classroom and asked if I had any other such works. 'Lots,' I replied, not thinking, and promised to show them to him. This was a promise that I never kept, however, because on looking through my poetry I realised it was mostly of the whimsical variety that I described earlier. There was very little written in the style of the work he had seen, and to show him my old work would have been too embarrassing, I felt.

An older boy caught me on the stairs after having read the published poem, grabbed me by the scruff of the neck and screamed, 'So that's what life's like when you're a Queer is it?' He shouted with such malice, his face turned maroon with anger. Luckily, in the rush of boys going home, he lost his grip on me and I fled. Just another close shave with a bully. This I had got quite used to, even come to expect. At least he had bothered to read it, I thought. At least he understood something of my life.

The attention from the English master kept me going into school for a while, but by the fourth year Honey Heath's and my truancy had become dangerously regular. Our parents were eventually notified by the local Education Authorities. After the initial drama, it was suggested that we should both make weekly visits to an Educational Psychologist. Honey Heath's parents agreed to this, but Eric mumbled something like, 'No son o' mine is goin' to a psychiatrist'. Horror of horrors, to admit that a Johnson may have needed professional help.

On his first visit Honey Heath was shown some pictures. One was of a man's face. 'What's missing?' he was asked.

'Nothing,' he replied. The psychologist gave him a searching look. What was missing, in fact, was the man's eyebrows. Honey Heath had recently shaved his off, in what we thought was a radical fashion statement. I shaved mine sometime after. When I tried to grow them back a few years later, they grew outwards at an odd angle and have never been the same since.

* * *

During the early and mid Seventies, there were three programmes on television that were of particular interest to gay people. One was the wonderful 'A Naked Civil Servant' which, as most people know, was based on the autobiography of Quentin Crisp, published in 1968. John Hurt's portrayal of the outrageously effeminate and eccentric character was an inspiration. Instead of shouting 'Queer' or 'Puff', boys would shout 'Quentin' at me from cars or buses or from the other side of the street. It was through this programme and after reading the book that I became acquainted with henna.

Henna is a vegetable dye that is mixed with hot water and applied like mud to hair or skin to achieve a strong orange-red colouring. The longer you leave it on, the stronger the colour would seem to get. I think it was Pete Burns from 'A Cut Above The Rest' who told me that if I applied the henna then wrapped my head in cling-film before going to bed, a most vibrant colour would be achieved. This I did several times, ruining my pillow cases in the process. Parental detection was inevitable, and I suffered Pat's and Eric's wrath. But what did it matter? I had the brightest, shiniest red hair for miles around.

The second of these television programmes was a documentary about a Liverpudlian called Joe. He had agreed to participate in what the programme called Aversion Therapy. Joe was a gay man in his late twenties or early thirties who was obviously unhappy with his sexual orientation or, more correctly perhaps, had been made unhappy by an ignorant and hostile heterosexual society. He would attend regular clinics in a special caravan where he was shown, alternately, pictures of naked men and naked women. Whenever he expressed excitement or pleasure on seeing a picture of a nude man – 'Nice arse!' he said in reaction to one blonde model – a short, sharp, electric shock would be administered to him. Joe was, of course, a volunteer. He hoped that the treatment would work. This idea of homosexuality as an illness, treatable by Aversion Therapy, was a terrible thing for me to watch in my mid-teens, as I tried to come to terms with my sexuality. I doubt that this treatment has ever been successful, and anyone consenting to it must be pitied, as their desire to conform to a mode of behaviour alien to themselves is to deny their God-given instincts and desires. Never will they find a moment's happiness. Self-loathing and shame are the gifts that Christianity and heterosexual society try to thrust on to the male homosexual.

The third of these programmes was *Johnny Go Home*, which chronicled male prostitution or rent boys in London in the early Seventies and the murder of a young man lured into the web of an unscrupulous warden who picked up young runaways at Euston railway station and offered them accommodation in a hostel. The first half of the programme showed an amusement arcade in Piccadilly called Playland, which was apparently a well-known place where young homeless boys would sell their arses to older men. The second half was more sinister and told the story of a young man who had been found dead in a ditch after staying at the hostel. Male prostitution is always shown in the media as somehow more depraved and shocking than heterosexual prostitution, which is often portrayed as merely titillating. Instead of discouraging young people from running away from home, the publicity led many to go on a pilgrimage to this very place. And that summer, Honey Heath and I saved our money and took the coach to London to see the legendary Meat Rack in Piccadilly and to stand outside Playland, wondering which boys were prostitutes. Too scared to go inside, we searched for 'Bright lights, Soho, Wardour Street' as described in David Bowie's Anthony Newley-style song from the Sixties, 'The London Boys'.

'What would you do if someone asked you to wank them off for a fiver?' I asked Honey Heath.

'It would depend on what they looked like,' was the cautious reply.

We had seen London, we thought. I was convinced that people looked wealthier, happier, and the sun shone brighter in London. As the bus pulled out of Victoria Coach Station to take us back to Liverpool before our parents noticed we were gone, we both vowed that we would return one day to live in this exciting Metropolis.

Madame Menopause

Later, the relationship with Honey Heath started to change. We both started to make new friends through our night club visits, and he befriended a girl called Pam, who, although she was very nice, was only interested in him, not me. Perhaps I started to feel possessive. Anastasia had also fallen head over heels for Honey Heath, and decided that she would move to London and try to set up a flat for them both to live. She worked as a residential chambermaid in a hotel in the West End. My relationship with Honey Heath was not without trauma. As with all people who cling together, there were arguments. These became more regular as his relationship with Anastasia improved. I wasn't jealous of their relationship but I think that she was wary of my relationship with him. Maybe she tried to discourage it, I don't know.

While this was all happening I somehow managed to start an Art class at school, dropping Spanish (or Spanish dropping me), and pleading with the Art master to take me on. I had a certain aptitude for drawing. Not an extremely technical talent, but one above the standard of the other boys. I worked on a drawing at home for many months of a naked decomposing negress that I called Madame Menopause. The finished drawing I mounted on the obituary page of the *Liverpool Echo* and gave to Honey Heath. I was very proud of this piece of work.

For some reason the Art master, Mr Pitt, didn't tell me there was such a thing as an Arts Foundation course that could be applied for. As I was now in the fourth or fifth year of the Collegiate, careers information was being given, although in a rather half-hearted way.

This is something I have always regretted – not getting the right advice. Although I was a compulsive truant, I still managed to pass quite a number of the mock 'O' levels that I took in early 1976, including Art and English. This might have suggested to any interested parties the direction I should take in further education. But unfortunately there were no interested parties. The Careers Officer insisted that Liverpool was a centre of commerce and that a job in an office was the thing. This became my greatest fear: working in a job that was wholly uncreative. I decided in May of 1976, after an intensive period of revision for my mock 'O' levels, that I was not going to sit the actual exams. If I did manage to get an average amount of qualifications, I thought, then I would end up in an average and soul-destroying job. Although it may have been a self-justifying argument, to rationalise my natural laziness, I think there might also have been an element of *wanting* to disappoint my father, who used to bully me into doing homework, and who always put great emphasis on an education that he had missed out on.

Influenced by my sister and the fashionables at 'A Cut Above The Rest', I did entertain the idea of becoming a hairdresser for a few weeks. I even applied to the same technical college as Clare. But Eric forbade any idea of his son becoming a 'Teasy Weasy'. The fact was, I didn't really want a job. I was secretly convinced that I was a genius. It was only a matter of time before the whole world would know.

* * *

I remember that because of my truancy, I was not allowed to have a door key to our house, in case I let myself in during the day. In fact when I think back, my parents made every effort to keep me out of their house as often as they could. I spent many hours sitting on the doorstep waiting for Pat to come home from work. By this time she was working as an auxiliary nurse in a children's heart clinic in Myrtle Street Children's Hospital. At home she would spend hours complaining to Eric about the maltreatment she had to suffer from nurses, Sisters or administrators at work. To hear her talk, a day did not go by without a major insult or injustice happening to her. 'People can be so hateful,' I can still hear her say. The change of life was starting to alter her personality and her mood-swings had become more and more unpredictable.

In the early days I remember her going out drinking to the pubs in Old Swan with Eric on his nightly sprees. She even made a friend called Maria, a rather common (I thought), bottle-blonde woman who lived in the flats in Old Swan. (Pat and Eric would *never* live in flats.) But then, all of a sudden, Pat wouldn't go out with Eric to the pubs any more. She would sit in watching the TV, which was a drag for us, who would rather have got both parents out of the way. Occasionally she would have a week or so when she would go out again with Eric. On one of these occasions she collapsed in the front room and regurgitated a half-digested Chinese take-away all over the carpet. As Eric was already in bed sleeping it off, it was left to me to clean up the mess. I'll never forget cleaning up those undigested garden peas and the smell of lager and lime. I suppose this was Pat's revenge for all the wet sheets she'd had to wash for me as a child.

I remember her arguing with Eric, usually over money. She would sleep downstairs on the couch for weeks on end as some kind of protest. He was still taking a percentage of her monthly wages off her 'to pay the bills' as he put it. Whenever she got a pay-rise or did some overtime, she would hide her payslips so he couldn't detect the increase and she would have a few pounds to spend on herself. She tried running a mail order catalogue from which people would order things and pay her in instalments, but this never seemed to work and people would stop the payments after a few weeks. Her days as an Avon Lady were similarly doomed. She complained to me that she had been moved about from school to school as a child, and never had the chance to settle down and get an education. 'That's why I can't spell,' she used to say.

El Masquerade

In early 1976 a new law was passed that allowed pupils who had passed their sixteenth birthday to leave school in May rather than wait until the end of the school term in July. I don't know why this new law came in, but I acted on it. I left a school that had been a living hell for me and immediately signed on at the Social Security Office in Picton Road. Unemployment was rising fast in Liverpool at this time, and many young people left school and signed on the dole. Liverpool was one of the first towns to experience the post-industrial decline that is now, over fifteen years later, being felt in London and the rest of the world.

In my stupid, arrogant teenage way, I was certain I was going to rise above it all; and I didn't want a mundane nine-to-five job slowing me down. I wanted glamour, limousines, fancy restaurants, Andy Warhol parties, and, most important of all, I wanted revenge. Revenge for boys who had kicked me in the corridor; revenge for Eric's doubting I'd ever amount to anything.

With my first Social Security cheque in my hot little hand, and after paying Eric an allotted amount of rent, I went out and bought myself a pair of winklepicker shoes and some drainpipe jeans. Drainpipe jeans were quite hard to find in the Oxford bag days of 1976. The only place that had old stock from the Sixties was the Army and Navy store in town. They sold Lybro jeans that had pronounced white stitching. The winklepickers I bought from the 'old Jew man's shop', his stock left over from the Fifties. By this time I had started to experiment with the shape of my hairline, shaving it up at the sides and the back. I felt I was a star on any street I walked down. I even shaved my hair off completely at one point having given in to my William Burroughs's Wild Boy fantasy. When Eric saw what I had done, his baiting of me caused another one of my suicide bids, which only made me vomit all over the kitchen floor.

I started hanging around with some of the 'A Cut Above The Rest' crowd, particularly a striking oriental lesbian called Stella (the fella). She was very striking to look at; her skin was a pale yellow colour and her cropped hair was dyed blonde. She wasn't much older than me but had moved away from home and had her own flat. Her father had been particularly cruel to her, I think, and she had a lot of emotional problems to cope with. She would sometimes be very cold and abusive towards me and at other times, kind and friendly. Stella was a good hairdresser though, and started experimenting on my head. I would sometimes stay over at her flat, sleeping on the couch whenever we went out nightclubbing. Eric couldn't have been more pleased when he heard I was sleeping over at a girl's flat. Such was his desire for me to be straight, he convinced himself that I was sleeping with Stella. He started to be a bit less strict about my comings and goings.

A Liverpool poet called Pete O'Halligan had opened a clothes market and sometime theatre in Mathew Street called Aunt Twacky's. (Auntwacky was the slang word in Liverpool for old-fashioned or antique.) This was the start of the second-hand clothing boom. Fifties clothes like Hawaiian shirts or glitzy ball gowns were in vogue – a cheap way of dressing in recessionary times. There were lots of different stalls run by eccentric-looking people. One was a male to female transsexual who called himself Layla. Jayne, the bald receptionist from 'A Cut Above The Rest' left this job and opened a stall selling old clothes. I remember I was in love with a pair of gold winklepicker ankle boots on her stall. I used to go in and hang around her while I was playing truant in town. Gay people were always attracted to Jayne – she was the kind of larger-than-life woman that a gay man might want to be.

Once I went in to show Jayne a new liquid, theatrical make-up I had discovered. It was a kind of chalky, white powder suspended in water. She offered to apply it for me and slapped it on in a blotchy and haphazard fashion. 'You look lovely,' she lied

68

theatrically in her most patronising tone. It wasn't true at all. She was just saying it so I'd walk around town looking foolish. Which I did.

*   *   *

Since The Beatles there had been few if any internationally successful bands or solo artists coming out of Liverpool. Very soon however, The Real Thing, a black vocal group, would have considerable chart success. They had already come to the public's attention through an appearance on a television talent show, 'Opportunity Knocks'.

Deaf School actually got themselves on to the cover of the *NME* and signed a record deal with Warner Brothers. There were a lot of people in the band: two male singers, and two female singers, with other odd characters, mainly Art students. Most of them had exotic names like Enrico Cadillac Jr, Betty Bright, The Reverend Max Ripple and Frankie Average. I believe that this group influenced the later punk fashion for unusual stage names. The politics of the group seemed to be escapist and romantic, sub Roxy Music. It was rumoured that the soon-to-be famous Bromley Contingent, consisting of Siouxsie, Billy Idol *et al*, tried to get backstage at an early Deaf School show in London.

*   *   *

Around this time I made my first trip to Manchester with a party of hairdressers from 'A Cut Above The Rest'. I had progressed to wearing a mohair jumper (one that belonged to my first primary school teacher Miss Schofield, whom I had been in love with) with my drainpipes and winklepickers. Julian Cheep was one of the hairdressers whom I befriended, one of those tall, thin, fey creatures. He played me the Rocky Horror Show album, and would say things like, 'I love Russia because it's so bleak; I hate the French because they're so French'. Julian and I went to a gay club in Manchester called the Ranch, supposed to be in vogue at that time. It was a very small, typically provincial gay club, with the average clientele, except for two tiny girls who were Vidal Sassoon hair models and had the most fantastic look I'd ever seen. One of them, who said her name was Coco, was wearing a pair of black PVC dungarees with a SEX label on the front – we were all dead jealous. This is my first memory of seeing someone wear Vivienne Westwood and Malcolm McLaren's clothes. Malcolm and Vivienne were just ahead of the game busy changing the name and style of their shop, from selling Fifties-influenced clothes ('Let It Rock'), to 'SEX' – selling rubber and PVC fetish- (and gay-) influenced fashions. There were still a lot of hippies about but they were starting to look rather tired.

By this time the Bear's Paw had stopped letting us in. The boys were wearing too much make-up and looking too weird. We tried Sadie's Bar Royal, another gay club, many times before we were let in. I, for one, was under age, and with my shaved head and white face make-up, was too much. Pete and Lyn, who had become a sort of couple by this time, seemed to have more money than everyone else. They started to make trips to London and came back with clothes from 'SEX'. Their look had become more and more extreme, rather influenced by Jordan, the legendary 'SEX' sales girl and muse.

At Sadie's Bar Royal, mingling with our crowd, I met for the first time Paul Rutherford – Rudderpuff as he was known in school. We must both have been about fifteen. He worked for Jayne in 'Aunt Twacky's' on a Saturday and was sporting a red check shirt look that Pete from 'A Cut Above' had just discarded. We didn't become friends immediately although we made each other laugh. Paul seemed shy then, hanging round with a fat girl called Gillian who was apparently his 'girlfriend'. They were Roxy Music fans, they said, and both tried to look attractive rather than strange. Paul insisted he wasn't Queer. He had a lisp and laughed like a hyena at my jokes.

That night I wore a black and white striped T-shirt with a black eyepatch painted over one eye, and carried a ticking pillowcase as a handbag. More dash than cash. On the way I had been searched by the police, who actually believed that the pillowcase was my swag-bag. Such was the level of intelligence of the Liverpool police force.

There was someone else at Sadie's that night who was to become a part of the Liverpool 'scene'. He was a bit older than all of us and quite attractive, despite the acne and the eyeliner. He eyed us furtively from a table on the other side of the club. He had his hairline shaved up above his ears, but with two bleached stripes on the sides. When everyone met up later in the toilets to fix make-up and gossip, away from the loud disco music, I said, 'Your hair's fab. I had mine like that two years ago.'

Frank fancied himself as a bit of a dancer and posed on the dance-floor. I can't remember how, but we became not quite friends – more verbal sparring partners. Years later I met his sister Margie, and he went on to write *A Letter to Brezhnev*, a fabulous, internationally successful motion picture – his words, not mine. It took him a long time to realise his talent – a wonderful – if provincial – sense of humour. I think maybe the reason we never really got on was because we're too alike.

When Stella, Julian Cheep, I and a few others started to go to El Masquerade (or the Massie) it was in a backstreet off Dale Street. It had a nightmare quality. We knocked on the door and were greeted by a strange-looking man called Harry, middle aged, with pale skin and unnaturally dyed black hair with long sideburns. He wore wide-lapelled suits and too many rings. When we first presented ourselves to him at the door of his establishment he looked a bit afraid. We were the new breed of young outrageously dressed Queers. We begged him to let us in. I inadvertently said the magic words, 'Sadie won't let us in his place.' Harry and Sadie had an ongoing feud, so rumour had it, so he let us all in.

Behind the bar were plastic clown masks, backlit with coloured light bulbs, laughing manically. There was a faded and dusty carnival aspect to the place. In the ladies' toilets where we always congregated, we met some gay women who worked as prostitutes. 'Me name's Jean and I'm a ship girl y'know. You

71

should see me coming off those ships in the mornin'. Staggering down the gang plank with me legs apart. I can 'ardly walk. Ha ha ha ha!'

I remember her short, blonde, overpermed hair, frizzed out in the heat and moisture of the basement club. She was one of the more friendly regulars, the others seeming to be there to 'cop off' (find a shag for the night) or get drunk. Occasionally you would see a kind of truck-driver transvestite or a fabulous black drag queen called 'Diana Ross'. We were all there to pose, dance, and have some fun. Harry soon got used to us and saw the advantage of our entertaining little troop in his nightclub. For years afterwards he used to whisper intimately into my ear, as I came and went from his club: 'Why don't you dress outrageoussss? Like you used to.' Once Julian Cheep produced some plastic flowers, and danced with me to Lou Reed's 'Vicious' ('You hit me with a flower . . .'), whipping me with the plastic bouquet.

There were a couple of records that they played which were the trademark of El Masquerade: one, by Doris Day I think, was called 'Masquerade', another one by a female vocalist whose name escapes me, was entitled 'Queer Things Are Happening To Me'. The last record of the night was always 'Spanish Eyes' by Perry Como. This was always the final dancefloor grope record – if you hadn't copped off by 'Spanish Eyes', tough luck.

Back then in the Seventies, gay clubs were carefully monitored by the police and a strict membership code was operated. I think that there were more false names and addresses on those lists than real ones, but I remember naïvely giving my real ones. I was lucky that the police never turned up on our doorstep.

How Common

Clare and Lenny managed to get a mortgage on a house in Aigburth. It was in need of modernisation, but was a fairly nice terraced house, suitable for a young couple. They also had a child around March of 1976, whom they called Ben. Clare recently told me that I visited her in hospital before Ben's birth with my hairline shaved into a Dracula-like point at the front. To accentuate the effect I had added an inch on to the point with make-up and had drawn a black line around my hairline. I might, subconsciously, have been inspired by a man in Liverpool who was bald. In order to disguise this, he spread black shoe polish on his head where hair would have been, and continued about his daily life, working in Lewis's the big department store in town. For his efforts he was given the nickname Cherry Blossom, although I don't know if anyone ever called him this to his face.

Clare wanted to go back to work soon after Ben was born, so she put a proposition to me. I had been unsuccessful in finding a job, something Pat and Eric urged me to do on a daily basis: 'Get a job ye' lazy, pfuckking goodfornothin' bastard!'

Clare proposed that if she took a job in the kitchens of the Bluecoat School around the corner, she could drop Ben off at my parents' home for me to look after, while she was at work. She would pay me a few quid a week for doing this. As Ben was only nine months old, I had to learn how to fold terry-towelling nappies into kite shapes, how to bottle feed him, and all the usual baby business. I quite enjoyed all of this, except for the times when he would scream uncontrollably for no apparent reason. Once, he rolled off the couch in the living room, when I went out of the room to make a cup of tea. He was unharmed – babies have a certain amount of bounce I believe. This bounce deserted him on one occasion, however. I was changing his nappy one afternoon when Clare returned from work. She rushed upstairs to the lavatory. Ben was crawling around nappy-less while I was locating and folding a clean one. He crawled out into the hall where I thought his mother was, and followed her up a few stairs, falling back down again and screaming very loudly. Clare rushed out of the lavatory and I rushed out of the living room to see what was wrong. He seemed to be all right, there was no blood or anything, but he would not stop crying. Clare took him to a casualty department where she discovered he had broken his leg. I felt so guilty: the poor child. He was to prove accident-prone however. The week he had his plaster-cast taken off his leg, he broke his arm.

So this little job didn't last for too long and I was back to watching daytime TV. Eric would come home for his lunch and harangue me about my unemployment. I was unemployable. There were already too many freaks at 'A Cut Above The Rest' and it was unlikely that any other establishment would have taken me on, looking the way I did. It's hard to imagine now but in those days people in Liverpool were not used to boys with dyed hair and earrings.

My left ear was pierced under unhygienic conditions by a Queen who wanted to supplement his supplementary benefit, with a stud gun, one evening in the Lisbon. There had been an earlier abortive attempt in front of the mirror above Honey Heath's fireplace. A needle was boiled, then an ice cube rubbed on the lobe. I managed to get the needle through without passing out but the hole it made wasn't big enough to accommodate the sleeper that I had 'borrowed' from my mother.

* * *

The *NME* started to report a strange phenomenon: just a review here and there at first, then things started to hot up. The Sex Pistols and the Clash were born, and in their wake a thousand bandwagoneers, who were inspired by the new 'Punk' attitude. Bands who could not even play their instruments would very soon be up on stage and have a record out. 'Anarchy In The UK' was released by the Sex Pistols. I had to pester my local record shop for weeks in advance to order it. I put it on the turntable and played it loud, unsure at first that I liked this guitar-dominated sound. I liked the reviews I had read and the photographs I had seen, but the sound? I wasn't sure.

The clothes worn by the Clash were more accessible to the unemployed youths they were singing for and about, but the Sex Pistols had the sartorial edge. The Clash were first to have an album out, which I bought and enjoyed – although I was disappointed that there was no lyric sheet. Bowie and Bolan albums had always had lyric sheets. Young people in their droves had been turning up for Roxy and Bowie nights at discos and it was all becoming a bit commonplace. What had earlier been a fairly exclusive obsession had become the mainstream. Bryan Ferry had descended into bourgeois lounge-lizarddom and had even made bitchy comments about Bowie in the press, so he was definitely out of favour. Bowie had done his 'Thin White Duke' and 'The Man Who Fell to Earth'. There was a need for something new.

What I did like about Punk was that, almost overnight, the abuse changed. Instead of 'Hom!' or 'Puff!', people would shout 'Punk Rocker!' at me. Whenever someone screamed at me in the street, I thought 'How Common'. 'Common' was a word Honey Heath's mother would have used. 'Common' meant betting shops, wearing gold sovereigns and sheepskin coats, smoking woodbines, putting Kraft cheese slices in sandwiches, and the men coming home pissed from the pub with brewer's droop. Heterosexuality is *terribly* common – to me Queers are infinitely more interesting. But 'How Common' was a phrase I certainly over-used at this time, in my teenage snob, daydream world. My elder brother John, who had now gone to do season work in Jersey, working as a barman or a steward on the ships, I always thought of as 'Most Common'.

'At least he's got a job!' my mother would scream.

'You,' said Eric, 'lazy, good-for-nothing bastard. Get a pfuckking job.'

'But I don't want to get a job. I want to be like David Bowie.'

'Then learn bloody music then.' Eric would say. 'I've never heard you play a single thing I recognise on that guitar that I bought yer.' He went on. 'David Bowie! 'ees got no voice whatsoever, what d'ye wanna sound like 'im for? Why don't you play the pubs – earn a few bob? Why caan't ye play like Johnny Cash or Waylon Jennings. "San Quentin I hate every inch of you", and that. Learn to pfuckking play!'

During the summer of 1975 Eric had come home with a wonderful shiny Epiphone six string acoustic guitar that I loved (I still cherish it). It wasn't Honey Heath's twelve string, but it was better quality. He didn't tell me where he bought it though, which made me a bit suspicious. It might have fallen off the back of a lorry, an extremely regular occurrence in Liverpool. It's the only time he encouraged my creative vent, although he was giving me a Country and Western guitar whilst I was accepting it as a prop for androgyny.

I wrote more songs on this guitar. I made a demo tape of some of these by using two cassette players and 'overdubbing' – playing what I had just played and sung on to the first cassette, while singing into the other cassette, which gave a crude double-tracking effect.

I sent the tape with a handwritten copy of the lyrics to EMI, who had just signed the then sixteen-year-old Kate Bush. I received a rejection slip with the usual blurb. I wasn't too disappointed though, as I had only confided in Honey Heath, so we were the only ones who knew.

After about six months the Department of Social Security decided that I had to go all the way to Green Lane in Old Swan to sign on. This was a drag – it not only took time, it cost money. Two hairdressers, ex-workmates of Clare, had opened up their own salon in Old Swan. One was a Greek boy called Jannis and the other was called Barry. I used to go and visit them after signing on and would sometimes help about the shop, doing the odd shampoo. Usually I would just entertain them with gossip. They were not Scene Queens, and seemed to have a stable relationship which I realised was quite unusual. Most gay men were single and a lot of them were Cottage Queens.

I never really became a full-time Cottage Queen, although the delights of tea-time trade are all wrapped up in adrenalin, anonymity and the instinctive fight or flight response. Some people can't have sex otherwise. I was warned by articles I'd read in *Gay News* about 'Agent Provocateurs', which I then thought meant a special branch of the police force who masqueraded as Queers and entrapped you in a toilet. I wasn't far wrong, was I? There was a lot of this kind of thing reported in the gay press, which was distributed only through gay clubs at this time. I was extremely disappointed that I didn't own a copy of the *Gay News* that included the famous so-called 'blasphemous' poem that garnered so much media attention in the Seventies.

I never felt that I fitted in on the gay scene and started to look around for something new. The flamboyant way I dressed was off-putting to people who didn't want to advertise their sexuality; campness has a low currency on the sex scene. Moreover sex didn't mean much to me then; I wouldn't stop wearing eye make-up just to cop-off with some Queer.

Around this time Jayne moved from her clothes stall in 'Aunt Twacky's' to a small self-contained shop by the side of St Luke's Church at the top of Bold Street. She was still commuting from Manchester every day, where she lived in comfortable domesticity with the accountant brother of the owner of 'A Cut Above The Rest'. She was definitely the type of girl who would always marry the boss, wherever she worked. It wasn't till then that we actually got to know each other and became friends. I knew it bothered her slightly that we had a very similar look – shaved heads with stubble, dyed blonde. I had started wearing boiler suits and khaki dungarees by then, which I felt covered me up. My weight was always up and down and could not be depended upon.

I started to go to a club called Eric's in Mathew Street that everyone was talking about. The Sex Pistols had played there, and it was gaining a reputation. Eric's was situated opposite the site of the Cavern in Mathew Street, now Cavern Walks Arcade. There was a plaque/statue commemorating the Beatles on the wall outside the club, which tourists would come and photograph. It wasn't a gay club and in the early days the bouncers on the door gave people who looked strange or young a lot of hassle. Sometimes they tried to stop us coming in. It was good to go with Jayne as her gift of the gab always got us in without paying – which could be a major expense if there was a band on. Fairly soon an elite group became established, who didn't have to pay and who were part of the furniture.

I would get ready at Stella's flat as usual. She would maybe cut my hair, and we would then go to Eric's. On one occasion I pestered her to do what was then called intercutting – that is, cutting lines into short, cropped hair just like the designs that you see on every other young, black kid today. Then it was new, and only one hairdresser in Liverpool had tried it. I arrived at Eric's that night and in walked Jayne with an almost identical design cut into her hair. She gave Stella, who had done the experiment, an extremely loaded look.

Stella, like many young and adventurous people, started to get itchy feet and wanted to move down to London. She was like me in many ways, but more emotionally damaged, with fierce independence and ambition fuelled by her sexuality and parental problems. The boys I met at Eric's fancied Stella like mad. They couldn't really comprehend the fact that such an attractive girl could be a lesbian. She meanwhile got more and more frustrated with the lack of young dykes on the Liverpool scene.

Eric's became a second home for a lot of us. Someone once said, 'You could have a nervous breakdown in Eric's and no one would notice.' I actually did notice one night a particular person slouched on the floor against the wall of the room where the bands played, jabbering into his plastic pint of lager in a very depressed state.

If you got past the bouncers and the front office, there was a small lobby and a staircase going underground. The club was split up into three areas: the bar and seating area with a small juke-box room off it, then the main room with a dance floor, stage and DJ booth, and a small kitchen at the back. In the daytime it had a most disgusting smell – I always wondered where the smell went at night.

Through going to Eric's I met lots of interesting people including Sue and Lori Larty who were two beautiful young sisters who had moved to Calderstones, not far from where I lived. They became good friends who I used to go and visit at home and at the Art school in town. I also met Julian Cope who was a nice, respectably-spectacled, middle-class boy from the Midlands when I met him; far removed from the public image he later cultivated. He went to C. F. Mott Teacher Training College. Julian was a Stranglers fan and told me he was a bass guitar player. I became more friendly with his girlfriend Cherry, though.

Around this time a girl (it might have been Cherry) told me that some of these so-called straight boys liked girls to stick one of their fingers up their arses as they were reaching a sexual climax. I didn't really believe it. I thought that maybe these straight boys were not that straight after all!

It was strange going to a straight club and seeing straight boys starting to dress up. They may have been liberal enough to wear unusual clothes and a bit of eyeliner, but they were still a bit uncomfortable about real live Queers. I had a few conversations with Les and Will (later to become Echo And The Bunnymen) about forming a band, but I think that their homophobia got the better of them. They were friendly enough but I began to get the feeling that however much liberal, straight people pretended to accept homosexuality, which was now approaching its most fashionable peak, they still did not, deep down, accept it as a normal and valid way of life. It was once said to me, 'You could never be one of the lads.' At the time, this summed up the Eric's scene for me. Very few musicians were gay, I soon discovered.

Generation X

It was through going to Eric's that I met Paul Rutherford again. Jayne seemed to have a kind of crush on him, he was most unlike the gay clone he later became. His hair had become very spiky in a carbon copy of Johnny Rotten. He'd even managed to get his mum to buy him a genuine bondage suit from 'Seditioneries', Vivienne Westwood and Malcolm Mclaren's new King's Road shop. Though he was on the dole like everyone else, Paul had a talent for sponging money to buy expensive clothes. I maintained that it was a bit unoriginal to buy a ready-made 'look' straight out of a shop, but I was probably jealous. I definitely wasn't a punk, I often repeated, 'I'm an individual.'

He was, and is, a very sociable person – people always loved his sense of humour and his look. I did too, but not in the way he thought I did. His narcissism knew no bounds. A year or so later in the Grapes, a pub in Mathew Street, when he was coming to terms with his sexuality, he said: 'Well I do think now I might be gay, but I could never fancy you.' I laughed haughtily and said, 'Don't worry dear, I've never had my sights on your knickers.' He apologised for being so presumptuous and misconstruing my friendship with him, although this particular type of arrogance was typical of this completely spoilt mummy's boy.

Paul also had a talent for being friends with lots of different people who didn't really like each other. For example, Pete and Lyn didn't (on the surface) like Jayne and would do cruel, but hysterically funny, impersonations of her: her particular way of speaking, the suppressed Liverpool accent, the lapsing into American slang and such. Whenever they met up, false, toothy smiles would abound. People in this scene were rather bitchy about each other, especially those I seemed to meet among the ranks of the trendy and the wannabe pop stars.

Paul had certainly come out of his shell, and became quite extrovert. He would smile and show his rotten and broken teeth – as a spoilt little kid he'd been given too many sweets – now that Johnny Rotten had made them fashionable. He became a great exhibitionist and entertained everyone with his dance floor antics. I was a bit more self-conscious on the dance floor. I spent hours in front of mirrors perfecting a kind of robotic dance style, Liverpool's answer to Lyndsey Kemp.

I remember Generation X coming to Eric's and playing in front of about thirty people. At that time Billy Idol was the prettiest thing any of us had ever seen. Most of the audience were quite static and a lot sat on Eric's carpet, but not Jayne. She was up and dancing in her charming but not-quite-in-time-to-the-music style, and making cow-eyes at Billy Idol. She got to talk to him after the show. Jayne has a special talent for getting in on just where the action is, with just the right people. This talent I have always admired in her. She was like the Social Secretary or Hostess for the bands who came to town, sometimes having to put some of them up on her living room floor. Jayne and Paul followed Generation X to Leeds, which I thought was rather uncool. He was pretty, but the band weren't that fabulous. Later, when he started to be more open about his homosexuality, Paul would sometimes come with me to the Masquerade, which had now moved to Cases Street in the centre of town and had become the number one gay club in Liverpool. 'Let's go the Gay Way!' one of us would say, and off we'd merrily go. I thought gay clubs played better music – Reggae had become terminally trendy at Eric's.

* * *

One night, while I was at Eric's, I helped to smuggle in (through the back door) a young girl and boy who must have been only fourteen. The girl was small and had an impish charm, but was very cheeky. The bouncers at the door wouldn't let them in as they were obviously under age. I sympathised with them, as I had been in the same position, so I hid them in the ladies' lavatory until the coast was clear. The girl told me her name was Cathy and she became known as Little Cathy or Cathy Psycho. She had short, spiky, black hair and was a first generation punk. I had seen her before, hanging round Pete and Lyn, who had opened up a shop called 'Extremes' in Cases Street.

Little Cathy became a member of Pete and Lyn's entourage. Later, they moved their shop to the back of Probe Records at the entrance to Mathew Street. I became quite close to Cathy, who lived off Smithdown Road, not far from my parents.

Pineapple Rings, Jam and Rice Krispies

I can't remember much of my home life around 1976, probably because I was there less and less. My parents were becoming more and more peeved with my unemployment and the hours I kept. Arguments seemed to occur daily. I remember physically fighting with my mother (who I was convinced was mad) on several occasions, and a Christmas tree falling over. There were complaints from the neighbours about the language that was being used in our family discussions. 'You fucking cunt, you shower of shite, you're all the bleeding same,' would penetrate the net-curtains.

'I've got kids in bed up here, and I don't want them listening to *that* sort of language,' the neighbours would interject.

I have always been fairly placid, taking abuse up to a certain point; but when pushed too far I have quite a bad temper, although not a really violent one unlike some of the members of my family. Many Liverpool people have a violent side to their nature, a kind of familiarity with violence. Being able to fight is something people are proud of – if a wrong word is spoken or a look at the wrong person lasts too long, then a fight often occurs. I had been through all this at school and felt that people who fought in the streets were peasants. Somehow I managed to avoid being beaten up too often on the streets of Liverpool, which was strange, considering the way I looked.

Sometime around 1977/8, Paul persuaded me to accompany him when he visited his dying mother in hospital. I felt uncomfortable about this as I had never met his mother but he wanted me there for moral support. She was emaciated when I met her, but there remained the traces of a once-handsome woman with Romany blood. She was sitting up cheerfully in bed, with her long raven-black hair hanging down, and a substantial gold chain and crucifix hanging round her neck outside of her nightdress. She entertained us with her scallywag charm. Perhaps she had been sucked dry by the many children she had mothered? Years later, Paul told me that on that day she'd taken him aside and said like a gypsy soothsayer: 'Stick with that lad, and you'll be alright.'

Paul was extremely unbalanced by her death. He had been her favourite. I remember going round to her house, where the coffin lay in the front room, and Paul was having conversations with the corpse. 'Come here and touch her hand,' he said. 'Doesn't she look lovely?' I found it hard to touch the dead body decked out like a shrine with all manner of Catholic regalia, but I stayed over with Paul. I had been spouting atheist doctrine at Paul for quite a while and he had always warned me that God was listening. The non-belief I had at that time was based on the Christian rejection of homosexuals, as by then I had accepted my sexuality. Paul had not quite left that first closet yet, although now he too wondered if there really was a God.

* * *

I remember one night painting my face white and wearing a black ski jumper with a multi-coloured yoke, below which I wore a pair of red ballet tights and ballet slippers. I somehow had the nerve to go to Kirklands dressed like that.

Kirklands, a wine bar in Renshaw Street, was a kind of multi-racial hang out with snooker tables and a long bar downstairs, and an upstairs disco. The place attracted a rich mixture of people: black, white, gay, straight; quite a few rough urban types as well as trendier suburban types. Here the Seventies' fashion for bottled lager and Jazz Funk were played out to the hilt – a complete contrast to Eric's. The co-owner, a character called Bernie Start, had an appreciation for 'characters' and used to let in for free people who were members of bands that had played there. He also had a sense of Liverpool's continuing culture, and once he started talking, there was no stopping him. He seemed to be a throwback to the Sixties Liverpool scene: a bit like Roger

McGough, Adrian Henri and Sam Walsh, who were by this time the Art Establishment of the city. In our opinion they were the 'Boring Old Farts' or 'Hippies' – the New Wave names for people over thirty. They had all known The Beatles; 'Yawn, yawn,' was our attitude. Although there was a hidden respect for and curiosity about what that generation had achieved, we were too cool to applaud those who we thought applauded themselves.

Brian Patten was my favourite 'Liverpool Poet'. I had secretly bought an anthology of Liverpool poets and liked his work the best. I also loved Sam Walsh's Pop Art paintings that I would see occasionally in the Walker Art Gallery. They reminded me of Andy Warhol's work, but instead of using photographs, Sam painstakingly reproduced portraits of Alan Ladd or old ladies using airbrush and other techniques.

Pete O'Halligan closed down Aunt Twacky's and transformed it into a theatre. One of the first productions was The Science Fiction Theatre of Liverpool's production of *Illuminatus*, which I never actually saw. It was directed by an unemployed actor who has bit parts in a BBC situation comedy. Jayne had a part in this three-day 'happening'. It was while she was doing this that she met Bill Drummond and Ian Broudie, who had been roped in to 'do the music' and help with the scenery.

* * *

Around this time Paul was approached by three 'Woollybacks' (people from St Helens or Warrington) to join a punk band, as the singer. As a bandwagon punk band they weren't too bad. I had a crush on the bass player called Trip so I used to go to the rehearsals. It was a long time before I realised that he might have been Queer or bisexual. Physically, he was everything that I wasn't. He was well-built, slim-hipped and lantern-jawed, with dyed black hair – a bit menacing, the type who could either kiss you or beat you up. Sexually attractive to both men and women, he fancied himself as a bit of a Jack Kerouac figure.

My feelings for him turned into something more than a crush however. Trip was twenty-two and didn't have a proper place to live – maybe he crashed with friends in St Helens or something. Sometimes, he would crash at Jayne's flat. Whenever Trip stayed at Jayne's I managed to stay too, sleeping on the same beanbag arrangement on the floor in the living room.

Jayne had moved in with a bohemian woman called Peonie and a posh student from Sussex called Merry; they had a large flat in Huskisson Street in the heart of Toxteth. Carla Lane could not have imagined a more unlikely threesome for a situation comedy. Peonie had had a stormy relationship with a man called Adam, whose clothes she had thrown out of the window when she ousted him for some misdemeanour. She had long, blonde hair down to her waist and had read Jean-Paul Sartre years ago. She was in her early thirties, wouldn't shave her armpits, drank wine in bistros and worked as an artist's model at the Art school.

Merry, from an upper-middle-class-type background but without the cash, was in Liverpool to study English Literature. She told me she had failed Oxbridge, a term that I didn't quite understand at the time. She was spotty, and slightly dumpy with a stocky, boyish build. She spoke with what sounded to me like a huge cock in her mouth. I was watching 'Wimbledon' on the TV in their spacious living room. 'Do you play at all?' she asked.

Peonie would sometimes get a bit uptight about Jayne's friends and acquaintances hanging around. And vice-versa. I would occasionally visit Linden who had the huge flat below all to herself, except for a large fierce-looking Samoyed bitch called Fang. Linden was a Geordie who had lived in Manchester. She was very striking – six feet tall with a shock of jet-black frizzy hair – and was of a slightly older generation to us. I would ask her questions like, 'What was LSD like?' or 'Who was Alastair Crowley?' and she always had the right answers. She was on the dole like me at the time. She smoked exquisitely thin roll-ups.

Linden told me that she had moved to Liverpool because a famous Mancunian TV presenter had stolen her boyfriend. She had worked in the Virgin record shop which her boyfriend had managed. She had records by groups like the Doors which I'd never heard before. 'The End' became my favourite song. About this time, I read *The Doors of Perception* by Aldous Huxley about the mescaline experience. Linden had a friend called Yvonne Gilbert who was also a Geordie and a successful illustrator/artist. Yvonne was the only person we knew who actually earned money.

One of the nights I was sleeping over at Jayne's, Trip said something like, 'Will you be my boyfriend?'

I started to cry. He was taller than me and had big hands, and a strong, angular face, his skin a bit acne scarred. His hair was dishevelled. His voice had a slight St Helens lilt, and he was very scruffy in appearance. I was pretty inexperienced sexually, having been completely celibate since my teenage sex experiments. Trip seemed to me to be a grown man in the physical sense, and he was the first *man* I was really interested in sexually. Somehow I didn't trust him though; I didn't feel that he was completely sincere about the situation, but I ignored these feelings and jumped in. As I got to know him better he told me that he had lived with a rather camp hairdresser, who had thrown himself out of the window of their first-floor flat in an unsuccessful suicide bid. Trip had been dyeing his hair at the time and had had to go to the hospital with black rivulets running down his face.

He had shaved his eyebrows and legs for some reason, and I remember this only endeared him to me more. I followed him round like a puppy for a while. I became so possessive that soon he was trying to end the relationship.

He didn't try hard enough.

Paul had somehow secured a bedsit in Gambier Terrace, which he and Trip were going to share. Paul knew how much I liked Trip and said, if I liked, I could move in too. There was only one small problem. We all had to share one double bed. From the first day Paul had to get used to me jumping on Trip and having sex with him. Still, it was mainly done under the bed covers – only once or twice in full view.

One afternoon when we were very bored I had sex with Trip in full view of Paul. I discovered that the hole in a pineapple ring was too small to fit over Trip's rather large cock, so I tried spray-on cream, and when that ran out I tried jam which I sprinkled with rice krispies and then sucked the whole lot off. I just thought this was an interesting thing to do. Paul even made some suggestions. He was slowly becoming more open about his sexuality.

Later that night in Eric's, we told Jayne what I had been up to. She had the 'news' right round the club in ten minutes flat. I told her she should have kept her mouth shut. She replied, 'You shouldn't have told me something like that if you wanted me to keep it quiet.' It wasn't that I was ashamed of what I'd done. It just bothered me to learn that friends couldn't be trusted to keep things to themselves.

*   *   *

It was an adventure leaving home, which I just did without telling anyone. I started to sign on at Renshaw Hall in town at 9.30 on Wednesday mornings, now that I had changed neighbourhood. I had to go through the whole rigmarole of registering for work at the Jobcentre in Williamson Square. I signed on as a musician or a poet, or some profession for which they were unlikely to find me a job. By this time I had taken to writing slogans on the side of my skinhead-short bleached hair – usually my Social Security number WK372455B. Sometimes it was 'Psycho' or 'XL5', after the cartoon series. Occasionally, if I wasn't careful I would write things backwards, instead of reversing things in the mirror.

I used to travel with The Spitfire Boys in their transit van. On one occasion I took my acoustic guitar and did a support act. It was a wedding in a Midlands New Town, for which the band had been booked – by mistake, I think. I sang 'My Death' by Jacques Brel, the only song (except for my own songs) which I could remember all the way through. It was my first audience, and to my surprise I got a cheer and a round of applause from the drunken crowd. I got off quick, not believing my luck. The Spitfire Boys got bottled and booed off the stage after two loud punky numbers.

At this time I started to wear a long green flasher's mac that had two very large pockets inside. When we were starving in our bedsit I would go out shoplifting things, like jars of jam and small loaves of bread. One night when we were really hungry a straight roadie we knew, called Terry, came round and said that if one of us would give him a wank, he would give us a quid so we could buy something from the Chinese chippy. So Trip and I took the pound note and left one of my assembled friends to do it (which neither of us witnessed). He was shy, he claimed, and told us that he had done it in the cupboard in the dark, with a polythene glove on – the kind you get in home hair-dyeing kits.

Trip would very occasionally sleep with a girl he knew from St Helens. I would pretend to be blasé about it, but was secretly hopping mad. I started to get possessive again, especially as Trip would write long letters that he would leave around the place. We once had a fight in Jayne's flat which ended in me sticking a fork in his arse, which was very out of character for me. I can't remember why I did it. I got a rather long letter after that one, complaining about my violent behaviour. It was a clear case of my feelings for him far outweighing his feelings for me.

The Spitfire Boys got a record contract of sorts and released a single. Record companies were like flies around shit with Punk bands at this time. Some awful bands got signed and better ones got lost in the stampede. Anyway, a tour was arranged.

Trip's mini-affair with Paul started on this tour, although Paul had his eye on Sean the van driver, I remember. I got pretty mad with them, especially when they both started staying with an acquaintance who had a flat at the top of Princess Avenue, another of the many fag hags who had a crush on Paul over the years. These girl friends always came in handy for providing him with a place to stay or a night out on the town.

Trip started to get more and more obsessed with Paul. Apparently they were having sex behind my back when I got up early to sign on – something Paul told me about a year later. I remember feeling that Paul had stabbed me in the back. He laughed with that familiar lisping hyena laugh 'Tss ssss sss sss sss ss' when I told him that he had betrayed me. He said I was being a bit dramatic.

Trip had been my first boyfriend, and I was very upset about the relationship ending, and how it ended. When you're seventeen years old and have moved away from home to live with someone you are crazy about, it seems like the end of the world when it goes wrong, even if the relationship has only lasted a few months.

Big In Japan

At 17 I played in my first band, Big In Japan, which was already formed when I joined. Jayne and Kevin Ward were both vocalists, although Kevin had been doubling as bass player. Bill Drummond played rhythm guitar, Ian Broudie lead guitar, and Phil Allen was on drums. (Phil's brother Steve, a.k.a. Enrico Cadillac Jr, was the lead singer of Deaf School.) Big In Japan had started by using Deaf School's equipment and rehearsing in Eric's. Anyway Kevin wanted to be free to sing, so the band had to find a new bass player.

I was approached by Jayne and Bill. Jayne knew that I wrote lyrics and poetry, and that I played the acoustic guitar and sang. Perhaps she also realised that I needed a distraction from my situation in the Gambier Terrace bedsit. I told them that my lyrics were perhaps a bit whimsical for the kind of thing their band was doing, but the truth was I was really too shy to show them my work. I was familiar with only one song of theirs, the band's theme tune 'Big In Japan', which actually I thought was dreadful, though I understood the tongue-in-cheek aspect of it.

Still, I felt that it might be fun. Also I knew it was a way of getting in to Eric's for free. Being a bass player in a New Wave band had never been part of my big plan; but it could be a kind of apprenticeship.

I went through a series of little auditions – one with Ian Broudie with my acoustic guitar. Ian checked out my playing ability, which compared to his was pretty minimal, but I did quite a good rendition of Jacques Brel's 'Amsterdam' – Bowie had sung this song on a B-side in the early Seventies.

The next audition was with Bill and Ian in Eric's. One day they gave me Kevin's bass guitar, a blue Fender Music Man. It was hell to play, but somehow I managed to perform a piece they taught me. Bill and Kevin were ten years older than I – they seemed ancient – and Jayne was twenty one. I think the nearest in age to me was Ian who was about eighteen, and by far the most accomplished musician and arranger. My obvious advantage to the group was that I looked like a male mirror image of Jayne, with my shaved head dyed blonde and the black eye make up. It gave the band a strong visual identity without a doubt.

I learned the songs by rote, in the manner Kevin had played them, not really understanding the musical style or the function of the bass guitar that much. I did manage however to have an influence on the lyrics.

Jayne would say 'let's write some lyrics,' so I would dictate lines that I had already written back at the flat to her, adapting them to her personality, since she would be singing them. I often rewrote lyrics to existing tunes. 'Suicide A Go Go', 'SCUM' and 'Nothing Special' were written in this manner. Looking back, I think they are some of my favourite lyrics.

Suicide A Go Go
Sidestep from the bar on to the street
Creatures of the Fairground,
Naked in the heat
A Penny Arcade Peep Show
Suicide A Go Go

'Suicide A Go Go' was inspired by William Burroughs's *The Wild Boys* that I was still carrying around with me as if it were a Bible. Jayne and I would give impromptu readings from it in pubs, just to get up people's noses. We added the 'Buy Me, Try Me' chorus as a handle for the song.

Nothing Special
I'm Nothing Special, the star of the show
The hottest thing on video
I spend my time, Interviewing me
With the aid of, trick photography
Me, me, me. I, I, I.

92

My, My, My.
Egomania, Egomania.

'Nothing Special' was inspired by Andy Warhol, one of my biggest heroes. His book *From A to B and Back Again*, actually written by Pat Hacket and Bob Colacello, gave rise to the idea for a TV show that he would call 'Nothing Special'. Another idea culled from this book was SCUM, The Society for Cutting Up Men, a feminist manifesto that was to spawn the shooting of Andy by Valerie Solanas.

S.C.U.M.
We'll cut you up, we'll shoot you dead
Look out Andy or it's in the head.
Society for cutting up men
Don't know where, Don't know when,
We're a tribe of Amazons
and we don't need silicon
Infiltrate key positions of state
The male race, Obliterate!
Society for cutting up men . . . etc

I lent Jayne a copy of the book and from the chapter called 'Taxi' she wrote, unaided, the lyrics of the song of the same name.

The demos of these songs were mainly recorded at Amazon recording studios in Liverpool, and some in a small studio in London.

The Eric's label was very much influenced by the Stiff record label and the Punk and New Wave explosion in general. At Eric's we saw bands like Talking Heads, The Ramones, Generation X, Siouxsie and the Banshees, Iggy Pop, The Human League (who played twice to an audience of about ten people) and Joy Division (who played to an audience of less than five people).

There were also appearances by a few of New York's campest acts like The Cramps and the American transsexual Wayne (who later, with the aid of plastic surgery, became Jayne) County, famous for the record 'If You Don't Want To Fuck Me Baby, Fuck Off!' Cherry Vanilla performed there too, supported by The Police. These people were slightly glamorous because of the people they knew (Andy Warhold and David Bowie) and because they came from the myth-land of Manhattan, New York.

In fact we were extremely spoilt musically and spent a lot of the time posing round the bar, in our latest Anti-Fashion fashions. We became very blasé, not even bothering to watch these bands half the time.

As Manchester was nearby we played there quite often, at a club called Rafters. There I met Pete Shelley from The Buzzcocks, whom I liked. I liked him more as he was the only musician I had ever met who displayed any sympathy for Queers. Otherwise I felt quite isolated in this very hetero music scene. Some of the time I felt I was merely tolerated by the male members of the band. I think I scared Ian Broudie once by putting my arm around him affectionately. We were standing at a bus stop and he had just told me that he was a Jew. I wasn't really sure what a Jew was at that time. I knew about Hitler but had been more concerned that he had gassed over 200,000 homosexuals. He said 'Some people don't like Jews'. So I put my arm around him and said 'Ahh'.

I would always fall asleep in the back of the transit van that Bill used to hire and drive, my head stuck between two amplifiers. There was never much thought of earning any *money* from all of this, as many musicians will know. Often we were out of pocket, but that seemed the least of our worries. It was something I didn't consider anyway, being the youngest; the serious stuff was left to the others. I didn't even own any of the equipment. Bill told me to pick out a bass combo that I liked in Rushworth's music store. It must have been paid for by Eric's club management or the group. And on stage I always felt perfectly at home, moving with a certain cocksureness that contrasted with my shyness off stage.

I did get the feeling that some of the other members of the group were very serious about it all, and my indifference to being a bass player soon got on their nerves. I got bored very quickly, feeling confident that I could sing a lot better than Jayne or Kevin. A 'How To Play Bass Guitar' manual was left for me at the door of Eric's, I was told. By a well wisher, I thought not. It was the kind of bitchiness that so typified the Liverpool scene. This whole generation of would-be creative people from Liverpool completely lacked any sense of community. All those immense egos were too busy being jealous, vying to become famous first.

* * *

So as in all groups politics started to rear its ugly head. The first target was Kevin, Jayne's on-and-off boyfriend. Bill Drummond and Jayne got together and somehow managed to get Kevin voted out of the group. I remember being quite shocked at the way Jayne helped engineer this. She claimed that Kevin tried to undermine her; maybe he did, I might have been too young to notice things like that. Bill had a theory that in matters like this, pop groups had to be ruthless. It was a bit like the popularity contests that I thought I'd left behind in school. Next it was Phil Allen's turn.

The Spitfire Boys' drummer 'Budgie' was one of the best in town at that time, and somehow Phil was out and Budgie was in. I didn't mind that much as Budgie had been my friend. Budgie was nice and one of the least homophobic musicians. We would keep each other company in either his or the Gambier Terrace flat. One week when I had ran out of Social Security, he fed me with lentils and let me stay at his flat as I couldn't feed myself or the electric meter. He even encouraged my bass playing, saying that I was a much better bass player than the one he'd been playing with. Budgie had been a student at the Art College like many of the musicians around town. He taught me about complementary colours. His flat was painted blue and orange that vibrated together. His nickname Budgie arose one night at Gambier Terrace. Paul and I were slagging budgies (the birds) and their keepers and Pete said, 'I've known some really nice budgies.' That was it: he was Budgie from then on.

95

The Sausages from Mars

A couple of months after my leaving home – or being driven out, which was how I saw the situation – Pat and Clare, with Ben in a pushchair, turned up on the doorstep of the Gambier Terrace bedsit. I hadn't seen them for a while and my mother seemed to be two stone heavier than usual. I, on the other hand, had become skin and bones. She invited me for Sunday dinner. At first it seemed strange going back to the old address, but I would often go back there for Sunday dinner after that. It was probably the only decent meal I got all week. My Social Security was usually wasted on drinks at Eric's or the odd piece of clothing.

At one point, Jayne made me a wonderful pair of tartan trousers on Linden's sewing machine. The tartan was a white background with red and yellow printed plaid. I loved them. With these I wore a pair of steel-toed brogues dyed pillar-box red. I somehow acquired a pair of red-and-white satin basketball shorts that I wore over the top of my tartan trousers. I also wore a collarless motorbike jacket I'd bought off Paul, often with no shirt underneath.

In order to get me out of that flat and its unhappy memories, Jayne hatched a plan. She and Merry were getting unwelcome vibes from Peonie, and as Roger Eagle was moving out of his little cottage situated at the side of a large house in Livingston Drive, Sefton Park, Jayne arranged that we three – Jayne, Merry and I – could move in there. Which we did. It gave me a chance to get away from the loneliness and misery of that scruffy bedsit.

As soon as I moved out of Gambier Terrace, Trip moved back in. At the same time, The Spitfire Boys started to lose their momentum and were coming to a natural and welcome end.

It took me quite a while to get over the experience with Trip. I felt that it would be quite a while before I could expose myself emotionally to another person again.

Ten years later, after I had become rather successful, Trip, fat, married with children, and according to rumour, working in a country pub, sent me a two-line letter. It said simply 'I need your help'. I grinned as I dropped the letter into the dustbin. Five years after that, one of my 'friends' gave my phone number to him and he rang up, asking to speak to me. But I didn't want to talk to the person I had known, and what would I say to the person that I now did not know?

I've heard more recently that he has become a faith healer.

* * *

It must have been the Autumn of 1977 when we moved into that drafty, leaky cottage in Livingstone Drive. I remember us all trying to get a taxi one night on Princess Avenue. We had some of our possessions with us, and Merry was carrying a broom (a most appropriate accessory) so we could clean up Roger's dusty home. Taxis wouldn't stop for us and we were freezing. Merry shouted out theatrically, 'And it all ended in a triple suicide pact!' I hadn't really noticed her having a sense of humour before, but this comment did sum up the situation. We were all misfits of a different kind.

Roger, who lived very much like a bachelor, had left the cottage a few weeks earlier. It was a mess, and the clean-up job took quite a while. None of us was particularly domesticated, especially me. I had just moved out of a hovel and was used to living rough by now. The two girls were more practical, dealing with the cooking and other things. Although they cleaned the house more than I did, they didn't seem to wash *themselves* as much as I washed myself, which I thought was odd.

I took Jayne home to my parents for tea one day. We had been decorating or cleaning the cottage. For months afterwards Eric kept going on about how dirty Jayne's nails and hands were. 'I've never seen a girl so filthy in all me life,' he would repeat.

* * *

Jayne painted lots of things black in the cottage: walls, doors, even her lips and toe nails. Black was her colour. I remember her painting a round raffia place-mat black. She stuck on top of this an artificial yellow Easter chick and with a piece of elastic it became a hat: an Easter Bonnet. This was inspired by Grace Jones's hat on an LP cover, designed by Jean Paul Goude. Another of Jayne's eccentricities was a scarf tied up in a bundle and carried on the end of a long twig that she had sprayed black. This Dick Whittington accessory got bigger and bigger, turning into a giant bundle if we had to go away anywhere. Not to be outdone, I started to carry an old wooden violin case as a handbag. It was shaped like a miniature, hand-carved coffin, most unlike modern violin cases.

Jayne and I had a bit of difficulty getting the Social Security to pay our rent. I remember miserable hours in the waiting room at the Social Security offices in Aigburth, drenched by the greyness of the building and the city sky outside. The landlord didn't want to accept our tenancy and wouldn't issue us with a rent book, which complicated matters further. Merry had an Education Authority grant so she didn't have the same problem.

We would occasionally throw dinner parties with blue spaghetti and jelly, as we did for my eighteenth birthday party. Merry's then boyfriend Graham, an artist, kindly gave me a silk screen and a Squeegee for my birthday. He showed me how to use it, making a quick stencil of Chairman Mao just like Andy Warhol's. I started to print on newspaper and old T-shirts that I turned inside out. Lyndsey Kemp's eyes cut out from a magazine was my most successful design. This same screen came in handy later when I was to apply for a place at the Art College.

Graham later did a schizophrenic drawing of both Jayne's and my facial characteristics in the same head. To look at it was disconcerting for both of us. Paul and I embarrassed Graham once by pulling his trousers down in the middle of Eric's, partly as a prank, partly to see what his cock looked like. This was typical of our behaviour then. We were all young and determined to be as obnoxious as possible.

People used to ask me what Jayne looked like without her heavy and expertly applied make up. I only saw this once or twice, as she seemed to put a new layer of make up over the one that had just worn out. When it all came off she looked ten years younger, to me anyway. I remember her inventing black-wool imitation dreadlocks which she braided into the front of her own short hair. When we saw a black and white photograph of this new style, it looked like someone had shot her in the head and the blood was trickling down her face. Very Punkette.

One of Jayne's relations came round and did something to the gas meter, so that instead of the gas units clocking up forwards, they went backwards. This solved the draft and damp problem, as we could now afford gas galore: we even left the oven on with the door open. Knickers and tights were often dried in the oven after that.

Meanwhile, Big In Japan were getting a bit of a reputation. Paul Morley, a freelance journalist for the *NME*, came over from Manchester to interview us. It took place in Eric's club one afternoon. He asked his usual awkward questions. 'What do you hope to achieve by all of this?' and 'What will you do when it's all over?' I think Bill answered that he would like to take a trip down the Amazon. I replied flippantly that I would like to open a chippy.

This small article enabled us to get further bookings up and down the country. We played some polytechnic or other, supporting Penetration. Their singer Pauline Murray had a good voice and could dance well. She also had a pair of proper 'bondage kecks' (Liverpool slang for trousers). 'Don't Dictate' was their best song. We also supported The Buzzcocks when they played the Mountford Hall in Liverpool. We only did a few numbers as we were drenched in spittle from the audience. A similar incident happened at Preston Polytechnic. Cans of lager were hurtled at us on the stage by ignorant students: we ducked these for two numbers, and left the stage.

Our visual presentation depended on the contrasting characters in the band. Bill would wear his kilt. Jayne would wear yellow nappies over a black leotard suit with a plunging neck line. She had always had a heavy decolletage and used it to its best advantage. On her head she would wear a yellow terry-towelling nappy that she had transformed into an Arab headdress. She had her black eyes, black lips, and black toenails that showed through her open-toed platform 'fuck me' pumps, worn to compensate for her small stature. Budgie had his shock of blonde hair behind the drums and Ian was just Ian in his John Lennon specs. I was wearing a tartan dinner jacket (Jayne found it for me in Layla's shop '69a'), and black footless tights or my tartan trousers. It was not really a punk look like all the other bands of the period, so we didn't really fit in. The music wasn't punk either, and we would often get in trouble with audiences who were there to spit and pogo.

Jet Records (owned by Don Arden, who had brought The Electric Light Orchestra to the world's notice) showed some interest in us. We went to London to have a meeting with them, and I remember an A and R man saying, 'Can you guarantee us a hit record?' We laughed and said how the hell can we do that! They arranged for us to do a showcase at the Marquee Club supporting some dreadful band. We got paid £25 for the show which had cost us £150 in travelling expenses.

We even got a TV slot on Tony Wilson's Granada TV programme 'What's On'. The Sex Pistols had played on it the year before, so we thought we were pop stars. Tony was a friend of Roger Eagle's and used to come and commune with him in the Eric's tiny office, which was always filled with the smoke of menthol Kools. I used to describe people of that generation as 'Stoned since the Sixties', the decade that they all claimed had liberated everyone. All it had actually liberated was the mouths of the thirtysomethings who all claimed that they had changed the world.

To relieve the serious aspects of Big In Japan, and so that I could get a chance to sing, Jayne and I started to do impromptu performances as The Sausages From Mars. I would strum my acoustic guitar and we would both sing. We never really rehearsed much, which was apparent from the performances. Our main song was Lou Reed's 'I'm Sticking With You' – an old song of his for a male and female voice.

One night Stiff Records came to town and put on a kind of

New Wave talent contest, so Stiff could check out provincial talent. At the end of a night of very boring acts, Jayne and I got up to do our little number. Even though I broke a string on Ian's electric guitar as soon as I got on the stage, we went down rather well. My baritone was a perfect foil for Jayne's high-pitched squeak.

A week or so later someone from Stiff records rang Pete Fullwell (who was in some sense Big In Japan's manager), offering The Sausages From Mars a singles deal. Although I didn't witness anything, the other members of Big In Japan got rather bitchy about this. I was up for this opportunity for fun, but Jayne didn't want to upset the other band members.

As The Spitfire Boys had more or less run out of steam, Paul was at a bit of a loose end. He had started following around an all girl Punk group, The Slits. Arianna the precocious fourteen-year-old singer had a strange individual style, twisting her hair into dreadlocks, which went along with the Reggae/Rasta fashion of the time. Paul idolised 'Ari-Up' as she was known, and started to imitate her style, thus transferring his hero worship from Johnny Rotten, who Ari's mum Nora was then going out with (and still is, I believe). I went to London with The Spitfire Boys once or twice and met members of The Slits: Palmolive the drummer, Viv Albertine the guitarist and Tessa the bassist. They all had a particular and wonderful dress sense. I went to Seditioneries in the King's Road. On one of these visits I wanted to buy one of Vivienne Westwood's creations. This was the first time I had seen Vivienne. She was dressed in a bondage suit, but had diverted one of the straps that ran up the arms and across the chest, and had it on her head.

Paul got a part in the chorus of the gothic opera *The Case of Charles Dexter Ward* when it went to the ICA. He had to stand with the small orchestra at the side of the stage wearing a black hooded robe. He taught me the Gregorian chant incantations which I loved. One went something like, *Yaing ah yog sototh, He'l geb phai throdog uahhh*. This had to be sung in a very nasal manner for the full effect. Some of the chorus sang into lengths of drainpipes for an eerier sound, and expensive incense was burned to create an atmosphere. A microphone was stuck out of a window and the street sounds were amplified into the audience as a kind of background noise.

Going AWOL from Big In Japan rehearsals, I drove down to London with Paul, Timmy the transvestite clarinetist and Ella (from the backstage crew). We stayed in a squat in Butlers Wharf, Tooley Street just near Tower Bridge. Timmy shared this squat with Keith Allen and a few other people. It was a grotty squat, no way of having a bath except for a weird public shower that you had to walk two blocks to. But when you're eighteen years old, things like that don't seem to matter too much.

That wharfside squat was right next to the warehouses where Andrew Logan and Derek Jarman lived. We saw the locations where Derek's film *Jubilee* had been shot. That movie sums the period up so well for me. It had all the more interesting London characters of the time in it: Jordan, Little Nell, Adam Ant, Gene October – even Lindsey Kemp made an appearance.

I returned to Liverpool after a few days to resume rehearsals with Big In Japan, which was becoming a bit like an unpaid job. Bill seemed to have some kind of Presbyterian work-ethic inherited from his father, a Scots Minister. This meant we had to rehearse every day in Eric's, where we were allowed to store our equipment. Still, more bookings followed – places like the Wigan Casino, Halifax Roxy Club and a pub in Bradford where the racist landlord said that we shouldn't worry because he didn't let 'Pakis' in.

We often would turn up at Eric's at one thirty in the morning to store our equipment, while the nightclub revellers were still there. One night Lori Larty introduced me to a handsome young man called Jake. I had been eyeing him up as I loaded my bass amp into the lock-up. He on the other hand thought, 'Who is this camp creature with the black eye make up?' (or so I learned later). He had black hair and golden brown skin, with a sultry, sulky-looking face. I thought he looked like a young matinee idol. It turned out that he was in the process of splitting up with Trip, who had given him a bad time, not unlike my own experience.

102

Initially my intentions may have been to make Trip jealous. I invited Jake back to the cottage to stay the night, dropping in on Trip on the way home. Jake, who was still a bit obsessed with Trip, almost weakened and got into bed, but realised there was no future in that relationship.

He was shy and a little bit naïve, and didn't realise the effect he had on people. He was very good looking but insecure, so I could boss him into bed. When you're eighteen, you're horny all the time. I had a massive crush on him, so I didn't notice it, but people later told me he was rather camp.

We developed a strange but very close relationship over the next few years. Jake was discovering himself and his sexuality at the same time as I was discovering myself. Jake liked older men on the whole, but at eighteen, resistance to sex is hard, even if the other person isn't your ideal type. Jake's soft golden skin, massive cock and extra-hirsute legs lent him, when naked, a Pan-like appearance.

Like Paul he was another Catholic boy struggling with guilt over his homosexuality.

Jake, Paul and I would occasionally all go out together to the Masquerade trying to pick up men. Jake was so good looking it was hard to get a look in. Paul still looked a bit effeminate for the gay scene with his long hair that he refused to comb in hope that it would become dreadlocks. It was a kind of Gypsy Queen look he was cultivating.

Jake was another apprentice hairdresser. Young girls would come to his house to get their hair done, giving him longing looks and sighing. He wouldn't even notice – young girls were the last thing on his mind. Jake, like me, didn't like staying in. He was always lending me a quid or two so we could go out. We could go to Kirklands and buy two ciders (25p each) and get pissed. That would last us most of the night. Jake introduced me to his friends, Alexandra Pigg, later star of *Letter To Brezhnev*, then a precocious fifteen year old who wanted to be an actress. Another friend of his, Colin, had a flat in a council block called Tommy White Gardens. 'Aare ye cummin t' Tommy Whites?' Colin would say and we'd all go back to his flat and stay up half the night gabbing or trying to get into Jake's, or someone else's, knickers. All those impromptu parties.

At one of those parties, there were various lesbians trying out various sexual techniques in one room. In another there'd be Queers like me putting their willies up fag hags, just to see what it felt like. One night a particularly homophobic teddy boy known as Bon'ed begged Jake to fuck him up the arse in a dark cubbyhole. It was that kind of party – there was no drink and you had to make your own entertainment.

Colin would later do a fabulous drag act at the Masquerade, miming to Connie Francis records such as 'Who's Sorry Now' and 'VACATION'. Colin was a drag legend – on Saturday nights in Kirklands, anyway.

One night when I got back late to the cottage with Jake, Jayne was there, depressed over something or other. Whenever she was depressed she went to sleep a lot, sometimes in the big armchair. Jayne didn't like Jake particularly, because he wasn't arty or part of the 'in' crowd. She said there was some food left in the oven then fell asleep. I ate with Jake, who said, 'Who does the cooking round here?' I said, 'She does,' pointing at Jayne asleep in the chair. Jake laughed. It was true, Jayne could cook better than I did, so she did it more. I didn't think any more of the comment.

It was either later that night or the next day that Jayne kicked off on me, accusing me of being sexist. She said she hadn't been asleep and had heard every word. I felt she was overreacting. She said that she didn't want to share a flat with me any more, that she and Merry were moving out, and that I had to move out too, as Roger was going to get into trouble for letting us move there in the first place. I was a bit peeved at this as it would have been no skin off her nose to let me stay on at the cottage for a while.

Jayne and I had another argument in the van going to or from a Big In Japan show. She had a habit of lapsing into a little girl's voice when she wanted to persuade 'men' to do something for her. It was just something that she had learned to do, so she tried it on me one day, in front of the rest of the band. 'Don't try that little girl voice on me dear, it just won't work,' I said sternly. 'You've just lost a friend, Johnson!' she replied in an attempt to wound me. People usually didn't stand up to Jayne in that way and she wasn't used to it. With men she did usually get her way, especially with Bill, who according to rumour, had a secret crush on her.

The fact was we were in each other's company too much and familiarity was starting to breed contempt. Maybe it was true that I didn't help much about the house and took things for granted. I certainly had very little experience in keeping a household together and managing money in a sensible way.

Much of the real reason for Jayne acting strangely may have been her seeing Kevin again. He always messed her head up – it was one of those relationships that were sexual dynamite but emotional suicide. According to Jayne, Kevin was a bit gregarious sexually, and the relationship was making her unhappy. She was also several months pregnant. She would come in at night and lift up her clothes to look at her growing stomach in the mirror, then pull them down again and pretend it wasn't happening. I came home one night after we hadn't really been speaking to each other. I found her sitting on the stairs in full drag and make up.

'Phone for an ambulance, I'm having a miscarriage,' she moaned. I got her in a taxi and took her to Sefton General Hospital. She was put in a wheelchair and wheeled off to the women's ward. She started to sing the Devo song 'Mongoloid, he was a mongoloid' as she was wheeled away. We both laughed. It was one of our private jokes.

The next day I went to visit her. I walked over the park and through the cemetery next to the hospital. On the way I collected some daffodils off one of the graves as I had no money to buy fresh flowers. We screamed with laughter when I told her where they had come from. It was somehow appropriate. Flowers for the dead.

At least all this seemed to get us over the hump in our friendship. We started to talk again, although it didn't change the flat situation. Jayne and Merry found another flat near Ullet Road and Jayne suggested I moved back to my parent's house. I wasn't in a financial position to put down a deposit on a flat of my own, so off I went, tail between my legs, back to Mother. At least my brother John had finally moved away from home and I no longer had to share a room. I was eighteen now and had tasted independence, so it wasn't going to be easy for me to fit back into Pat and Eric's regime.

From Y to Z and Never Again

Pat and Clare came to see a Big In Japan concert at Kirklands. They both cheered the loudest, and my mother danced the rest of the night away with Martin from The Yachts, a good-time pop band from the Art school. I squirmed with embarrassment as usual.

My position in Big In Japan was shortly to end. I never knew exactly why. The band's politics had just swung in another direction. At the same time the music scene in Liverpool was moving on. Lots of the people who had been in the audience of Big In Japan shows stopped sneering at us for a moment and formed their own bands, thinking, 'We could do better than them'. Echo and The Bunnymen was one example. Their first show at Eric's was chaos – they only had one song and played it for twenty minutes. The drum machine was the only thing that could play. Another new band was The Teardrop Explodes – Julian Cope stopped just talking music and started playing it. Even Pete Burns eventually started to try and get in on the act. He stopped looking in the mirror long enough to form first The Mystery Girls, then Nightmares In Wax, then Dead Or Alive. Others included Dalek I Love You and Orchestral Manoeuvres In The Dark, who came from across the water on the Wirral. These were part of a new generation of bands, some of whom were strongly influenced by the Eric's scene.

I visited Jayne one day at her and Merry's new basement flat in Grosvenor Terrace. She burst into tears and told me that the boys in the band didn't want to work with me any more. I was a bit stunned, but didn't think that it merited such histrionics. In fact I was disappointed that Jayne had allowed this to happen; her position in the band was quite important after all. It may have been due to my indifference to being a bass player, though years later Jayne claimed a bit of homophobia was involved. I didn't know, and couldn't care less.

Still, my sense of identity was taken away from me a bit. I had grown comfortable in the situation. People around town knew who I was and what band I was in. Now all of a sudden I was 'out', and I stopped going to Eric's.

The next incarnation of Big In Japan (with Dave Balfe as bass player) did not last long. They had started to rehearse in The Open Eye, a bookshop/cafe-cum-arts-centre near Mathew Street. After about three months they decided to split up and that was to be almost the end of Big In Japan. I was invited to play the bass for a few songs at the farewell concert, which I did.

A few months after this Bill Drummond and Dave Balfe decided to start up their own independent record label and Zoo Records was born. The first release was an EP of Big In Japan demos, 'From Y to Z and Never Again'. Three of the tracks on this I had played on or contributed to creatively: 'Nothing Special', 'Suicide A Go Go' and 'Taxi'. 'Sindy and the Barbi Dolls' was Bill and Ian's song that I disowned because of the 'Chipmunk' vocals. I think the initial two thousand copies sold out.

Also the Open Eye, which had a small recording studio and video facility, released an LP which contained a Big In Japan instrumental track. John Peel wrote the sleeve notes, which said that Big In Japan was the quintessential Liverpool group and the cornerstone of an era. Or something to that effect. And John Peel subsequently invited Big In Japan to do a Peel session. Coming from Liverpool, John Peel like to encourage Liverpool groups. He was already a hero of mine as he had been a supporter of T Rex and Marc Bolan, even contributing a speaking voice on an early Tyrannosaurus Rex album.

I was asked to be a part of this reformation of the group for the Peel session. I think all the members of the band were in agreement that I should be asked back for this last event, realising now that my removal had been a mistake. This Peel session was probably the best and most polished thing that Big In Japan ever did.

Then one day I got a call from Jayne who said there was to be a meeting at the Open Eye about the Big In Japan EP. Apparently the original run had sold out due to the efforts of Bill and Dave and maybe the extra publicity that the Peel session had generated. I got the bus into town with Bill, who was squirming a little. I said I didn't know what was going on really.

It turned out that Bill and Dave had ordered a further run to be pressed without informing the other band members. This had been discovered by one of the Open Eye organisers who had answered a phone call meant for Bill. It was very much Jayne's meeting. Accusations of ripping people off were bandied about. Bill claimed he had planned to give everyone fifty quid when the profits had come in, but I don't think he was taken seriously. Bill and Dave were now considered ruthless businessmen – laughable when you consider the small amounts of money involved.

Another thing happened that did concern me, however. Dave Balfe told me that my signature had been forged on a publishing contract, assigning the Big In Japan songs to Warner Brothers Publishing. This had been done in return for the recordings being paid for by them. Rob Dickens, then head of this company, loved Big In Japan. Dave implied that Bill had signed my name on the contract, but explained that I was credited for most of the songs, even the ones that I had not contributed to. So for years I believed this to be true, mildly resenting what I thought was Bill's action. It was not until fifteen years later that I discovered who had forged my signature; Wolfgang witnessed the confession. The culprit claimed it had been for convenience's sake, as I knew nothing about the signing of the contract at the time. We both laughed (me through my teeth) about it when I showed the culprit a copy of the forged signature that I obtained recently. They had even spelt my name wrong. It amazes me how I repeatedly forgave this 'friend'. 'It's only Holly, he won't mind', was the general attitude towards me. I must have a forgiving nature: either that or I just look like a doormat.

A Threesome

While all this was happening with Big In Japan, I became friends with Little Cathy. I had started to talk to her sometimes when I met her in town. Cathy was blonde now and was experimenting with make up; bright yellows lit up her cheeky face. She was so impish. For some reason we would just look at each other and fall about laughing. There was a chemistry between us, a rebelliousness and a shared sense of the absurd. I used to visit her at her mum's. Cathy had similar problems with her parents as I had with mine. She used to show me her poems and I would play the songs that I had written to her. We started to smoke dope together, getting stoned and giggling all night. She was a Syd Barrett fan. There was a self destructive, almost malicious wild streak in her personality though.

When we had no money for cigarettes, she devised a plan. The idea was to go into a local tobacconist and ask for twenty ciggies, then when the shop assistant placed them on the counter to ask for a packet of Red Rizla. This usually meant the shop assistant had to turn round and bend over for the Rizla. At this point the cigarettes were picked up and she or I were out of the shop and half way down the street. Cathy was an expert shoplifter, a skill which she developed more and more as time went on. I introduced her to Jake and we would sometimes go out together at night.

Jake meanwhile had started to go out with a man called Gerald who lived in or near Prescot. I was a bit jealous of their relationship, but would sometimes go up to Gerald's with Jake. Jake started to experiment sexually with the older and more experienced Gerald, and would tell me about their adventurous sex life. Gerald was fucking him up the arse and he discovered he really enjoyed this. They would do it in front of mirrors, in costume and things like that. Jake seemed to enjoy giving me detailed descriptions of what went on. I was obviously curious about all of this, but a bit put out as I still had a yearning for Jake. Gerald once even suggested a threesome, but that did not appeal.

One night I left Gerald's house and walked home in the dark – about ten miles or more. On the way I wrote a song in my head. It was called 'Treasure Island' and summed up my feelings about the situation I had just walked out of.

'Wasn't it enough to hurt me with the fact
You wanted me to lie and listen to the act?'

This was the first time an idea for a song had come to me in this way. Usually I would sit with my guitar trying to put a melody to poems that I had already written. Now the lyrics and the melody seemed to come to me all at once. Over the next few weeks I worked out a few simple chords on the guitar to accompany myself.

Jake and I had started to get a few items of leather clothing made, including some leather trousers for me. These were shaped rather like jodhpurs – reminiscent of Tom Of Finland drawings. We later found a lovely old man called Fred who made S and M clothing for the Northern Chapter of a gay Leather Men's club. He used to show me dirty magazines. 'What do you think about that then?' he'd say, eyeing my crotch. 'Ooh, I'd love one of those.' 'Are you into rubber?' he'd go on. 'I've got lots of rubber in the cupboard. Rubber sheets.' Jake, Paul and I would drool over one or two members of this club that met sometimes at the Masquerade. They weren't ostentatiously leather-clad, just leather jackets with jeans. It was a masculine look that we preferred to the Queeny Vanilla types. But when we got talking to these men, we realised they were just the same as everyone else; in fact they were self-consciously trying too hard to look masculine. I got Fred to make me a leather peaked cap that I studded at the front. This was the beginning of my leather phase. It was a 'look' rather than a sexual thing though.

111

One night Jake and I were in the Masquerade when two men who were not regulars walked in. The taller and younger one, who had a short back and sides and looked a bit ex-Army, kept smiling at me. I was going through a skinhead-in-camouflage-trousers phase which was a bit off-putting for the regular type of queens (on the Liverpool gay scene at that time, it was all Bee Gee blow-dried hair do's with highlights), so I was pleased by the attention. The older of the two men, John, gave me a phone number, so I rang them a week or so later. They lived 'over the water', the Wirral, in other words. I arranged to get the train over the next Sunday. I wore a rather-too-baggy pair of trousers tapering to narrow bottoms that Jake had made. The younger one of the two, 'Tom', met me at the station. He was in his mid twenties and about six foot tall, very well built with dark, poker-straight hair. Since our last meeting, he had shaved off his moustache. He said he and his friend lived a bus ride away. As we were waiting for the bus he asked me, 'What do you like to do in bed then?' I suppose this was my cue to have him salivating with detailed descriptions of my sexual preferences, but I was a bit shy of answering and said, 'Anything really, as long as it's not painful'. I'd heard of S and M by this time and was worried about what might be expected of me. We talked about tattoos, he telling me he had a few I could see when I got back to his flat.

We boarded the top of the bus and sat at the back. He asked me again what I liked to do; again I didn't know how to reply. A bit inexperienced, I had only really indulged in oral sex or mutual masturbation. The most adventurous thing I had done was letting someone put his cock between my thighs and move up and down on top of me – this I had found very exciting. Jake had, of course, told me about a few things that he'd done. He said he had once been fucked in the mouth and had nearly suffocated, but had got a real thrill from the experience. We arrived back at their unremarkable, cosy flat. I noted John, the older one, had grown a moustache. He was short and stocky in his early forties with dark skin. I didn't really fancy him that much – not because of his age, I just preferred Tom. John said, 'A friend of ours is on telly this afternoon, I hope you don't mind if we watch it'. It turned out to be a strange drama series called 'The Owl Service' that many people had a problem following. When it was over Tom pounced, sticking his large tongue down my throat and in my ear. I was interested in his short hair which I kept feeling at the back of his neck. As I was necking with Tom, John came over and started to pull my pants down. 'Let's go into the bedroom,' he said.

I managed to get Tom's trousers off. He was wearing a black Cire G string which he must have bought mail order from an advert in newspapers or magazines. I took his massive, thick dick out of the pouch and started to suck, hoping he didn't want to fuck me with it. But then, while I was engaged with Tom, John was trying to fuck me. He kept telling me to relax, but I had no idea how to do what he expected of me. We all managed to come eventually and then got dressed. Afterwards we had some tea and chatted while they told me about some of their experiences. It occurred to me then that they often had these afternoons. One or the other would click with someone, who would then be invited over for a threesome. I was told the time of the trains and at about six o'clock I made for the door. They both started to grope me again, then remembered that on Sunday there was a reduced service. They told me to give them a ring sometime.

I met Jake that night in Kirklands to give him all the gossip. We laughed our heads off at the whole idea. I had enjoyed the experience, although had felt awkward about it. I didn't ring them again. I don't know if it was because I lost the number or didn't fancy it. Jake was pleased that I had a sexual outlet though; it meant that I kept my hands off him for a while. On the other hand, when he felt like it, he would exploit the fact that I was eager for sex with him, asking me to 'bath' him when his parents were out, or fuck him (awkwardly) when I stayed the night at his house. It was a strange friendship.

We would argue quite a lot, falling out with each other every five minutes; two highly strung Aquarians with sharp tongues and quick tempers. Aquarians go out of their way to appear different and unusual. One night a gaggle of Queens including Jake and I were walking down Hardman Street away from Kirklands. At

113

one point I said something to Jake that he didn't like, so he punched me on the side of the face. I hit him back, and we started to fight. All of a sudden a police-woman grabbed me by the neck and pushed me against the wall. I shouted at her to let go of me. She did but only to pass me to a tall plainclothes policeman who was a bit on the rough side. He accused me of being 'a shaved-headed punk rocker, making trouble on his patch'. He dragged me along the floor and was pretty abusive. Jake had somehow got off scot-free. He must have looked like the innocent party, even though he had started the fight. I was pretty shaken, and walked off when the policeman let me go. I sat on a bench behind St Luke's Church to catch my breath. One of the Queens we were with, a hairdresser, followed me and persuaded me to rejoin the party.

Monged!

Dykes and Queens seemed to live in fairly close harmony on the gay scene in Liverpool. There were not enough clubs for segregation to exist. If there were any fights in the clubs, the Dykes usually started them. There was one particular Dyke who looked like an extra from 'Prisoner: Cell Block H'. Her name was Marie and she was very butch. People were petrified of her. A Queen known as Josie was also quite rough and was known to pick fights with anyone. Being a pansy did not always mean being fey and retiring, especially in Liverpool. I was glad I was taught who to keep away from by older and wiser friends.

One of these friends was a mixed-race woman called Grace in her late thirties. She had short hair and an athletic, boyish figure, so much so that some people mistook her for a teenage boy. She was full of energy and was always surrounded by young people.

Grace had four children that she had lost the custody of. A bigoted female judge had given custody to their father. According to Grace, both the father and the judge claimed in court that as Grace was a lesbian, she was not a fit mother. The Judge considered allowing her the custody of the male child, but not the three girls. This was particularly painful for Grace as she was brought up in Welsh orphanages and craved the security of family life. According to Grace, her husband had previously enjoyed her lesbian activities, sharing a bed with her lovers and her. He would often wank himself while watching them. But when the divorce came, he claimed *she* was the kinky one. Grace had never felt guilty about her sexuality, and didn't know the word 'lesbian'.

Grace lived in Falkner Street off Hope Street on the border of the town centre and Toxteth, just around the corner from Kirklands where she worked as a chef. She had befriended a young Italian boy, Mario, at catering college. He had an acute literacy problem and she had helped him pass the exams. She was also a friend of Frank Clarke. All these people became my new friends and acquaintances, as I became more involved with the gay scene rather than the music scene in Liverpool.

It was very much a dope-smoking clique, though I was not really a dope smoker by this time. One of the first times that I got well and truly stoned was with Steve and Sarah Slingback. Steve lived in a hard-to-let tower block in Huyton. The council were going through a stage when they were giving young single people two- or three-bedroomed flats in high-rise buildings instead of putting families or old age pensioners in them. It was the kind of place where the lift was covered in graffiti and smelt of piss.

Steve (along with his sister Sarah) had attended the Liverpool Stage School. Steve was, I suppose, a theatrical. His interest was mainly in dance though he didn't seem to be pursuing any particular profession. It appeared to me that he saved up all his energies to pursue sex. Sarah lived in a low-rise council estate literally two minutes from Steve, with her husband Johnny and her son Thomas, who must have been five or six years old at the time.

Steve had a plant growing in one of his spare bedrooms. Whenever he ran out of hashish, he would pluck a few leaves from the plant, grill them like toast till they were dry, then roll a joint and smoke them. As Steve got stoned he would dance around his flat to tapes of Kraftwerk and Tomita, early electronic music.

'What do you feel like doing when you get stoned? I like to dance,' he said. Not being very experienced at 'being stoned' I was trying desperately to appear as though I knew what he meant. I didn't feel stoned at first but then Sarah turned up and it hit me. I went into fits of giggles. Every second I felt I was waking up into a new unfamiliar world; I even suspected paranoidly that I had been spiked with LSD. My vision seemed to flicker like an old silent movie. All of a sudden Sarah was laying on the scally charm.

'Ay 'olly, do us a favour. Go round to me flat an' ask our

Johnny if he'll sell yer a two quid deal on tic. He wont give it t' me an I caan't smoke that 'ome grown shite.'

To use one of Sarah's phrases, I was gobsmacked. I really didn't want to go. I hardly knew Johnny, and in my then state of dope-induced paranoia, I could not even imagine negotiating the lift. What was worse, I had to ask for the two-quid deal on credit. But doing the errand must have been preferable to saying no to Sarah, so I somehow managed it. Saying no to one Slingback is possible, but when there's two in the same room, you don't stand a chance.

'Go on 'olly, don't be mean.'

When I finally staggered over to Sarah's flat Johnny asked me if I'd ever been stoned before as I was acting strangely.

'Not like this,' I replied, laughing nervously and hysterically.

'I'm monged," I said – to use a typical Slingbackism.

* * *

Another girl-about-town I remember was Margi Clarke. She had bright red hair and a penchant for green eye shadow. She had been a bit tied down by domestic life and was dying to break out on to the scene. 'Breaking in' would be a better description. She made several attempts at forming a band, none of which were particularly fruitful for long. One of her bands later played Eric's – she called herself Margeaux (pronounced Ma-gox). What she lacked in singing ability she made up for with a spunky attitude and uninhibited imagination. She wrote a couple of interesting songs, 'Jimmy's Grin' and 'Angel Fish Dream', and her answer to the inevitable hecklers was, 'Why don't ye go and take yer face fer a shit,' and other choice phrases.

The book *England's Dreaming* by John Savage touches briefly on the Liverpool scene of this period. He quotes Margi saying that she wore an apple round her neck on a piece of string and carried a kettle for a handbag. I remember the apple but not the kettle. He also quotes her as saying that I wore a Tampax for an earring and wore a chocolate box on my head as a hat. It's true I once wore one of my mothers Lillett's hanging from a sleeper in

117

my ear. This was my reaction to the razor-blade earring trend of that time. If women could wear razor-blades in their ears then I could wear a jam rag.

I remember Margi coming round to my parent's house in January 1980 to try and write a song with me. Songwriting had always been a bit of an introspective thing for me. Not being a 'Muso' (trained musician) in the typical sense made it difficult for me to respond to her in the way she needed. She came out with a string of weird and wonderful ideas for songs. 'Abstract Ice' was one of them. She also told me the basic outline of *A Letter To Brezhnev*, which I presume Frank had told her, and which she tried to turn into lyrics. Sitting up in my bedroom with my acoustic guitar trying to strum along to Margi, however unfruitful it was as a songwriting exercise, is an amusing memory. She 'charmed the boots' off Pat and Eric, who always liked it when girls came round to see me.

BIG IN JAPAN

Little Cathy

During one of the lapses in my friendship with Jake I started hanging out with Little Cathy a lot more. We planned to move to London away from Liverpool and its village atmosphere. We were going to busk in tube stations. A few rehearsals of 'He's A Rebel' and Twinkle's 'Terry' didn't come to much though. Cathy couldn't stop laughing long enough.

On one occasion Cathy and I hitchhiked to London for the night. I took her to the Colherne, the famous leather bar in Earls Court. On the way down Earls Court Road she asked if she could wear my green flasher's mac. I said 'No!' She then explained angrily that she was about to start her monthly period, and as she was wearing white trousers this could be embarrassing. I lent her the mac immediately. She tried to get me to go into a chemist's to shop-lift a packet of Tampax, as we didn't have much money. I don't know how I managed it but I did it.

When we arrived at the Colherne, this tiny girl was dwarfed by a host of leather-clad queens. I saw a blonde, six-foot-four Texan cowboy, a flight attendant for the now-defunct Branif Airlines, whom I had met once before in Liverpool at the Grapes in Mathew Street. A friend had introduced us then; he'd been showing him off in fact, as he couldn't believe his luck in having this huge Texan hunk interested in him. The Texan had had an idea that my friend looked like John Boy Walton. Now, on this evening in the Colherne, the Texan said to me in his best Southern drawl, 'This is no place to bring a lady'. He was right.

Cathy and I spent the night hanging round Trafalgar Square and Piccadilly: no place for a lady either, and we were moved on by the police a few times, cold and hungry. Hitchhiking home the next day Cathy's forlorn, Dickensian waif-like appearance helped our cause on the motorway. By contrast, my leatherboy look was a bit off-putting for most motorists. Still, we managed to get home safely.

Jake and I also used to hitch to London for a bit of excitement. We had heard of the Black Cap, a gay pub in Camden Town where drag acts played regularly. We managed to get to London easily enough, but it was now approaching closing time at the Black Cap and we still hadn't 'copped off' or found a place to stay. Jake was not the type to rough it and hang round Trafalgar Square. As the crowds dispersed outside of the pub, he persuaded a man in his thirties to put us up. There was what seemed like an unending tube journey to somewhere called Plaistow where the man, Randy, lived. The three of us got into his single bed and the inevitable happened. As in all threesomes, there was one who felt left out. This time it was Jake. I think he couldn't lose his inhibitions in front of a third party even though he was dying to get fucked by Randy.

Jake told me this resentfully the next day as we tried to hitch home, finding that two eighteen-year-old boys in full leather gear did not have the hitchhiking cachet of a boy and a waif-like girl. The further north we got the more difficult it was to get lifts. It was a very cold winter and just as we were dropped off by a lorry driver outside Pontefract, the sky turned pitch black and it started to rain. The wind was howling and the traffic had reduced to a trickle. And we were on a part of the motorway where it was hard for motorists to see us. Slowly the realisation that we were stranded dawned on us. We started to argue – Jake was a bit of a whiner in these situations. It got colder, and the rain started to lash and burn our faces.

I had noticed a caravan sales park at the side of the motorway, about a mile down the road. We trudged along the motorway narrowly missing death from a lorry who refused our signals. Desperate measures were needed. If we had stayed out in this weather we would have died of exposure. I found a brick which I used to break the glass of a caravan door. Afraid that we might be discovered, we huddled on the floor of the aisle of the caravan, scared to lie on the beds in case a passing night watchman discovered us. Jake blamed the whole situation on me.

I thought that having sex might take our minds off our predicament, but he slapped my hand every time I tried to get his pants down.

The next morning we crept out early and walked into Pontefract town centre. We looked terrible. Not only were we dressed bizarrely by Pontefract standards, but we looked like a couple of drowned rats. People stared at us, making openly disapproving comments. We thought that we had better get out of the place before we got into further trouble, so I phoned someone to tell them our plight. They told me to go to the Police Station and ask the police to phone our parents, to request that they lodged the train fare home at a Police Station in Liverpool. The police gave us a bit of a hard time, questioning us about where we stayed the night before and such, but we got the train eventually. Eric was pissed off as he had had to part with the seven quid to get me home. He has also had to take an hour of his precious time 'on the road' to go to the Police Station. I was not a popular person that night. 'So what's new?' I thought.

*   *   *

My next London adventure was with Cathy. I wrote to Timmy, the clarinet player at the squat in Butlers Wharf, saying I wanted to move down to London; I may have omitted to mention Cathy. He wrote back saying I could move into his old room, as someone had moved out and he had moved into their room. So Cathy, my guitar and I, and all my worldly goods in a suitcase, headed for London. We were planning to sign on in London as soon as we got there, as it was quite common in those days for people to travel around looking for work, and claimants were allowed to sign on at any Social Security Office in the country. I was always using this one as an excuse for signing on a day late. 'I was looking for work in London, honest.'

Timmy was friendly enough when we arrived, but everyone at the squat seemed to be a bit down, especially as there was no theatre production to inspire anyone. Camilla, another squat inhabitant, was writing a piece to be performed in a church. She said she and Timmy used to busk. We never got that far however. Cathy started to slag me off as I urged her to rehearse with me. She said that my voice sounded too 'Opportunity Knocks', and she wouldn't make the effort to learn the lyrics of 'Treasure Island'.

During one of my early trips to the Colherne I met a young man called Jason. He had golden brown skin and a cropped short afro hair. He was hanging around outside after closing time, as many Colherne regulars would if they had not found someone to go home with. Jason wore the gay leatherboy uniform of black leather jacket, white T-shirt and blue Levi 501 jeans. Despite this he stood out, as I had never seen a coloured man during my few visits to leather bars. We chatted in a friendly way, walking around the block. We saw other gay couplings in doorways, leatherboys fucking in front gardens and down the stairs to basement flats. Speaking with a pronounced cockney accent, he told me that he had relatives up in Liverpool, family who lived in Toxteth, Liverpool 8 – where else? He took me back to a flat. I was always very curious about what it would be like to sleep with a coloured man, wondering if the myth about their massive cocks was true.

We went to the small bedroom that just contained a single bed and a pine chest from which he took a pair of leather trousers, and he put them on after stripping naked with his back to me. He had a golden-skinned body, athletic but not over sculpted (going to the gym was not so compulsory for a young hustler in those days). He asked me what I liked to do. I started to suck his hard uncircumcised cock that protruded out of the leather trousers. It tasted slightly different to white cock. He was pumping his cock into my face while I held on to his gorgeous arse. Then he threw me on to the bed, withdrawing his cock from me as a kind of punishment. He sat on my chest and rubbed the head of his cock over my face, not letting my mouth around his ample cockhead.

'D' yer want me to fuck you?' he said.

I told him that I had never been fucked up the arse, and that I was scared of it.

'Maybe you like oil then,' he said, producing a bottle of

Johnson's Baby Oil which he poured on to my chest, the cold oil a shock to my warm skin. He started to slip and slide all over me like an animal, spitting into my face.

'You fucking bastard, you want me to fuck you!' he kept repeating. This I found rather disturbing; what was this? It may have been one of his fantasies, but it had never been one of mine. After the spitting episode he got wilder and wilder, trying various things from his sexual repertoire in an attempt to make me come. Eventually he rubbed his cock against my stomach until he came, thick and white, all over my chest. Part of me was glad that it was over. His sexual style was a bit too sophisticated for me.

Keith Allen cornered me one day at the squat: he had got a 'gig' at the Marquee Club and would I play bass guitar for him? I explained I didn't have a bass guitar or amplifier and that I wasn't the type of bass player that could play along spontaneously without rehearsal. Nonetheless Keith seemed to think it would be alright on the night. This was very much the attitude of the times: musicianship was secondary to bravado. I didn't fancy it though. Apart from the technical aspects, I also didn't want to be just someone's bass player ever again. I had learned that lesson well.

London was not the same as Liverpool, where people were interested and spoke to each other on the streets. It wasn't that the people at the squat were unfriendly, they just had their own problems to deal with, and didn't have the time for two runaway teenagers from Liverpool.

So after about two weeks of not knowing our way around or having the money to get the tube anywhere, we decided to hitch home. At the start of the motorway we met some gypsies who were living in a caravan. They asked me to sing them a song which I did, trying to get Cathy to sing along. In return they made us some jam butties wrapped up in silver foil and gave us cups of tea. They were nice friendly people, a pleasure to meet.

I was wearing a bowler hat, which didn't help us get a lift, so I made Cathy put it on. Cathy started to moan and make her usual digs at me, saying I looked like a Queer and that's why we couldn't get a lift.

* * *

Back at home, Cathy became obsessed with a boy called Jammo, part of a crowd of drop outs and students. They seemed to me to be rather negative. Their attitude was 'society stinks, so we're going to take drugs and get fucked up'. They weren't unintelligent, just negative. They seemed to lack any ambition, preferring to shoplift bottles of whisky from an off-licence and get pissed.

I started to see less of Cathy as she got more involved with these people, and we started to argue more regularly. She made one of her biting comments about me in front of her new friends, which must have touched a sore point because I hit her in the eye. I regretted doing it immediately. I felt terrible and kept apologising. We left the flat we had been visiting, which was on the top floor of a big house. I had my acoustic guitar with me. When I reached the top of the stairs Cathy pushed me so I started to fall down the stairs. By some stroke of luck I managed to stop my fall after a few stairs by grabbing the banister with one hand while still holding on to my guitar with the other. Cathy fell into fits of manic laughter. I got the impression it wouldn't have mattered to her if I'd have broken my neck.

Sometime later Grace got me a part time job in a pizza restaurant as a pizza chef. One night Cathy and a friend of hers, Fat Ella, came in. All the waiters and the manager knew she was a friend of mine. I could tell she had her mischievous head on, as she kept giggling and looking in my direction as I worked. They were ordering lots of drinks, vodka, pizzas and banana splits, stuff like that. They ran up quite a bill. I noticed that they chose to sit near the door. Obviously they planned to do a runner when their waiter turned his back. When they took off, some of the waiters ran after them but I think they got away. This was pure Cathy – embarrassing me and getting a free night out into the bargain.

Over the next few years I saw less and less of her. I would see her running through town with store detectives at her heels. She had become a professional shoplifter. She would steal perfume or expensive fashion magazines. In Liverpool, there's no shame in shoplifting, and the goods are sold later in the pub, at half the retail price. Everyone's on the fiddle.

I met Cathy only once more. It was near my parent's house. She told me she had been raped by two men in a flat in Princess Avenue. I felt it might have been symptomatic of the people she had chosen as friends. Her boyfriend had been close at hand at the time I think, locked in an adjoining room, but unable to stop the rape.

The next thing I heard was that she had thrown herself off the landing balcony of the fourteenth floor of a tower-block in Greenbank Drive. Pete Burns's wife Lyn told me the news one night in Pickwicks, the night club. I couldn't believe it at first. Apparently she hung herself over the balcony and maybe changed her mind, but in the scramble to save herself fell to her death. There was something just too vibrant and bright about Little Cathy. Unfortunately for her there was 'No Future', just like in The Sex Pistols song. Poor Cathy, I hope she's happy now.

My Cowboy Period

I seemed to drift without direction for a while after Big In Japan, though still wanting to be a star, still writing songs on my acoustic guitar in between my social activities. At this point, Jayne kindly persuaded Pete Fullwell to record a Holly single. I creamed my jeans. I was going to make my very own record. This is one of my few memories of feeling truly elated. I was given a whole day in Amazons' eight track studio, which I was determined to make the most of. I recorded three songs: 'Treasure Island', 'Yankee Rose' and 'Desperate Dan'.

'Treasure Island' was meant to be the A side. Ian Broudie was going to produce it, but he had to drop out due to other commitments, though he did give me some good ideas for arrangements, bass lines, backing vocals, etc. I got Lori Larty, a good friend of mine at that time, to do backing vocals. Pete Wiley contributed a bit of guitar on 'Treasure Island' but didn't really understand the calypso feel of the song. I also got Wah Heats' keyboard player to add a string synth line.

To create a cinematic sound-scape on 'Yankee Rose' I got people in the studio to play Cowboys and Indians. Pete Fullwell got down on his hands and knees and made horse noises with coconut shells. It was a bit unorthodox but a lot of fun. I would point at one set of people like a conductor and they would do their allotted thing. Someone tinkled on an out-of-tune saloon piano and Wiley played harmonica. I used a tape loop to create the cowboy-on-the-range bass line as it was too difficult for me to play the monotonous line over and over in perfect time. Lori's 'Yankee Rose' vocal line was meant to conjure up memories of 'Johnny Remember Me'. Her voice really added something special. Pete Fullwell thought 'Yankee Rose' the best of the three songs, and I let him persuade me that it should be the A side, although 'Treasure Island' was a better song in my opinion.

126

I think I got an extra afternoon to mix everything, then there it was. For the sleeve, Bob Wakelin, a cartoonist and illustrator, created a drawing of my head with a glinting tooth smile. Lynched cowboys formed the background. I did some publicity photographs and created a photocopied mail out. The single got a favourable review in either *NME* or *Melody Maker*, but without a band I had no way of promoting it by playing live dates. This was a problem which I knew had to be solved eventually.

* * *

Due to lack of money I would often go out for the night and then walk home instead of getting a taxi. On one of these occasions I was wearing a Seditioneries cowboy T-shirt that Paul had discarded. It showed two cartoon cowboys, trouserless, their cocks almost touching. I'd had it hidden from my father for quite some time, though Pat knew about it as she had washed it for me once. To finish off my look I had borrowed a pair of ornate spurs to wear on my cowboy boots. It was not a cold night so I had my leather jacket draped over my shoulders.

I was almost home and had reached the junction of Smithdown Road and Ullet Road where there was a public toilet on a traffic island. It was about 2.30 am. Suddenly a police car sped out of a side road and two policemen got out – they had been lying in wait near the 'cottage'. I quickly folded my arms to obscure the T-shirt. One of the policemen – old and not very pleasant – asked me where I had been. 'The Masquerade,' I stupidly answered.

'So you're a Queer then, are yer?' he growled.

'I don't know what you mean. officer,' I replied in my best voice.

'You're probably too young to know yet,' he snarled in his most intimidating manner. He then started telling me that the spurs I was wearing were offensive weapons and that he was going to arrest me. I was told to get in the back of the police car. Somehow I got in without unfolding my arms. I couldn't even put my jacket on to cover the T-shirt in case he saw the huge Tom-Of-Finland-style cowboy cocks. He asked me where I lived and

127

then they drove me home. He rang the bell and woke my mother up. He explained to her about the spurs and told her that he would 'let me off this time'.

The next morning I found the T-shirt ripped up in the bin.

On another eventful night I was walking home during my leather phase. A man in a car stopped me along Smithdown Road and asked me if I wanted a lift. I got in. He was a business man type in his forties, who drove with one hand and got my cock out of my trousers with the other. He asked me if I minded if we went past where I lived and had a bit of fun. I was a bit drunk and game for anything. He took me up a secluded alley somewhere and asked me to fuck him, which I did in my inexperienced way. I didn't even like him, never mind fancy him. It was his brazen attitude that excited me. He then dropped me at the bottom of our street and drove off quickly. I was left wondering to myself, 'Did that actually happen?'

While I was still living at home a couple of new gay clubs opened in Liverpool – Stevie's and Macmillan's. Stevie's was a large club that later became the Warehouse, a venue for bands and the inheritor of the Eric's scene. There I managed to cop off with a lad of about twenty-one that I had fancied for ages. I had spoken to him before and he had told me he was a park ranger over the water. He was short and blonde, brown-skinned, and had a compact muscular physique. He was covered in blonde hair on his arms and chest, and his face was lit up by an open, innocent expression. He said his car was over the water, parked at the entrance of the Mersey Tunnel. So we got the Tunnel bus, picked up his car and drove back to my parent's house. He said that he couldn't take me back to where he lived, so I sneaked him up to my bedroom and had his clothes off in seconds. My hands and mouth were all over him, I couldn't stop myself. I had kept the harsh electric light on so I could see his beautiful brown body. I caressed his cock and skin with my hands and mouth. He was shy and asked if we could get into bed and turn the light out. I did, and got into bed with him. I did everything I could to try and please him, but he just lay there motionless and seemed unable to do anything. Was this what necrophilia was like? I thought.

(Necrophilia had been the subject of one of my teenage poems. It described just such a blonde man laying on a marble slab, and the detailed description of what I would do to the body.) I wondered if perhaps he wanted me to fuck him, which I stupidly tried to do without any lubrication. It wasn't a very exciting experience for either of us ultimately, even though I was very attracted to him. The next morning I woke up and he was gone. Just as well. It might have been a bit difficult to explain to my parents.

I bumped into him occasionally over the next few years but we only nodded to each other over crowded, throbbing, dance floors. I never managed to find anything but the occasional one-night stand on the Liverpool gay scene. I'm not saying that lasting relationships are the only way to live, but the lack of them on the gay scene of my youth was a very isolating experience.

Fucked!

It must have been the summer of 1978. I had become friendly with Merry after taking an interest in what she was studying. I became a sounding board for her ideas on English Literature which she spewed out relentlessly. Half of them just confused me but I nodded reassuringly anyway. She invited me to London to meet her family. Their house was wonderful, huge but homely. She seemed to have endless brothers who talked quickly and incessantly with the same public-school accent. I became self-conscious about my Liverpool drawl and my lack of education.

They had all been brought up on the grounds of a public school in Sussex, where their father was the art master, living in a pretty cottage on the edge of the grounds.

One afternoon Merry was trying to study in her room while I was singing with my guitar in the garden. She came out and asked me to stop. 'Your voice is lovely Holly, but it's very distracting,' she said in her Queen's English.

I walked off in a huff and went for a walk in the grounds of the old school. Once a monastery, it was still run by monks. I fell asleep in the hot summer sun and got sunstroke. My fair skin turned the colour of beetroot and I was very sick. Afterwards I lay in one of the quiet bedrooms for hours, hallucinating, delirious.

I remember talking to one of the more handsome boys through the dormitory window. He laughed when he saw the colour I had turned. I felt like Scudder in the Merchant Ivory production of *Maurice* – the working-class boy with his face up against the sexually charged shop window of blonde, youthful privilege.

Merry was having a flirtation with a sculptor called Charlie who was planning a trip to Paris. I said I wished I could go to Paris with him. He said, 'You can, and to pay for the trip you can work with me in Wapping as a labourer when we return. The job should last six weeks and you'll get a hundred quid a week in your hand.'

I was going to Paris for a week, getting out of Liverpool for three whole months and getting paid for it -- fantastic! Charlie had friends called Trish and Adam we could stay with in Paris. They had a tiny flat on Boulevard Beaumarchais near the Bastille.

I'd had to get a quick passport done at Petite France. For the necessary photographs I wore one of my home-made leather neckerchiefs that I was sporting at the time, over a white collarless shirt, slightly Hitler Youth. Somehow the sunstroke didn't show up on the black-and-white image. I had inserted 'Holly' as my middle name. It was now official. I put my occupation as artist, which I felt was appropriate.

I took to wandering the streets of Paris on my own. Jake had made a pair of baggy black-and-white striped pirate trousers that he felt were too loud for him, so I had inherited them. I got my head shaved to the bone in a Parisian barber's shop, all done with a pair of manual clippers. In the Rue Saint Denis I bought a sailor's hat of the American Marine variety – I must have been trying to live out some kind of Jean Genet fantasy. I loved the Rue Saint Denis with its prostitutes parading in black leotards and fish-net stockings in broad daylight. But I also remember being petrified by the harsh Military Police who stood motionless with their loaded machine guns on the pavement, a disdainful look in their eyes. Vile warriors. I saw the biker rally at the Bastille on Saturday night when we took Trish and Adam out to Chatiers, the students' restaurant, as a 'thank-you' for letting us stay. Adam lent me his leather biker's jacket for the occasion, which I wore with my Tom Of Finland leather cap.

Travelling in the open back of Adam's pick up truck, I remember thinking, 'it doesn't get much better than this' as we drove down the Champs-Elysées in the sunshine. People waved at me and shouted *'Salut Marine!'* Was I breaking out of my rut of being an unsuccessful musician in Liverpool? I had been finding the 'village' aspect of Liverpool's music scene claustrophobic; Liverpool is a very hard place to leave.

I returned in a pink raw silk suit and with a bit of money in my pocket, but not much. I went to see Grace at the Pizza restaurant, where she was now working as a chef. Somewhere along the line she got me a job doing the Friday and Saturday night shifts that no one else wanted to do. The pay was lousy and the waiters didn't share the tips with the chef. I wasn't great at the job either but I could do it. Unfortunately the wife of one of the owners took an instant dislike to me. She hated the leather trousers I wore, and if I greased my hair she freaked. I hated her back, of course. 'Stuck up bitch,' I thought.

Everyone I came into contact with seemed to smoke dope – even the waiters would sneak out to the back of the kitchen. It was considered an everyday sort of thing. Some of the waiters were friendly and if the manager (Dick the Prick) was out we could have a good time. This job supplemented my Supplementary Benefit for the short period that I had it.

I was still going to Eric's occasionally to see Pete Fullwell. I persuaded him to record another 'Holly' single I'd written called 'Hobo Joe', which was recorded at the Cargo sixteen-track studios in Rochdale. I remember seeing Mark Smith from The Fall sitting in the small reception area. The lovely Gary Dwyer, the drummer from Teardrop Explodes, kindly played drums for me. Ian Broudie produced and played guitar and I played bass. We thought the result was quite good. Almost commercial.

Meanwhile Steve Lovell, a guitarist then in his mid-twenties who worked at Virgin record shop, rang me at home to ask me if I would sing on a songwriter's demo. He had heard 'Yankee Rose' and liked it. He then asked me if I wanted to form a band with him and Ambrose Reynolds, a bass player who had been in The Walkie Talkies, and had also played on 'Black Leather' by Pete Burns's Nightmares in Wax, which had a great disco bassline and fabulous trashy lyrics.

We rehearsed in Hambi's basement with a drummer called Phil. Ambrose had the idea that I should play bass as well to create a rhythmic counterpoint. We booked a 'gig' in the Masonic pub in town, but needed a name for the group in order to do this. In our rehearsal room someone had stuck a page from

Guy Peelhaerts' book *Rock Dreams*. It was a painting of a newspaper front-cover, and the headline ran, 'Frankie Goes Hollywood'. Underneath was a picture of Frank Sinatra getting off a plane. I added the 'To' so that it scanned better, and we had a name.

Ironically this show never actually happened. I didn't really feel happy with the music we were making. Ambrose was a bit upset but accepted it in good grace. I planned to work further with Steve though. He seemed to me to be older and more sensible than most musicians I knew in Liverpool, so over the next few months I kept in touch with him.

Sometime during 1980 Grace decided to search for her GI father in America. She had a nice Liverpool Housing Trust flat in Falkner Street. It was all beige fitted carpets and mirror tiles in the bathroom. In order not to lose her tenancy she needed someone to continue to pay rent while she was away. I needed desperately to move away from home, so I was very grateful.

Shortly after I moved into Grace's flat in Falkner Street, 'Hobo Joe' was released, and got a few favourable reviews. It was the week that John Lennon died. I remember not really being affected by his death as I had not been of the generation who had idolised him. Marc Bolan's death had upset me more, even though I realise now that Lennon had a far greater influence on pop culture.

I was listening endlessly to 'Remain In Light' by Talking Heads, 'Scary Monsters' by David Bowie, and 'I'm Coming Out' by Diana Ross – produced by Chic, the Seventies disco phenomenon. I also played 'Love And Affection' by Joan Armatrading incessantly – a masterpiece. I would often go out alone now as Paul had gone to stay with his family in America, and Jake and I had drifted apart for a while. I used to go out alone and dance to George McCrea's 'Rock Your Baby' and other disco classics.

One night I saw an unfamiliar face. Tall, with straight dark hair and a dark complexion, he had a lean-looking body. I rather fancied him. I approached him a bit later and discovered his name was Jock. He was a Scot, in his late thirties and living in

Manchester, where he worked as a headmaster in a primary school. He looked much younger to me. He went to the YMCA gymnasium, so he could keep fit. His friends whom he was visiting called Bill and Charlie were ex-lovers, now sisters, and both lived in Liverpool. I took Jock back to the flat that night, together with Tweela, a fashion student I knew well and a boy he had picked up. I had promised to give them a mattress in the living room as they had no place to stay. I was sporting a bleached blonde flat top that I had had done at Max's Barber Shop where all the Rockabillies went. Jock was wearing a blue-and-white striped Rugby shirt and, I suppose, he fulfilled a fantasy for me. The masculine athlete, a bit like my former English teacher. He was a bit of a liberal and kept going on about proportional representation, but his enthusiasm for sex took me by surprise when I led him to the bedroom, although his preferred activity was rubbing cocks together. I certainly enjoyed his hard, lean body. The next morning he left to go and have lunch with his friends.

I became friendly with Bill and Charlie, partly due to my interest in Jock. Charlie worked at the Gas Board. I saw him there when I was asking for time to pay my bill, a regular occurrence – I was always in trouble with money. Bill worked for the council as an electrician, and showed me how to fiddle the electric meter as a twenty-first birthday present. He had his own flat, hi-fi, video camera and car, one of the first gay men I knew who was not on the dole. I was impressed with the way he held things together in a straight world. They took me to Heroes (a gay club in Manchester) a few times where I met Jock again; this time however he had his boyfriend with him and I was rather disappointed.

A few months later he came to Liverpool again and slept at my flat. This was the first time I remember being fucked. Jock was the first person I suppose I wanted to do that particular thing with – he was handsome and a figure of authority. He looked a bit like the headmaster who had caned me. I can't remember if I was twenty or twenty-one by then: maybe we broke the law, maybe we didn't. I requested a repeat performance the next morning, and was sorry to see him leave. Later Bill explained to me that my crush on Jock wasn't a good idea as he already lived with someone in Manchester. Bill persuaded me to stay over on the couch at his flat one night when Jock was also staying, so that Jock could see I was one of Bill's friends and not just a convenient sex partner for Jock when he happened to visit Liverpool. Although I had fun with Bill and Charlie, the experience with Jock soured things a little for me. I wrote a song about the self-pity that I went through after this experience, called 'Bring On The Violins'.

I started to write more and more songs at Falkner Street, sometimes borrowing a TEAC four-track to record them on, sometimes just using a cassette player. 'Boyfriend Sixty Five' was one particular favourite from that era.

A Nice Wet Wank

During the final days of Pete O'Halligan's little theatre, a group of unemployed theatre technicians and actors got together to form the ill-fated Black Box Theatre Company. Chris Bernard was to direct a play with dialogue by Frank Clarke, and I was supposed to write some songs for it. The set was to consist of an ingenious revolving black box that contained the set for each scenario.

The play was based on a book about a pair of male Siamese twins who had an extra dormant head. I was asked to play the subservient twin to Frank's domineering one. The idea was in order to get publicity for the play, Frank and I would spend a week or two tied together, something that I wasn't looking forward to. He kept taunting me that I would have to share a toilet with him – a malodorous idea.

I wrote a song called 'Boys Of The Head' that everyone seemed to like, while Frank came up with a few pages of dialogue. The female lead was to be played by Gilly Coman, the most experienced member of the cast. Unfortunately she was absolutely the wrong person for Frank to be working with. The minute she heard his dialogue, she freaked. Frank had written a line that contained the phrase, 'Why don't you go and have a nice wet wank?' She thought it was disgusting and unnecessary to use such language. She later came to public attention as the Aveline character in Carla Lane's 'Bread'. The situation developed into a row between her and Frank, and she started talking me down too, saying I couldn't act. There were a few other hiccups, and eventually the whole thing came to a halt.

Around this time, I picked up a stocky young boy in the Masquerade and had nowhere to take him. Frank said that I could come back to his high-rise flat in Everton as he had a spare bedroom. After cups of coffee and late-night chat I was directed to the spare bedroom, which had a window looking out on to the large balcony. All I could see out of it was a slice of moon and the sequin stars twinkling in the night sky. We both got into the bed and during the proceedings, I started to hear extra noises, sounding a bit like suppressed laughter. I ignored this until I distinctly heard a whisper, 'I think they're wanking each other off!' I looked up and there was Frank and a couple of friends, known as the Frankettes, standing on the balcony outside watching through the window and recording the proceedings on a cassette. 'Fuck Off you bastards!' I said. They succeeded in damping any attempts at passion for me and my friend that night.

* * *

Around the time 'Hobo Joe' was released, someone from Granada Television came to Eric's in Liverpool. They were looking for Northern bands to play on an arts programme called 'Celebration'. I was chosen on the strength of my two singles on the Eric's label. Pete Burns's band were also chosen, but I can't remember what they were called at the time.

The day of the TV recording was Thursday, 30th of October 1980. I still have the daily call-sheet that Granada printed. It has my name at the top, then below, a cast list for 'Coronation Street'. It was such a good experience for me, learning to react to a camera. The director had set up a rocking horse for me to sit on to sing 'Yankee Rose'. On a blue screen in the background was projected an old Western. I sang in my quasi-cowboy outfit, playing an acoustic guitar, while the rocking horse wore sunglasses and had an arrow through its head. It was all very tongue-in-cheek.

I came home on the train elated by the experience. I had spoken briefly to the handsome Ray Langton from 'Coronation Street' and I had even caught a glimpse of the legendary Elsie Tanner (Pat Phoenix). On the other hand, witnessing one of the ageing actors fall asleep between takes was a bit sad.

Sometime later Steve Lovell turned up at my flat in Falkner

Street and announced that he had left his girlfriend and moved out. He had no real plans about where he was going to stay, so I said he could sleep on the mattress in the living room.

One day, Steve Lovell brought home the Saturday boy from the Virgin Records shop in St John's Precinct. Steve knew I thought this young lad was cute. He was in his late teens, short, with dark hair and black cherry eyes, and a slim, athletic wiriness. He had a particular charisma and way of dressing that was very 'scally', as young, straight and slightly trendy Liverpuddlians are called. For some reason I nicknamed him Buddy Mate.

We all got on very well. There were three generations of young men: Buddy about sixteen, me about twenty one, and Steve about twenty six. We would talk about music non-stop. They used to bring back all the best records, new and old, from Virgin, and we amassed a great record collection.

On our trips into town we would get paralytic on vodka and orange or Tequila Sunrise cocktails, our chosen drinks. We preferred smoking dope though. It was cheaper and we didn't suffer hangovers from it. We would sometimes 'score' dope in the Masonic Pub, where bands played, sometimes being sold beeswax by the black drug dealers – particularly annoying if it was your last fiver. Lured into the toilets by two physically substantial black men, I wasn't going to confront them when I realised that the black lump they were handing me looked slightly suspicious.

For some reason we had just started to experiment with LSD – there was a period when blue microdots were being sold in Liverpool. I had been introduced to 'Acid' in summer 1980 by a photographer friend, Jon. I dragged him into a sinister looking space-invader arcade, where I showed him my favourite game 'GORF', which I played to 'Space Commander' level. We later wandered around the Roman Catholic Cathedral (known to many as Paddy's Wigwam). I started laughing at the people sitting in pews, having a 'religious experience'.

Steve Lovell was someone who I felt I could trust when I took acid, and did so a couple of times. He was a kind of not-so-sensible 'uncle' figure. Once, when tripping and trying to record in Hambi's studio, I threw an old transistor radio against the wall and said to Steve, 'Record that sound!' as if it were a vitally important thing. Steve quickly took control of the situation and got us out of there before any real damage was done.

Unfortunately we introduced Buddy Mate to drugs and because of his addictive personality, this developed into a serious problem, like with so many other young people in Liverpool around 1984. All of a sudden, cheap 'smack' was everywhere. Chasing The Dragon (smoking burnt heroin through a cardboard tube) became the 'in' thing. It was as if there was a progressive infection seeping through the city, one that began with unemployment and ended with heroin addiction.

Meanwhile, Steve, Buddy Mate and I started rehearsing in 'The Ministry', a well equipped rehearsal room set up by Billy and Mike. Our band was to be called WIN (World Intelligence Network), a name taken from the puppet series 'Joe 90'. Eventually however, Steve and I decided that Buddy's bass playing wasn't slick enough. Rather guiltily, we sacked him.

I had started to come under pressure from the DHSS to get a job, due to a particularly nasty supervisor at Kinglake House who dealt with my claim. He threatened that if I did not go on a residential rehabilitation course to learn soft toy making or gardening, he would have my Social Security Benefit stopped, which he eventually did. He claimed that after having been on Social Security for so long, I was unemployable and needed reintegration into society. I of course had other ideas. One Friday, my Giro just didn't arrive. 'The bastards!' I thought. I was sure that this wasn't legal but they did it regardless. I couldn't believe that this was happening. How was I going to eat and pay the rent on Grace's flat?

Luckily for me, an old acquaintance turned up in Liverpool that week. Camilla had written the gothic opera *The Case Of Charles Dexter Ward*, performed a few years previously at Pete O'Halligan's small theatre in Mathew Street. I knew some of the chorus parts as Paul had taught them to me when he had a job in it during its ICA run in London. Now it was to be performed at the Everyman Theatre, Hope Street. Camilla gave me a part in the chorus for £25 a week, a bit less for rehearsals. This was a lifesaver. Camilla asked me to help her choose some young performers from the Everyman Youth Theatre to augment the chorus. I chose a young schoolgirl punkette. She wore a trademark teabag as an earring, and became known as 'Teabag' for years to come. We became close friends.

When the production ended I was able to sign on the Social Security officially as 'available for work as a singer', which scuppered the plans of the Kinglake House SS Supervisor. I can't begin to describe the special kind of grey-suited, supercilious arsehole he was. I can just see him spying on mothers of one parent families on income support after dark, the next morning, checking if the air valves on their boyfriend's car tyres have moved since the night before.

I had now been living in Grace's flat for over a year and been paying rent to The Liverpool Housing Trust (via the DHSS) even though it was in Grace's name. I started to worry that when Grace returned I would be homeless again, so I applied for a flat through the Housing Trust, which by law they had to give me. They gave me a wonderful two-bedroomed flat in the attic of a large refurbished building, 46 Catherine Street. It was all odd angles and if you stood on your toes, the Anglican Cathedral was framed perfectly in the Velux window of the living room. I couldn't believe my luck – it was a beautiful flat. The rent was about eleven pounds a week or something ridiculously low. In the summer I used to open the windows in the roof and sit out on the slate tiles with the record player's speakers up there, listening to The Drifters 'Up On The Roof'.

Subway and Gomorrah

A few months after we asked him to leave our group, Buddy Mate formed his own band, out of a group of young scally teenagers. His still-at-school girlfriend Julie played keyboards, Brian Nash (Nasher) played guitar, Buddy played bass guitar, Peter Gill (Ped) played drums and Ged O'Tool (Mark's brother) sang. They used to rehearse in The Cells, a disused prison behind the Hollywood Club in Duke Street, ten minutes' walk away from my flat. I used to go down the hill and watch them rehearse and I even named them – The Dancing Girls.

Eventually, at a friend's suggestion, I replaced Ged as the singer. They thought I was hip as I'd had two singles out on the Eric's label and had been in Big In Japan, a group that some of them had seen as kids at Eric's Saturday matinees. Nasher had a job as an apprentice electrician with the council, and Ped, having just been made redundant from Hygena, had used his redundancy money to buy himself a better drum kit. They were all around sixteen or seventeen years old. I was an 'old man' of twenty-one or twenty-two.

I tried to rewrite the songs that they had, putting new lyrics to their backing music. We eventually got a spot on a local Granada TV show as 'Sons Of Egypt' which became our name for some unknown reason. 'Shake, Shake' was one of the songs. The performance was quite good, but the songs in general were not.

As well as dope, Buddy got interested in amphetamines (speed), and would book into a room at the Holiday Inn for all-night talking sessions which just became too much in the end. He had also started to get a bit bossy. He was the self-appointed leader of the band, financing most of the social events, buying the drugs and paying for most of the equipment, courtesy of Virgin Records where he now worked full time.

I had realised I needed to get a live band going if I was ever going to attract record company attention. Eventually Ped and I decided to leave Buddy's band and form another with Mark O'Tool as bass player. We felt a bit guilty leaving Buddy in the lurch, but we knew that his bass playing and his attitude were holding things back.

Almost on the first rehearsal we wrote 'Love Has Got A Gun', a song that appeared on the first Frankie Goes To Hollywood album. Mark had an energetic bass playing style influenced by Bow Wow Wow and Spandau Ballet – fast and funky. Ped had a solid drumming style and an appreciation for what was becoming fashionable at the time from a percussive point of view (we liked the rhythms of The Hicksons from East Anglia and 'In The Name Of Love' by The Thompson Twins).

I wrote lyrics and melodies over this rhythm section. This was how 'Two Tribes' was written. Mark had a Russian-sounding bass line that he played, an adaptation of a Bow Wow Wow bass line. I suggested that we broke it up with an American funk bass line, as an extreme cultural contrast, for a verse, and there it was. The lyrics were inspired by the Armageddon scenario described by a voice-over at the beginning of the film *Mad Max 2: The Road Warrior*, and the threat of the Falklands War. Quite a few songs were bashed out, just like this, by the three of us. Sometimes we would drag the equipment out into the sunny yard at the back of the building. Anyone who joined the band later would have to accept that we had written most of the songs.

At this time *Sounds*, a pop-music newspaper, printed a family tree of Liverpool bands in which 'Frankie Goes To Hollywood' somehow appeared. This was the band that had never played live, with the line-up of Steve Lovell, Ambrose Reynolds and Holly Johnson. We decided to take this name, one I had created for my old band, as the name for the new one.

We tried out a few guitarists from the echelons of Mark's family. There were two brothers who could both play, Vinny and Ged, the latter becoming the guitarist for the first performances, though neither was a very important part of the sound which was dominated by the rhythm section. Ped and I had tried to get the guitarist from The Jazz Babies to join, but without success. I played maracas while singing at these early rehearsals to fill out our sparse sound. We eventually also added a girl singer, Sonia M, to do backing vocals. She also added visual interest. She was a short rotund girl of Eastern extraction who told us she collected semen and urine samples in a clinic in the Liverpool Royal Hospital. She had a red satin dress that she had made herself, with a small padded devil's tail safety-pinned to the hem at the back. She was the kind of girl whose stiletto heels came from wire baskets outside shoe shops. Her voice could be described as overpowering. Her style was rather 'Frank 'n' Furter Goes To Kwik Save'.

*   *   *

I had been working very hard at these band rehearsals for over eighteen months, having to socialise with these bloody teenagers. Meanwhile Paul Rutherford had been raving in London nightclubs while he shared a flat with my old friend Jake. He would come and visit me, telling me what a wild time he was having on the gay scene in London. Earlier he had come home from a holiday in San Francisco with a new gay clone look. He cut his hair and started to wear leathers, which were not unlike the clothes that Jake and I had been wearing a few years before.

On one occasion when I was visiting Paul in London, he took me to the Subway, a notorious gay club in Leicester Square. His job, collecting used glasses there, prohibited him talking to me or dancing with me, the kind of stuff that we would normally do together in gay clubs up north – we had been dancing partners for years. But things had changed a bit and whenever Paul now showed me round the gay scene in London he would often take me to a club then waltz off with his new London friends, meeting up with me again at the end of the night.

With no one to talk to, all there was for me to do was drink or listen to the music. There was a room off the dancefloor that did not seem to be the toilet, but men would disappear into it sometimes, not coming out for quite a while. One man who went in and out looked like a well-known singer. He was many women's dream lover; my sister-in-law for example, a thirty-year-old bank clerk, had a crush on him. One of his albums had been TV advertised, though he was not really a pop star, more of a cabaret act. The amount of times he entered this room made the situation all the more interesting. I hung round the entrance, wondering. Then Paul came swishing past laden down with beer glasses.

'What's in there?' I asked him. Somehow he heard me over the loud disco music.

'I wouldn't go in there if I were you,' he replied with a laugh, then was off again. I was much too curious and merry from the beer to take any notice, so I entered the dark portal and waited until my eye got used to the dim light. I'm not sure, but I seem to remember flashes – visions – of an orgy going on every time the door was opened and the strobing disco lights momentarily lit up the scene. There were blue jeans round ankles and white vests or T-shirts scattered about or rolled up over the heads of uniformly crop-headed, moustached men.

This was my first back-room experience; but it was not my last. Other rooms like this were to be found in the future on other drunken or drugged nights in other European cities – Amsterdam, Paris or Munich.

* * *

After hearing 'Two Tribes' in our rehearsal room one evening while on one of his visits to Liverpool, Paul got rather excited and started to hang around me more often. I definitely knew I was on to something then.

With Steve Lovell's help I arranged some support dates on the Hambi and The Dance tour, the first at Pickwick's, a Liverpool club. Paul got a job doing backing vocals and dancing with Hambi and The Dance. What he actually did was deliberately and professionally upstage Hambi at every show. When a performer has no real musical role to concentrate on fully, he can play around and distract the audience quite easily. Paul's occasional backing vocals would always sound effortless against Hambi's lead, breathless after singing a whole set, and Paul's dancing, honed in the gay discos, was something a straight rock audience had never really seen before.

At our Pickwick's gig, Paul enthusiastically jumped on stage with us. I was in the centre, with Sonia on the right. I had taken LSD which, after the PA had failed to work, made me feel rather paranoid. But we generated a lot of energy and immediately after the show we were approached by Janice Long to appear on her Sunday night programme 'Street Life' on BBC Radio Merseyside.

The next show was at the Leeds Warehouse club, where Paul joined us on the stage for the whole performance. Mark's bass playing was very distinctive without a doubt, and with two mad Queens and an Eastern-looking 'Sex Dwarf' (as we had nicknamed Sonia), we made a strong impact.

Soon after, I arranged, with the clandestine use of my parents' phone, another show at Leeds Warehouse, this time supporting Leeds group Vicious Pink Phenomenon, whose only claim to fame was that they knew Marc Almond who had attended Art College there. One obnoxious girl at the front kept screaming through our set 'We want Vicious Pink!' I bent over from the stage and said to the girl, 'Have you got something to say?' Just before she had the opportunity to shout her message into the microphone I smacked her in the mouth with it. Paul shook my hand immediately – it was rather comic. She gave us no further trouble. The smack is clearly audible on a live cassette of the concert as was Sonia's rather overpowering and tonally-flat backing vocals. Soon after, I was the one who had to ring her up and sack her.

Not long after these first shows we all went to a Bow Wow Wow concert in Sefton Park. The crowd were going wild for Anabella Lwin, the young Lolita that Malcolm McLaren had discovered. I had taken a Unicorn's Head blotting paper impregnated with LSD. In between fits of paranoia to the effect that the crowd was going to avalanche into the lake at the bottom of the hill, I had an idea. Malcolm McLaren was right: people wanted sex and spectacle. They wanted to be entertained. I spoke to Paul (a willing accomplice) about it and we decided to go to Jodie's Gothic/Punk night and find some girls who dressed in leather to decorate the stage.

I had already been strongly influenced by the Mad Max post-Apocalypse scenario when I wrote 'Two Tribes'. We decided to incorporate the *Mad Max* Warrior look with Tom Of Finland and create a kind of post-Apocalypse, S and M punk look. We were bound to get attention and have lots of fun that way. Paul was a great help in finding new bits and belts to dress the whole thing up.

Soon the Larks In The Park, an annual open-air event for the local bands, came up. We made sure we got a place on the bill, and planned our appearance down to the last detail. We would have a delayed start when we would play car crash sounds from the *Mad Max* soundtrack which Paul provided. I wore a pair of old leather chaps with a G string, which meant that my arse was exposed at the back, and I got someone to paint one cheek pink and the other blue with oil pastel crayons. A black-and-white publicity photo by John Stoddard of this made it look as if my cheeks had been whipped with a riding crop.

Paul and I each dragged a 'Leather Pet' on to the stage, pulling at a chain attached to a dog-collar around their necks. The two sisters from Kirkby (the Muscatelli sisters, Julie and Marie) posed as captive slaves for us. Slowly we chained them to the drum kit, then launched into 'Two Tribes', which we also played at the end of the set as it was our best song. We had only about eight songs at the time, if that. We sometimes did an impromptu version of The Mickey Mouse Club song to lighten things up a bit: 'M.I.C. See ya real soon. K.E.Y. Why? Because we like you – M.O.U.S.E.'

I walked down the ramp on to the lake during one of the first songs. When I turned to return to the stage there was an audible gasp from the audience, provoked by my exposed arse. Near the end of the set I asked the audience if we should release the Leather Pets. We did, and they came gyrating to the front of the stage. Dancing wasn't their strong point we realised, so for subsequent shows we kept them tied up for as long as possible. People left the park bemused, but still talking about what they had seen. The photographs taken by John Stoddard that day gave us further ammunition to assault people's senses with.

When we later played Jodie's bar downstairs, we filled the whole club with dry ice and so were obscured for the first few numbers. This was the last time I took LSD to go on stage. I realised it was not a good idea for performing, although it did seem to loosen my tongue a bit in talking to the audience. Jake came to this particular concert and warned me that Paul was constantly trying to upstage me, just as he had tried to do to Hambi. I wasn't bothered about that, though: the harder Paul tried to upstage me, the better the spectacle.

Jake started to visit Liverpool again and invited me to stay with him and his boyfriend Tim in Stoke Newington, North London. I would stay with Jake and Tim for the weekend or longer, then return to Liverpool almost penniless. Jake introduced me to his friend Karl, a British Airways steward who shared a beautiful house in North London with Tom, his older boyfriend, a CSO for British Airways. I was rather impressed by these older, successful and attractive gay people. I had a big crush on Karl. All these men had moustaches – this was the age of the clone look – and I felt a bit left out with my skinhead mohican.

Karl would make DJ tapes of the latest disco records, mixing them so they ran into each other seamlessly, a hobby of quite a few Disco Queens. He also brought the drug MDA over from New York. MDA, nicknamed 'Mary Don't Ask', was a forerunner of the drug Ecstasy (chemical name MDMA). There was also a drug called Crystal which we would snort for Saturday Night at Heaven, the famous gay disco under the arches at Charing Cross. This scene had an influence on the music I wanted to make. I would pester Ped to play fours on his bass drum, just like the disco records I'd heard in London. I saw Madonna do a PA in Heaven to promote the release of her first single 'Everybody', one of my favourite records of the time, along with Sharon Redd's 'Beat The Street' and 'In The Name of Love'.

I spent one New Year's Eve in Heaven. I had positioned

myself on a riser at the edge of the dancefloor so I could see the action. Ten seconds before midnight, a twenty-foot flaccid penis was revealed on stage, and a countdown started: ten . . . nine . . . eight . . . The huge cock rose in jerks, becoming more erect each second. At the stroke of midnight, it ejaculated some kind of party snowstorm. At the same moment the centre of the dancefloor erupted with champagne corks, streamers and party poppers wielded by young, body-builder Queens who had staked out the centre of the floor.

'Look at all that energy, Holly!' shouted someone over the noise. A thousand gay men were going apeshit.

A second later a man standing on the floor below me, his head level with my crutch, pulled down my jeans and started to suck my cock. Happy New Year!

The London gay scene, trendy and influenced by the New York and LA scenes, was a new experience for me. Heaven was a mecca for handsome muscle-bound creatures, snorting poppers and ethyl (chloride), dancing under the laser lights to pumping rhythms and disco divas. It was this dangerous, perhaps even threatening style – the fetishes and the eroticism – that was to form the 'Frankie' style, introducing something new into mainstream pop culture.

* * *

Back in Liverpool, Steve Lovell had moved out of my Catherine Street flat. We had drifted apart as Frankie Goes To Hollywood was taking up more of my time. His girlfriend and production projects were taking up his. He gave me no real warning of his departure, suddenly leaving me a note saying that he was moving to London and that the money I owed him was his contribution to the upcoming gas and electricity bills. Steve had been generous, lending me money over a long period of time, but I was left well and truly in the lurch. Soon the electricity was cut off as I had no real way of surviving day to day and paying bills.

'Teabag' took pity on me and would come round and cook a kind of risotto out of rice and a packet soup, filched from her mother's kitchen. She was waiting for me in my flat one day when the gas board called to cut my gas off. She paid them for me. She had got a cameo part in *Brookside* (then the new soap opera) and during this time, she was extremely generous and rather motherly. I was not very responsible as far as money was concerned. I would spend my Giro on a new pair of jack-boots rather than buy food. I got a cheque for two month's back rent and spent it on a pair of Church's brogues which I bought in Bold Street, once Liverpool's Bond Street.

After the weekend glamour of Heaven, I was coming home to a grey, rainy Liverpool and harsh reality. I would visit my parents when I was starving and spirit away tins of beans, soap or shampoo. My sister Clare, who had now moved to the same area as my parents, would help out with a pint of milk here and there. As the popular Human League song of the time said, these were 'Hard Times'.

Krisco Kisses

By this time Eric's, the night club, had been raided for drugs and closed down by the police, while Stevie's had become The Warehouse, taking over as the place where bands now played. We booked ourselves in for a concert and spent all the money we were to be paid on dry ice and a tiny red laser light – fairly extravagant for an almost unknown band. We saved the Leather Pets to the end of the show, when they caused quite a sensation, rubbing themselves up against the band members. I wore just a pair of leather knickers and a hat. This was the first time that I began to worry that the spectacle overshadowed the music. We were definitely the most talked about group in Liverpool though, which, after all, was the desired effect.

Although I knew that this new band I was in seemed to have something extra, and was worth all the trouble we took, I was tired of signing on the Social Security. So I decided to create a portfolio of artwork, so I could apply for an Arts Foundation course and get a grant from the Local Education Authority. A lot of my friends, from as far back as 1977, had gone to the Art School over the years and I was familiar with the standard of work. I knew if I applied myself I could do it, despite not having an 'O' Level to my name. Over the next year or so I started to keep a sketch book, as all my friends at Art School had done. I also worked on silk-screen prints with the simple equipment that I had been given for my eighteenth birthday. I was particularly inspired by an exhibition of Gilbert and George's work that appeared at The Walker Art Gallery in the early Eighties. I even plucked up the courage to ask how much money one of those large photopieces would cost. I was told £6000, which was more than a little out of reach for a social security struggler.

* * *

I had been given some 'speed' by a friend one day and was late for rehearsals. I had no money so I had to walk all the way from my parent's house to town. Walking down Princess Avenue, I started to sing something to myself to make the journey go faster.

Relax, don't do it, When you want to go to it.

Relax, don't do it, When you want to come.

I laughed out loud at the last line, which I kept repeating, with its simple tune, over and over in my head. When I got to rehearsals Mark and Ped were jamming on a simple one-note bass line and my little tune seemed to fit perfectly. Because of the simplicity of the repetitive chorus, we created a convoluted middle eight in a different rhythm, but we later dropped that for the simple but climactic middle eight that ended up on the record.

Bob and Sharon Johnson, who had recently become our London-based managers, arranged for us to make a video demo of two songs. Bob had a friend at Arista Records (Simon Potts) who invested six hundred pounds. We recorded 'Two Tribes' and 'Relax' in a sixteen-track studio in Clapham. A while later Bob hired a video camera, which was operated by a photographer friend of his. We used the basement of the Hope and Anchor to record our performance. During the recording, the manager of the venue drew Bob aside and accused him of using the premises to make a porn video. We had really gone to town on the bondage look. I wore a pair of leather knickers and an old Seditioneries cropped T-shirt, with unzipped nipple holes and bike tyre pieces on the shoulders, that I had inherited from Pete Burns. Paul purloined a pair of leather thigh guards that strapped at the back, which left his arse completely bare. He also waved around a fake Luger. We dressed the boys in denim shorts with the odd bit of leather. Mark wore a black 'Lone Ranger' mask and denim shorts. The Leather Pets were there in studded leather mini dresses and suspenders holding up laddered stockings; we chained them to scaffolding. To top it all, a friend of ours from San Francisco, Elyse, or Queen Cat as she was once known, donned her best Hollywood party dress and bubble-point blonde beehive. She announced us with a clapper board. To create a visual tension, I threw her Good Fairiness off the stage.

We created a very seedy and tacky performance video in just a few takes. There are some very comical moments when Paul and I seem to do a Pan's People routine. There's also a bit of simulated sodomy that I perform on Paul. For any era this video was outrageous. Unfortunately it didn't have the desired effect. Bob Johnson hawked the video around several record companies, to no avail. The younger A and R men seemed keen but didn't think they could persuade their older bosses. Island's Chris Blackwell supposedly sent a telex saying something like 'Not in my lifetime'. Simon Draper at Virgin allegedly said 'We've already got one old Queen we can't sell, why do I need another one?'

There was a similar reaction when Bob Johnson organised our first London gig at Cha Cha's, the tiny Cellar Bar at Heaven. The band had to perform behind a grill, in a cage suspended above the dance floor. The poor Leather Pets had to stand outside the cage near the audience, on top of the PA columns which were stacked below us on the dance floor. The support act was a huge man who ate fire and drove skewers through his face, which scared half of the A and R men away before we even appeared. One man from the Cowbell agency actually got beaten up by two leather boys in the line, waiting to get in. Then, as soon as the first bars of 'Two Tribes' struck up, I knew Ged O'Tool's guitar was completely out of tune. The show was a complete disaster, and the hyper-trendy audience was no help as they were all far too cool to applaud.

We did secure a John Peel session, however, and an article in the *NME* written by Dave Dorell. The Peel session was a great way of recording free demos and publicising our existence. I think we recorded 'Two Tribes', 'Relax' and two other tracks. The video also eventually got us some interest from Tyne Tees Television. They were starting a new programme in the winter called 'The Tube' to be presented by Jools Holland and Paula Yates. However, they considered our video too lewd to be shown, so they came to Liverpool and filmed us at the newly opened State Ballroom, Liverpool's glitziest disco. We had the use of the laser lighting, which then was the latest thing, and the camera men loved doing soft focus crutch shots of The Leather Pets. It was a resounding success when it was shown later in the year. The camera somehow liked me. A member of Yes, who was recording 'Owner Of A Lonely Heart' with Trevor Horn, brought the clip to Trevor's attention. Trevor claimed that he could make a number one hit out of that song, then promptly forgot all about us.

*   *   *

Back in Liverpool, Tweela, now an ex-fashion student from the Art School, moved in to share my flat. This was meant to help with the bills. He was also a friend of Jake's and we would all meet up in London sometimes to go out on the town. Jake and Tweela both sported the clone moustache and had practised the art of looking available in dark corners. There was a bit of peer pressure on me to grow a moustache which I attempted, but couldn't stand the in-between stage.

Frankie Goes To Hollywood did a further photo session with John Stoddard in his studio, pulling out all the stops, using all the bondage clothing we could find. One particular photograph has me in profile with a knife in my mouth. The knife was tucked down Paul's belt that held up a pair of knickers. It comes across as a kind of fellatio with a knife. It accompanied an interview Paul and I did for the *NME* with Dave Dorrell, among the huge Egyptian relics at the British Museum in a naïve attempt to make the event more epic, more Hollywood.

Jake was now on the periphery of a kind of older, fist-fucking fraternity. He was fascinated by this clique and would fantasise about what they might get up to. These men had, I assumed, taken so many cocks up their arse that they were no longer satisfied and needed bigger things to excite them. He told me about slings in which men would be suspended from ceilings; he told me about the home movies, made with video cameras, showing his friends fist fucking each other. He wanted to be a porn star and had all the qualifications except one – a real confidence in his looks and body. He showed me his collection of rubber sex toys, dildos, butt plugs and other things. He had a huge tub of Crisco, an American cooking fat that was used as lubrication for fist fucking. 'Sex is my hobby,' Jake would always say as he flicked through the pages of American porno mags illegally imported courtesy of Karl, Jake's friendly neighbourhood air steward. How Jake had changed in the last few years! He was no longer a teenager struggling with Catholic guilt over his sexuality; now he even saw himself as a kind of concubine, kept by his businessman boyfriend. This hobby of Jake's eventually inspired me to write the lyrics of a song called 'Krisco Kisses': 'You fit me like a glove, my love, a little puppet glove.'

Although I was, like Jake, fascinated by the imagery of S and M, I never really got involved in its hardcore 'scenes'. Once when I picked up a male hustler in the London Apprentice (Jake's local), he took me back to a council flat and took me to his playroom that was lined in heavily textured black rubber tiles and sex aids. He was about twenty five, tall and sturdy – a bit like a Welsh rugby player. He asked me to insert a large black wooden truncheon up his arse. It amazed me how effortlessly he took this thick, smoothly rounded piece of ebony.

On another occasion I picked up a German chauffeur. He had a sleek black Mercedes outside which was probably not his, and drove me back to a grotty council estate, where he begged me to whip him with a leather belt as he grovelled on all fours, naked but still wearing his chauffeur's hat. He seemed to enjoy it more and more as I whipped harder. I suppose I was working out my frustrations or self-loathing, since I would sometimes (as in this case) go home with men I did not find that attractive, just for a place to stay or simply for the adventure.

One British Airways air steward, called Brenda, who I was friendly with, took me back to his flat one night and nearly ripped my dick off with his highly developed arse muscles. He could draw a cock in, then trap it hard in the walls of his magic arsehole, only letting go when he felt like it. I met him years later cycling on the streets of London, on his way to the Kobler Centre perhaps. We talked about friends that we had lost. I told him that I was writing a book.

'What's it about?' he asked.

'Oh, you know, my sordid past and stuff like that,' I replied.

'Am I in it?'

You are now.

Zaang Tuum Tumb

Bob Johnson got us some support dates with a band called Fashion, who had a record deal and were booked into a few polytechnics. One of the first shows we did with them was the Manchester Apollo – our first theatre venue. At one of the polytechnic dates we only lasted a couple of numbers, then were booed off. Frustration started to set in, as we seemed not to be getting the record company attention we were so desperate for. I remember taking the boys in the band to the Lisbon one afternoon. Mark started to fantasise about who could produce us. 'Imagine Trevor Horn,' he said. Trevor had recently had success with Dollar, ABC and Spandau Ballet, not to mention the ground-breaking recording 'Duck Rock' with Malcolm McLaren. Trevor made the kind of high tech records we all loved.

By March 1983 it seemed we were never going to get a record deal. Bob and Sharon put us on at the Camden Palace. The ticket read 'SLUM IT IN STYLE, TRASH AT THE PALACE, every Tuesday 9-3am'. I remember Sharon Johnson covering two sets of wooden step ladders with tin-foil so that we could chain The Leather Pets to them. We didn't have the budget for scaffolding. We were hard, rough and sleazy. The Palace's laser came on momentarily during 'Relax' but I felt they were a bit mean with it.

Meanwhile I started to work much harder on my Art College portfolio. I did lots of silk-screen prints of male torsos in pastel shades, with gold writing on top and some detailed drawing. Yvonne Gilbert lent me her expensive art presentation folder for showing my work during the interview at the art college. I faced a panel of two lecturers and three students. The students said that my work was the best shown that day. The lecturers however

156

were dubious about accepting musicians – such people had a long history of dropping out of the course. Still, with the student vote I was accepted. I stuck the acceptance letter inside my sketch book. I was really pleased and felt that I had achieved something. Years of failure and unemployment can chip away at your self-esteem, and I had had more than my fair share of setbacks. It was encouraging to think that if I applied myself, I could achieve results.

Bob and Sharon pointed out to us at some point that Ged O'Tool could not afford to take further time off work as he now had a wife and child to support. We asked Mark's cousin Brian Nash (Nasher) to take his place, out of desperation more than anything. His guitar playing was not as good as Ged's, although he had a better sound.

Somehow we had managed to get a Kid Jensen session on Radio One – he then had a slightly earlier show than John Peel. We recorded 'Relax' again, plus three other songs. When the session was transmitted we were interviewed at BBC Radio Merseyside. Trevor Horn apparently heard the Jensen session on his car radio and was reminded of our previous 'Tube' appearance. He contacted us and said he was interested in signing us to his new label. There was one other offer in the air after that, from Beggar's Banquet, who would have provided us with a wage of about forty quid a week. Trevor's offer didn't include much money at all, a £250 advance between us for the first single and £5,000 for the publishing of our songs. It was put to us that without signing the publishing agreement with Perfect Songs, their music publishing company, there would be no recording deal. Normally, with a recording contract under its belt, a group could auction itself off to the highest bidding publisher. We could reasonably have expected to get many times more than £5,000 with other publishers. I later heard of a rival Liverpudlian group who received a huge (by comparison) advance at about this time. Paul was not a party to the publishing agreement, as he had not been involved in the composition of any music or the writing of any lyrics whatsoever; neither had Nasher for that matter, but later he was to contribute a little.

157

Bob Johnson introduced us to a solicitor called David Gentle who attempted to negotiate on our behalf, but without much success. Both contracts, we were told, had to be signed – or there was no deal. Many attempts at changing clauses were met with a resounding 'No!' from Jill Sinclair, Trevor Horn's wife, manager and business partner.

There were one or two preliminary meetings with Trevor Horn, Jill Sinclair and Paul Morley. Trevor was porky and short with huge spectacles and a slight Durham accent. Jill was a hefty, dark-haired blue-stocking with a school marmish manner. She reminded me a bit of Tina Charles, Trevor's former protégée. Morley, an ex-*NME* journalist, was employed as Artistic Director of the company. Jill, Trevor and Paul Morley took Bob, Sharon, Paul and me to dinner at the Hiroko restaurant at the Kensington Hilton. Paul and I went to another meeting at Sarm West, then a run-down studio owned by Chris Blackwell, proprietor of Island Records, who were going to distribute Trevor's label. Morley was there posing in Eighties black clothes and sipping some alcoholic beverage out of a metal flask. He told us that the label would be called ZAANG TUUM TUMB, after a Futurist poem. I think we were meant to be astounded at the originality of the idea.

We waited and Trevor eventually came to talk to us. He told us of his plans to refurbish the studio and building. We played him some new demos, including 'Welcome To The Pleasuredome' I believe, and he criticised my rhyming 'power' with 'hour' or something like that. Trevor said that we had to wait until the Autumn before he was free to record with us, and before his studio would be refurbished.

Later with my publishing advance – about £500 – I went for a weekend to Amsterdam. I went on a club crawl, getting into backroom sex, sometimes with more than one person at a time. The next morning I was woken up on a canal houseboat by a six-foot-six tall Elvis-impersonator who started to fuck me. He said it was the only polite way to wake someone up: 'what a cure for a hangover!' The sort of behaviour that in England had been confined to the Subway here in Amsterdam seemed an everyday experience. Everywhere, in dimly lit bars and nightclubs with cellars, all manner of secret sexual theatres were acted out. The freedom of buying hash cakes openly in Amsterdam was an inspiration. On the Monday morning, when the party was over, I missed my plane. My ticket wasn't the type that could be used on another flight, so I had to ring up ZTT to get their travel agent to book me on to the next flight. I was another two hundred pounds in the hole already.

I remember meeting a member of a new band called Bronski Beat in the London Apprentice. He said his name was Steve Bronski, and told me that ZTT had wanted to sign them but they had not liked the recording contract one little bit.

On another occasion, Morley invited me round to his flat in London for a celebratory drink of champagne. I was staying with Jake and Tim in Stoke Newington at the time. I made it over to Morley's flat, but I was taken ill with something mysterious, and couldn't drink the champagne. I somehow got the train home to Liverpool and went straight to my bed. I couldn't move from it for days. Tweela looked in on me and apologised that he could not look after me as he was going to London; he was preparing to move there very soon. Eventually I managed to drag myself out to a local doctor. He took blood for various tests, suspecting glandular fever or worse, but they were all negative, and he prescribed a course of multivitamins. He also questioned me about my lifestyle: did I take drugs? etc. He told me that there was a mysterious new illness affecting gay men with history of recreational drug use and a hedonistic lifestyle. This was the spring of 1983 and little was known about the new 'American' disease. The first I heard of it was when I turned up at Heaven with Jake, Tim and Karl. There was a notice there saying that Patrick Cowley, the famous American disco record producer and remixer, had died of AIDS in San Francisco: that night was dedicated to his music. But we still didn't know what this AIDS was or how it was contracted.

I lost about eight to twelve pounds, and recovered slowly. I stayed in Liverpool for the most part of that summer. I made a new friend, an attractive red haired woman of Irish extraction called Christine; she worked hard to keep her ten-year-old son in private school. Tweela moved to London and out of my flat so Christine invited me to stay in her Huyton council house, where I contributed what I could from my Giro. There was a lot of speed about in that house, as well as the occasional acid. Christine would be up all night, printing T-shirts or making clothes for people to make extra money – this was where the speed came in handy. I would help her with silk-screening T-shirts and creating stencils of Kabuki masks to print on white cotton shirts. She would pay me a part of the profits after she sold them to a shop in Mathew Street.

Christine had a high sex drive, and as I was the only person around, she would occasionally pounce on me when we shared a bed. Although I went through the motions I didn't feel comfortable with the situation. After about three or four of these – for me – unnatural events, I asked her to stop. Although I reached orgasm with Christine, I was not really excited by the softness and floppiness of a woman's body. And the noises that were made in the process seemed rather vulgar to me. We remained friends though. Then, at the end of the summer, her boyfriend returned and I moved back to my Catherine Street flat.

Due to the signing of the recording and publishing contracts with ZTT and Perfect Songs (Jill and Trevor's publishing company), I didn't apply for my education authority grant to attend the Art Foundation course on which I had gained a place. There have been many moments when I regretted this.

Relax

July 1983 was the month when Trevor eventually called upon us to start recording. Sarm Studios was still not ready so he booked us into The Manor Studios, Virgin's luxurious residential studio in Oxford. We all went down there; I even took Christine for one night. Trevor told me he could tell that Christine was very interested in sex, I remember. There was little for me to do but swim in the outdoor pool, while Trevor was putting the band through their paces. He did not like what he heard. Mark, Nasher and Ped were between sixteen and eighteen years old, and inexperienced as studio musicians. Trevor soon got tired of their playing and started to construct a rhythm track on his Fairlight (a then state-of-the-art sampling keyboard device). Trevor occupied 'The Lads', as they became known, by getting J. J. Jeckzalic, the Fairlight operator (and co-founder of The Art of Noise), to record samples of them jumping into the swimming pool, a sound effect which was to be their only musical contribution to the recording of 'Relax'. We were in awe of Trevor and whatever he said we went along with. As with the contract, we understood only that ZTT held all the cards.

Meanwhile the refurbishing of Sarm was completed so Trevor abandoned The Manor sessions, and resumed recording there. 'The Lads' – Mark, Ped and Nasher – returned to Liverpool. Trevor had me stay down in London at the Columbia Hotel, a regular record company hotel in Bayswater.

Trevor's second idea was to see how a professional session band would play 'Relax'. So he employed Ian Dury's Blockheads to record a version of the song, which he scrapped. He then employed Steve Lipson as an engineer and Andy Richards as a keyboard player and programmer. Andy had been working on a Robin Cousins ice skating tour playing Vangelis covers; he even gave us tickets to go and see the show. Steve Lipson said he had engineered for The Rolling Stones, but it was his guitar-playing ability that eventually came in most handy. So a hybrid 'Relax' was created using ideas from The Blockheads version, the original version, and some new ideas. Still Trevor was not satisfied, so this too was scrapped. 'Relax' was to be the first record released on Trevor's new label, and he was determined it was going to be a great hit. He was prepared to spare no expense – spending money that, of course, we would have to recoup from our UK royalty on the single of 6% of RRP. So this state of affairs was both to our advantage and disadvantage.

Trevor then scrapped the *third* version of 'Relax'. With the help of J. J. Jeckzalic, Andy Richards on keyboards and Steve Lipson on guitar, Trevor created a new, machine-like electronic version of the backing track. It was a hybrid of the kind of disco records I had heard in the gay clubs, but with a significant rock edge to it.

Paul and I were summoned to the studio at about eleven pm. Trevor played us the latest version. He told us to go to a club and come back later. Excitedly we went to a gay club, the Copacabana in Earls Court, then returned to the studio at about two am. After an hour of waiting, Trevor sent Paul home. After another hour, I was asked to sing. I always smoked dope in these sessions when it was offered to me. On this particular session I had a Nepalese Temple Ball (a particularly potent form of hashish). So, very stoned, I was positioned in front of a microphone in the huge, empty studio. The control-room window was framed with plaster Roman pillars, a design cliché of the early Eighties. I was very excited by the new groove that 'Relax' had, and finally I sang my heart out – at four am in the morning. I did some overdubs afterwards but the bulk of the vocal was done very quickly that night.

The next night, Chris Blackwell, the owner of Island Records, came down to the studio with two exotic-looking women. He commented on the lead vocals, saying that they sounded great. I was very flattered as this was the man who had produced one of my favourite records, The B52s' first album.

Trevor had the idea during these sessions to record 'Ferry Across The Mersey', the old Gerry and The Pacemakers song, as a B side. Although I was a bit reluctant, this was recorded quickly with Trevor playing bass and Andy Richards on keyboards. I did a vocal that surprised everyone, and for a while it was sounding better than 'Relax'.

Another night, when I got very stoned, Morley came to the studio and interviewed a giggling Paul and me in a very relaxed mood. Trevor told us that this was going to be the B side of the seven inch single. For his efforts Morley was awarded a percentage of the publishing royalties of the B side along with the rest of the band. I had composed an instrumental years earlier that was used as background music. Since B side Mechanical Publishing royalties are paid out at the same rate as the A side, this would prove rather profitable for Morley who was a non-share-holding director of ZTT. The usual way of making sure directors of record companies get good remuneration is to pay them points or a percentage from the record companies' profits, not to invite them to write part of the B side, thus getting the band to pay them. Although I later discovered that Morley was also paid a percentage of ZTT's profits.

During the recording of 'Relax' I had to return to Liverpool several times to sign on at the Social Security office there. If I was sometimes a day or so late I claimed, as I had done before, that I had been to London in search of work. In fact Ped, Paul and I were all signing on as the ZTT recording agreement provided such a minuscule advance. In my experience record companies would have paid the bands they sign a lump sum so the band could put themselves on a wage. So there I was, recording in an extravagantly decorated studio in awe of our millionaire producer (and studio co-owner), being charged nearly a thousand pounds a day for the privilege, and with hardly a penny in my pocket. This signing-on scenario eventually inspired Trevor to include a little spoken set piece just before the song 'Ferry Across The Mersey' (album version). I got my actress friend Teabag to play the part of the Social Security officer, and Paul played the dole-ite.

Paul: 'I've left me card [a UB40] ar' 'ome.'

Teabag: 'Well yer late as well, next time I'll put yer on daily signin.'

On one occasion Trevor said to me that he had considered sacking the musicians from the band, leaving just Paul and me to front the act. I protested gently, saying I didn't fancy being an Eighties version of Simon and Garfunkel. And I had enough loyalty to the band at that time to discourage the idea.

Finally 'Relax' seemed completed after a mix by Julian Mendelsohn. Trevor took me to the Townhouse cutting-room where I told him the vocal sounded too quiet. He said the last singer to tell him that was David Van Day from Dollar. Meanwhile work on the first twelve inch dance mix of 'Relax' began in Sarm East. I did a special whispering vocal, speaking a list of sexual peccadilloes and the names of Amsterdam leather bars. Appropriately this became known as the Sex Mix. It was not the most popular mix, though, as it did not include the song's familiar refrain. Also people were unsure what speed to play it at, as the speed instructions given were incorrect.

Our minds were now directed at a record cover. Our friend, the illustrator Yvonne Gilbert, had done some erotic illustrations for *Men Only* magazine which I had seen. I showed them to Bob and the rest of the band, and decided on one with a man on his knees and a red haired woman reclining on his back. This image was sent to XL to incorporate into a record sleeve.

There had been talk of whether the BBC would play the record. I was certain that they would, as there were no actual swear words in the lyrics. What's more, John Peel and Kid Jensen had already played it. There is no law against using the word 'come', although the imagined context might have a bearing. I suppose the record company may have had an interest in getting the record banned, but that didn't occur to us as a real possibility at the time.

The next thing was the video. Island Records set up a meeting between us and Bernard Rose in a production company office in Soho. Bernard was still at film school but had already directed classic pop videos for UB40. I told him my ideas about an innocent working-class boy being dragged into a Babylonian pleasuredome. Also the idea that 'Life was a movie and this was his audition'.

Bernard wanted Paul to play the innocent at first, but I insisted that I should. I had to assert myself in this manner quite often. I couldn't allow the backing vocalist to overshadow me, the central character and voice of the band, could I? Paul was used to being the centre of attention in most of his social situations, so I think he found it demeaning to play second fiddle within the group. This of course eventually had an adverse effect on our relationship. He was constantly vying with me for the spotlight, but always not quite managing it. He would even tell people that he was the lead singer. We decided at the meeting that Paul and I would go round the gay clubs and enlist the help of the best dressed Leather Boys and Drag Queens we could find. This was fun. I even got Jake to help us and act as an extra. In Heaven a few months earlier, I had met Mark Tyme, a black dancer who was with the original Hot Gossip at their peak. Sometimes I used to stay with him in his Oxford Circus flat. Mark and his friends Juicy Lucy, Space and Dougweena had a keen interest in glamorous drag, so we roped them all in. We asked 'Ange', a friend of ours from Liverpool: she was a tall, blonde international netball player who had done some modelling for Tweela. She plays the busty, basqued barmaid. Leigh Bowery even contributed some sequined masks. We also invited The Leather Pets, but they missed the train to London on the day of the video shoot.

Bernard Rose suggested using instruments of torture and a live lion on the set in an attempt to make the video epic and cinematic. I told him the title of our album would be 'Welcome To The Pleasuredome', which put him in mind of one of Kenneth Anger's films, *Inauguration To The Pleasuredome*.

We shot the video at a disused, half-derelict nightclub that had a balcony. I bought a Paul Smith Prince-of-Wales check suit so that I would stand out against all the 'Wild Ones'. It was an extremely long day, as video shoots invariably are. Bernard got one of the leather boys to throw lager in my face, then attack me.

I was pissed off as the lager went all over my new suit. After that scene, where I witness a girl being killed in an iron maiden, I take the jacket off, then the 'Fat Lord' on the balcony has me fed to a lion. The lion was a cub called Tessa who appears small on the screen, but in reality she was about four feet long, heavy and with *large* teeth. I was told to lie on the stage and the handler dropped her on top of me from about three feet in the air while the crowd of extras shouted 'Kill! Kill!' I felt that this was going too far, so I suggested that I just play with the animal on the floor and the shots could be obtained in that way.

The other ordeal was being strapped on a wagon wheel and being sprayed with a soda syphon, giving the impression that we were being pissed on by the 'Fat Lord'. Finally, at the end of the day, we were expected to film the opening shots of me arriving in a rickshaw being pulled by a flunky and led into the club by a rubber-clad rent-boy clone, played convincingly by Rutherford. Not surprisingly, I looked exhausted in these opening shots, and I was filmed from my worst angle.

Top of the Pops

Sometime near the end of October or the beginning of November 1983, 'Relax' was finally released. None of the reviews was especially glowing. Paul and I had posed in rubber-wear bought at the fetishist shop 'Expectations' for the cover of the *NME*, 5th November 1983, for which we were photographed by Anton Corbijn. The accompanying interview started at the Columbia Hotel where I was still staying. We were very honest about our sexuality and lifestyle, telling the journalist about our recent trip to Amsterdam and leaving out none of the details. We even took him to the Colherne. This was obviously just too much for the interviewer, who admitted shamelessly in his article that he was 'someone who just stopped reading *Picture Of Dorian Gray* because it was "too faggy", who would rather listen to half an hour of Mary Whitehouse than two minutes of Quentin Crisp, who'd never heard of homophobia, just "good sense"' (sic).

* * *

Rather than stay at the Columbia Hotel in the evening, I would go out to Earls Court pubs and nightclubs. Although the hotel staff were friendly I was extremely lonely, and one-night stands became a way of life for the three months at the end of 1983 that I stayed there. Paul was spending his time with Joe in Fulham and our friendship had already cooled to a degree, and Stoke Newington was a long way to travel every night to see Jake. I felt at a loose end.

Karl had fallen ill a few times, and Jake and I would visit him at his house. He had started to lose weight. We thought that maybe he had been overdoing it on recreational drugs but he claimed otherwise.

As 'Relax' had been released we had to find a way to promote it. Gary Blackburn at Island Records' promotion department suggested a PA club tour. About ten dates were arranged up and down the country. We were given a van and driver called Tony Pope, a friend of Gary Blackburn's.

As two of the musicians in the band were working at their council apprenticeships, only Ped was able to come along, while The Leather Pets seemed to have fallen by the wayside by now. We did invite Juicy Lucy and Ange, stars of the video, to come along with us. We also bought a blow-up sex doll, with a gaping mouth, to throw about the stage and into the audience. I think the first PA was at a small club in the Midlands: it had no stage so they had to clear the dance floor, but as the microphone lead only extended a short distance, my movements were restricted. 'Ferry Across The Mersey' was the low-key start to the act. The plan was that I would be on stage alone and during the song the others would join me one by one, then all hell would break loose during the 'Sex Mix' and the 'Relax' seven-inch version. On this first PA I walked out to find Morley looking like a complete idiot sitting in the middle of the dance floor, wearing Mickey-Mouse ears and holding the blow-up doll. Not really appropriate for a rendering of 'Ferry Across The Mersey', I thought. I was just very glad when that first PA was over. It had proved rather mainstream 'Sharon-and-Tracy' audience rather than the esoteric nightclub crowd we had played to before. For me, it was all rather embarrassing. Juicy and Ange looked extra glamorous in the same costumes they wore in the video, and few, I think, guessed that Juicy was a man in drag. I was still wearing my Paul Smith suit from the video; over the rest of the tour it somehow got covered in lipstick and cigarette burns from Juicy or Ange, who simulated fellatio with me on stage. Ped I think wore some kind of devil-mask. It was a freak show alright.

After this we went to Scotland and played Maestro's in Edinburgh and the Hootchi Cootchie Club in Glasgow, while in Edinburgh we were booked by Sam Piacentini who later opened the Sub Club. Juicy and I did the gay clubs afterwards, and I ended up with a handsome Edinburgh postman who had a bad back but a fabulous body. I always had a weakness for a Scots brogue.

Our PA at the Manchester Hacienda was fun. I was driven on stage by motorbike while the rest of the cast made mysterious shapes behind a back-lit projection screen behind me. For the Camden Palace show, we also had a motorbike to dress the stage. When I walked out to sing the first few bars of 'Ferry Across The Mersey', the backing tape started at half speed. Despite this, it turned out to be one of our best nights, though by now our blow-up doll was patched up with sticking plaster and my suit was looking very shabby. The best PA of all was the one we did at Heaven one Thursday night when I accidentally pushed Juicy off the stage. She was back on that stage in seconds, smiling and dancing like nothing had happened. Work it, Miss Thing!

Around this time the single had charted, but only in the low 70s of the Gallup chart. It even went *down* one place a week or so later. Luckily 'The Tube' came to the rescue and invited us to play 'live', as was their policy. We weren't in a position or indeed prepared to play the new version of the song live, so we used backing tapes without vocals, over which I sang live. This showing helped the single up to about number 35 in the Gallup charts, where it froze over Christmas.

I remember doing a phone interview with Ann Nightingale from my parents' phone – she kindly phoned me back, so I would not run up a huge bill. I also tried to organise a PA at Heaven for New Year's Eve. This was to be a paid show. The straight trio in the group didn't want to be in a gay club for New Year so they weren't included. Mark Tyme and Juicy did a bit of choreography, and Heaven manager David Inches hired two muscle men to decorate the stage. The show started with me behind a screen in a doctor's coat giving Juicy an injection. I come from behind the screen and the velcro'd doctor's outfit is ripped from me by Juicy and Mark. The introduction was played out to 'Moments in Love' by The Art Of Noise. I had started to sing a little line over these opening chords.

Dreams are like angels, they keep bad at bay
And love is the light scaring darkness away.

We had recently parted company with Bob Johnson, since I felt that he was so occupied with Aztec Camera and their hit 'Oblivious' that he couldn't look after us properly. I had a talk with him at the Columbia Hotel one evening and he said he would release us from his contract as we hadn't had legal advice anyway: he was very nice about the situation. I had become a bit monstrous or tetchy as I was doing all the liaising with the record company, something that wasn't easy when the record company was Jill Sinclair. I wasn't prepared to flatter her to get into her good books like the other members of the band, who would kiss her arse then slag her off behind her back.

I complained to Trevor that it was difficult to survive with just our Social Security money. He explained that his wife Jill didn't understand what it was like not to have a fiver in your pocket, as she was from a middle-class Jewish family. He said that he would talk to her about it. Thereafter an expenses system was worked out. If a member of the band was required in the studio, then he would get £10 *per diem*, and if one was just required in London then £5 *per diem* would be paid. So each day we would have to ask Gigi the secretary, who controlled the petty cash, for our *per diem*.

Somehow in the new year we qualified for 'Top Of The Pops'; they usually didn't go as far down as number 35 in the charts, so we were lucky to get it. We then explained to Jill and Trevor that if we did 'Top Of The Pops' we could no longer sign on Social Security: we would definitely be caught out as 'working' while claiming benefit. So ZTT agreed to put us on a wage of forty pounds per week, not including studio days *per diem*. But Jill often reiterated that they were taking all the financial risks and could not afford to pay us this wage.

On the morning of 'Top Of The Pops', which was to be transmitted 'live' later that week, Gary Farrow, ZTT's independent record plugger/promoter, whose job it was to get airplay for the record, took me into the Radio One offices to meet some DJs and do a short interview. I met Paul Gambaccini who said that he was amazed that the record was being played. He said no one had got away with such obvious sexual innuendo since Lou Reed's 'Walk On The Wild Side' (which has a line about 'giving head').

I didn't *have a thing to wear* for 'Top Of The Pops'. I borrowed a pair of leather trousers from Jake's boyfriend Tim, and Gary Farrow lent me his leather jacket. Paul, as always, had his outfit well sorted out weeks before. I think we hired tuxedos from Moss Bros for the three musicians. Unfortunately, we had an early call. If your band was first on the show, then you had first rehearsal at about eleven am. There are another two or three rehearsals of the entire show the same day and a lot of hanging around. The final taping (or in this case, live transmission) happened at about seven pm.

The small audience was herded from stage to stage in the large studio. Green-coated cleaning and catering staff trudged around on the periphery. A record company employee turned up with specially printed 'Frankie' flags bearing our logo that were distributed throughout the audience. He shouted from the back of the audience, egging us on as we performed the song. For this televised performance I had chosen to wear a yellow handkerchief in my back pocket, a signal in the S and M fraternity that the wearer is into 'Water Sports' or 'Golden Showers' (a sexual fetish that involves pissing on each other). Suddenly it was all over, and the cameras moved on to film another song. The result of this 'Top Of The Pops' appearance was that 'Relax' jumped from number thirty-five to number six in one week. The next week this momentum took the record to number two.

And that's when it happened, BANG! – the banning of 'Relax' from the BBC's airwaves. Rumour has it that the producer of Radio One DJ Mike Reid came home one evening to find his children rewinding and replaying the 'Relax' video which had already been denied further BBC airtime due to its controversial content. All of a sudden he understood the innuendo of the record. Apparently, the next day, January 11th 1984, he urged Mike Reid not to play the record. Reid complied with the request, calling the record 'obscene' on the air. Later a memo was sent round BBC local radio stations saying that the record should not be played, even though it had been played almost one hundred times on Radio One already. I am going on hearsay for most of this story, but I believe it to be fairly accurate. The record went to number one the next week. I actually believe it would have made it without the ban, but that's something we'll never really know.

ZTT immediately claimed credit for the band's success, claiming that it was Morley's misquoting of the lyrics on the record sleeve that had caused it. He wanted to appear in the media as the mastermind of Frankie Goes To Hollywood, instead of the journalist interviewing famous and talented people and feeding off their dreams.

Indiana Jones

The day after 'Relax' reached number one in the UK, the group were all immediately flown off to Germany, where we were presented with a giant red satin 'number one' cushion. We were booked in to do 'Music Laden' – a popular German music show – in Bremen as well as some other TV shows and interviews. The next few months were a blur of airports and European TV studios, restaurants and nightclubs. With the help of Island Records' licensees in European territories, 'Relax' became a massive hit throughout the world.

Wherever we went we were asked about our sexuality. I eventually became rather cagey about these questions, often accusing journalists of sensationalising or exploiting my homosexuality. I always tried to make it clear that I was not looking for the tolerance of bigots, nor was I setting myself up as a spokesman for the gay community.

We had already been attacked in the press by the cosy, cuddly Boy George, who had not yet come out at that time, and who claimed that our video gave gay people a bad name – 'Cheap, disgusting and very childish' (*Record Mirror*, 12th May 1984). This 'Widow Twanky' act was, of course, pure green-eyed jealousy. He no longer appeared even slightly controversial. His proclaiming that he would rather have a cup of tea than have sex was another way of confirming to the world that his suspect sexuality was something to be ashamed of. It was an exciting moment in time, and just for a moment, I felt all my years of relentless songwriting had at last come to fruition. Frankie Goes To Hollywood was to the Eighties what The Sex Pistols were to the Seventies. The politics that were thrust upon them were wildly different from ours, but the relationships that the two groups had with their particular decades and economic climates

173

were very similar. Frankie Goes To Hollywood might not have been a part of an identifiable movement as The Sex Pistols had been, but the ideas of stylish pleasure and guilt-free sexuality perfectly matched the mood of the time.

Of course ZTT were convinced that the record was a hit solely because of their expertise, a comment Jill Sinclair made more than once. She droned on about 'our marketing expertise', as if we'd had nothing to do with it. ZTT, it seemed, could not stand the thought that the group might be given one iota of credit. Perhaps this blowing of the ZTT trumpet was a kind of self-justification of the unfair contractual terms they had us under.

Since the Bernard Rose video was banned by the BBC in England, another video had to be made. Dave Robinson, owner of Stiff Records and then Managing Director of Island UK, set up a new video shoot in an empty warehouse that Stiff had used. It was a dreadful 'performance' video, done in cold damp conditions with a laser lighting rig as the only prop. I don't like it because of the way I look in it – pure vanity! Naomi the make-up girl went a bit over the top I thought. It proved popular though, and was used as a TV advertisement for the single. This TV advertising activated a clause in the agreement between Island Records and ZTT that if TV advertising was paid for by ZTT then we would only receive a half royalty worldwide, until the costs had been recouped, even if that advertising was in one TV region. This effectively halved our royalty rate to 3% for seven inch singles in UK and less in the rest of the world for a period, to be divided equally between the five band members. The industry norm at this time would have been about 11% for singles in the UK, minus 2% for the producer (half would have resulted in a 5.5% royalty).

Dave Robinson had the idea of multiple twelve-inch record releases to prolong the life of the record. This started off another round of controversy. We were accused of trying to rip fans off by releasing multiple mixes of the same track, when in reality the fans adored it. This eventually led to a 'Spitting Image' skit of the band. My Spitting Image dummy was peculiar, all mismatched eyes and huge lips. I was asked to actually sing the lines for the sketch: '*Remix, re use it*', to the tune of 'Relax'. It was an offer I foolishly declined.

Meanwhile Morley had seen us wearing Katherine Hamnett T-shirts and was 'inspired' with the idea of a baggy white T-shirt with a large, printed slogan. He created the slogan 'Frankie Says . . . Relax' for a giveaway promotional T-shirt. We bought the idea off him and got Tony Pope to find us a merchandising deal to produce Frankie T-shirts. We survived on the proceeds of these T-shirts for many months to come. Then all of a sudden ZTT wanted to take over our merchandising and started to make plans to sell merchandise with the forthcoming album.

No one could have foreseen the popularity of those T-shirts. Their appeal just escalated, so that by the summer of 1984 it appeared that the whole thing had all been carefully planned down to the last detail. By that point it was easy for ZTT to claim this to an eager press fraternity who already loved the idea of media manipulation and 'Frankie Puppets'.

* * *

I was tired of having to liaise with the record company and I asked Tony Pope to manage the band in an administrative sense for 15% of future recording, merchandising and touring royalties (excluding those on the already-released 'Relax', at Bob Johnson's request). I had also had a meeting with Simon Napier Bell who was then managing Wham!, but ZTT were very concerned that he did not become our manager. Morley, possibly primed by Jill and Trevor, appealed to me, saying that Napier Bell would just try and get a large advance out of ZTT so he could grab the commission. They didn't like Tony Pope much either. My guess is that anyone with the band's interest at heart would have been anathema to ZTT. While we had no strong direction from an experienced manager we were more pliable to work with. Perfect Songs Ltd had already lost our signed publishing agreement and got me to sign a letter accepting the second half of the advance so as to ensure that the agreement was enforced. Perfect Songs made a concession to up the royalty rate from 60% in our favour to 65% in return for our resigning a duplicate agreement. There was also a window through which we could have extricated ourselves from the recording agreement, but with the absence of management we missed the opportunity to at least renegotiate.

I had arguments with Jill Sinclair, who suspected that I might be troublesome for ZTT. She claimed to me on the phone on more than one occasion that I was 'not indispensable to the group'. My instincts told me she was campaigning against me with Trevor and the rest of the band.

I now moved into the spare room (the size of a matchbox) of an acquaintance in a flat in Egerton Gardens, Knightsbridge. The lease was owned by an Art Deco dealer called Tony. There were two lodgers, me and another young man of twenty eight called Richard, who was the fashion editor of a women's magazine. It was a lovely flat decorated in a queeny Art Deco style: Trash Deluxe. I had a crush on Richard at first, but we soon became good friends – sisters if you like. Richard was fastidious in his appearance and also kept the flat and my room immaculately clean. This was useful, as I was still as untidy as ever. He showed me how to iron my shirts for PAs and pointed me in the direction of the right designers to suit my look – he favoured Claude Montana over the Japanese designers then coming into vogue. He would also help me get my bags packed for our many European TV appearances. Tony would help occasionally too, joking that he was running the Lucy Clayton Grooming Academy. With Tony and others I discussed my fears that ZTT wanted me ousted from the group, fears that were perhaps justified I discovered years later, when a recording engineer I was working with informed me that he had witnessed a conversation between the recording of 'Relax' and 'Two Tribes'. According to the engineer, someone was urging Trevor to sack me from the band and replace me with Paul as the lead singer. If true, I suspect that this was because they were worried that I would be a disruptive influence. I was advised to form a company called Frankie Goes To Hollywood Ltd in order to protect my position. This would help insure that no one else could use that name without my permission. After all, it was a name that *I* had created.

Tony Pope had arranged for us to meet with an accountant, Ian Haring of Lubbock Fine at the offices of David Gentle (our solicitor). Ian had suggested that the group form a company called F.G.T.H. Ltd, but he'd done a search and discovered that I had already done this. The band looked at me accusingly, thinking I was planning to leave them in the lurch and take away the name for myself, which was never my intention. They became hostile. I didn't want to accuse them of trying to oust me, so I gave no reason for the incorporation of the company. I agreed to sign a letter which said that, if there was a member of the group leaving, then permission to use the name for the remaining members would revert to me, but I could not leave and take the name with me. This was to everyone's satisfaction, but it did begin a process of alienation between me and the rest of the band.

*   *   *

During my last days at the Columbia I had visited Karl in St Mary's Hospital, Paddington. I guessed that he might have this new disease AIDS, but it was never confirmed by Thomas his boyfriend. Karl was moved that I visited him, saying that I could have been out on the town being wined and dined rather than seeing him in an isolation room on the top floor of St Mary's. Karl had become a shadow of his former six-foot, attractive, muscular self. But I still loved him in my way and hoped he would get better. Treatment for AIDS-related illnesses at that time was non-existent in this country. The terrible epidemic that had started a few years before in San Francisco and New York was still largely ignored by the Government and UK media, as it 'only' seemed to affect gay men.

In April I was ordered to go on holiday by ZTT. I had become a pain, Jill and Trevor said, and a holiday would do me good. I think they were hinting that I had become big headed with the band's success. In my opinion it was their heads that were swollen. I had been burning the candle at both ends, although I had stopped taking chemical drugs by now after several bad experiences the year before. I'd had paranoid trips. The only drug I have touched since then is marijuana. I packed a bag and went off to Ibiza on my own. After a few days I met some nice provincial Queens who drove me out to the gay beach a couple of times. It was rather like Hampstead-Heath-On-Sea. I also went to a few gay clubs and generally drank too many brandy and cokes, cheap and generous there. And I managed to burn my face quite badly as usual.

I didn't start changing my behaviour because none of us knew how the disease was transmitted. We thought we were safe so long as we didn't sleep with Americans or take poppers. I returned home to the news that Karl had died. Some of the band had got hold of this information while I was away and actually laughed while they related it to me. I attended the funeral with Jake, Tony and Thomas. I couldn't relate to the coffin containing the person I had known as it slid into the crematorium. Thomas said Karl was probably one of the first thirty people to die of AIDS-related illnesses in this country.

Jake and Tim were my 'gay' parents and Karl and Tom were part of my extended gay family.

*　*　*

After 'Relax' had been such a huge hit, Trevor became very nervous, afraid that he would not be able to produce 'Two Tribes' to a sufficient standard to make it a hit. He was also scared that we might become just a one-hit wonder. He asked us to record a song called 'Slave To The Rhythm' written by Bruce Wooley and Simon Darlow. No one in the band was keen about the idea but it was hard for us to say 'no' to Trevor. A version was recorded, but to no one's satisfaction. Later Trevor cobbled together an electronically sequenced version of 'Two Tribes' that to my mind sounded fantastic. It wasn't up to his standards however, and was scrapped. Another three-month process began in which Trevor and his team worked on 'Two Tribes' over and over again. 'Two Tribes' and all subsequent Frankie tracks were recorded digitally, in contrast to 'Relax' which was recorded on one twenty-four-track analogue tape. I believe that on the 'Two Tribes' sessions, Steve Lipson learnt to use Trevor's new toy, the Synclavier (an extremely expensive instrument that was to replace the Fairlight as the premier sampling tool), for a while. During the recording of 'Two Tribes' Trevor would still ask me to come into the studio and sing at odd hours.

On one occasion he asked me to come in at eleven o'clock at night. I did not know what to do with myself till then, so to kill time I went to a gay bar in Earls Court called Harpoon Louie's, a meeting place for people who wanted to go to the Copacabana Club in the basement below. That night I met Wolfgang who was going to be very important in my life. I spotted him on one side of the bar and thought that he was very handsome in a Harrison-Fordish sort of way; like me, he had no moustache, an unusual thing in a gay bar in those days. I asked him where the cigarette machine was (not very original), then I returned to him to ask for change which he did not have. After getting the cigarettes I returned to him again and asked for a light. I think I had made my intentions obvious enough by this time and offered to buy him a drink. We both had a pint of lager shandy as it was a warm evening, and we chatted. I asked him for his phone number as I had to leave and go to the studio. I remember wearing an interesting shirt that night by Comme des Garçons – one of the sleeves had a contrasting type of plaid. Wolfgang suggested it would look good hanging on a chair in his flat.

Filthy Lucre

I arranged to meet Wolfgang about a week later outside the Reject Shop on the Kings Road. I was in my Katherine Hamnett cotton poplin suit, Yohji Yamamoto duster coat and Gianni Versace linen cap. I was reacting against having had to shop in Oxfam or secondhand shops for the last eight years. We met at the allotted time and had lunch at the Chelsea Farmers Market. I told Wolfgang about 'Relax' and its success. He told me that he had been in catering for years, had just sold his share in a business, and was currently involved in the design and management of two new delicatessen sandwich-bars in the City for two German associates. They were the first of their kind in London, the kind of place where you got a whole quarter of roast beef and salad on a choice of breads and could pay over five pounds for a Yuppie sandwich.

A fashion war had developed within the band, especially between Paul and me. Neither of us would be seen dead in the same thing twice as far as photo sessions or TV appearances went, which was expensive and time consuming. I dragged Wolfgang to this shop and that, trying this on one thing after another. He got so bored with this vain pop star that he walked off down the Kings Road in a huff. I was dumbstruck.

I walked home tail between my legs and told Richard what had happened. 'He obviously is not the right one for you,' he said. I was not convinced, so against Richard's advice, I rang Wolfgang and met him at his flat in Fulham later that afternoon. The relationship developed very quickly after that and within a few weeks I was staying at Wolfgang's flat every night. I was looking for some sense of security and stability. He wasn't a phony, like most people in the music industry or those people on the gay scene who wouldn't have looked at me twice till I was famous.

Wolfgang cycled from Fulham to the City every morning at five o'clock. At first I would get up with him at that unearthly hour, only to fall back into sleep when he had gone. Eventually I too bought a bicycle to get around London. It was the spring of 1984 and I had fallen head over heels in love. It seemed that the world was my oyster after all.

Fairly soon after meeting Wolfgang I was offered two free tickets to fly on Virgin Airlines' maiden voyage to New York. I asked Wolfgang to go with me but he declined, saying that he couldn't get time off work. Jill Sinclair had decreed that none of the Frankies should take up Virgin's offer of tickets, partly because rehearsals for a live appearance on 'The Tube' started on the following Monday. I explained to her that there was no way I was going to miss the opportunity. A trip to New York – home of Andy Warhol and The Velvet Underground – had always been my dream.

The flight was highly publicised, with paparazzi everywhere. On the plane I sat in front of Sandie Shaw and behind Bonnie Langford. I met Phil Lynott and Una Stubbs and, most memorably, Steve Strange (he'd had a couple of hits with Visage) who now became my official guide to New York's night life. He was a wide-boy and I liked him. Somehow the not-yet-famous Magenta De Vine had got a ticket too, so there were a few familiar faces on the trip.

Richard Branson, sitting a few seats away from me, kept saying the name 'Holly'. I would often turn around wondering why he was not looking in my direction, until I discovered that this was the name of his younger daughter. The in-flight entertainment was F.A.B. The Mint Juleps were hired to stand at the front of the plane and sing their acapella set. They were a wonderful vocal group of young cockney girls who coincidentally later signed to ZTT. There was also Simon Drake, a magician employed to do 'close-up' magic for the passengers. He had done magic and effects on Kate Bush's only tour and now has his own surreal magic TV show. Everyone on the flight seemed to get obnoxiously drunk on champagne, but perhaps only I did.

The hotel we stayed at was not elegant but adequate. My

companion Marco had brought a super-eight camera to film New York which – typically – he shot completely out of focus. We immediately walked out to discover the streets of New York. We found ourselves on Forty-Second Street with its lights, smells, hustlers and generally threatening ambience. We were petrified. I was wearing an expensive Gaultier suit (and carrying hundreds of dollars) and Marco was wearing jeans, and we both looked very muggable. An old bag-lady mumbled 'Mutt and Jeff, right?' We quickly walked back in the direction of our hotel.

The next day we went to Greenwich Village and SoHo looking at the natives in amazement and eating typical 'diner' food. That night there was a special dinner party for the Virgin travellers. We sat at a table with Kate Rabbet (actress and ex-girlfriend of Prince Andrew) and Steve Strange. Steve took us to Danceteria and introduced us to Diane Brill, The Queen Of The Night. She was the hostess with the mostest. I loved her bubbly personality and her larger-than-life look. On the top floor of Danceteria was an S and M art exhibition. I made the mistake of saying the leather-clad artist was cute. Steve Strange then embarrassed me by asking the artist to sleep with me. 'It's his first night in New York,' he shouted over the loud music. Luckily the artist was otherwise engaged.

We also went to Area, then the trendiest club in town. The unusual thing about Area was its use of performance artists as decoration and that night displayed on a pedestal was a pink-suited Jackie Onassis impersonator whose torso appeared out of a miniature car, waving to imaginary onlookers. I was photographed by paparazzi in a rather drunken state. I remember standing next to Kid Creole (August Darnell) posing for a photograph. The result was responsible for my almost totally giving up alcohol: I never wanted to look so 'glazed' in a photo again.

Steve Strange then took us to the Anvil, a gay bar after which he had named his last Visage album. Downstairs was a cruising area with dark and not-so-dark recesses where men had sex openly. I was very tempted, but now there was a bit more (mis)information about the new disease called AIDS. The word was that one got it from Americans.

holly johnson

Holljelujah
Holly Johnson
remix album

Dreams That Money Can't Buy

BLAST

liverpool
IMCD 13
FRANKIE GOES TO HOLLYWOOD

WELCOME TO THE
PLEASUREDOME

BANG!... THE GREATEST HITS OF FRANKIE GOES TO HOLLYWOOD

relax don't do it
when you want to
go to it
relax don't do it
when you want to
come

RELAX
FRANKIE GOES
TO HOLLYWOOD

FRANKIE GOES TO HOLLYWOOD
TWO TRIBES

Later we visited Washington Square and went to Macy's, like all good tourists, buying T-shirts and the then-fashionable haversacks worn over one shoulder by all trendy New Yorkers. We were fooled like everyone else by the New York City Tax which had to be paid on top of the ticket price. But what the hell – we were in 'New York City, Na na na na na na na now!' Just like a Lou Reed song.

We arrived home exhausted on Monday morning and I went straight to the rehearsal rooms. Trevor started to put the band through their paces and I fell asleep in a heap on the floor. Apparently while I was asleep Trevor put the microphone up to my face amplifying my snoring, to the amusement of everyone present.

At this time I tried to get an overdraft facility at the Knightsbridge branch of the Nat West. I wanted one of £500 so I could buy clothes for TV appearances etc. Sometimes ZTT would advance me money against my future publishing income, but I hated going to Jill 'cap in hand'. So, armed with a letter from her saying I would have substantial future income, and my Gold Disc (soon to become Platinum) for 'Relax', I walked into the assistant manager's office. I showed him the Gold Disc. He took it away for a few minutes, then returned, saying in a condescending tone, 'This is the one that got banned isn't it?', and handing it back to me as if it were contaminated. I was refused the overdraft facility. I moved my account from the Nat West immediately and was highly amused when they asked could my name be used in an advertising campaign a few years later.

I had another problem over money. My old friend Jake had been doing people's hair at their home, but he wanted to get back into salon work. He asked me to lend him £500 so he could do an intensive refresher course. I had already lent his boyfriend Tim £100 that I suspected I would never see again, but I didn't really mind as Tim had been very hospitable to me. The trouble was, I only had about £500 in the bank at that time, and I needed it myself. Jake was very sensitive and somehow jumped to the conclusion that I was accusing him of only hanging round with me for my money. We fell out, seeing each other only a couple of times after that. It was such a stupid thing to do. I really needed old friends like him.

Lending money to friends can be perilous, I discovered. When fame knocks, friends automatically think you are loaded. They borrow money and then convince themselves that they need not pay you back. It's not the money that matters, just the fact that they think they can abuse you in that way.

* * *

'Two Tribes' went through as many incarnations as 'Relax' had done. The wonderful bass line was eventually created from a series of sampled, sequenced and played elements. The sixty-piece orchestra was arranged and conducted by Ann Dudly – friend of Trevor's and a member of The Art Of Noise. I read in an interview with Ann that Trevor said to her that he wanted to spend lots of money on a huge string section. The orchestra certainly sounded magnificent. Trevor was now assured substantial income from 'Relax' so he felt that he now had *carte blanche* to Spend, Spend, Spend. On our behalf.

'Two Tribes' was released to great acclaim and went straight to number one in the UK. It then stayed there for nine weeks, equalling Queen's previous record with 'Bohemian Rhapsody'. For it we recorded about five different 'Top Of The Pops' performances. It almost became a bind, and certainly put a strain on our wardrobes, as we were determined to have a slightly different look for each show. While 'Two Tribes' stayed at number one, 'Relax' re-entered the charts and reached number two again. This had never happened to a new pop group before, the nearest event in living memory was The Beatles' early success. 'Relax' eventually sold over five million copies, and 'Two Tribes' over three million. Then Fleet Street really became interested in 'The New Pop Phenomenon'. *'They have the wit of the Beatles, the decadence of the Rolling Stones and the wildness of the Sex Pistols . . .'* wrote Mike Andrews of the *Daily Express* (Monday 25th June 1984).

* * *

With the success of 'Two Tribes', Fleet Street's interest in Frankie Goes to Hollywood escalated, typically exploiting friends and family. My parents had mistakenly spoken to *The Sun*. They were misquoted extensively according to them – and I can believe it. The centre-page headline on Monday 6th August 1984 said 'MY GAY SON – By Holly's proud dad', a line that I knew would never have come from my father's mouth. 'How embarrassing it must be for you,' said Jill as she smarmily unfurled the pages.

A week or so after the article appeared, *The Sun* sent my father a cheque for about a hundred pounds. He sent it back to them in disgust and never bought the newspaper again. These tabloids are the enemy of all homosexuals, sensationalising their existence and generally *over-emphasising* openly gay people's sexuality. There was a time when it seemed that I couldn't read my name without the prefix 'Outrageous Gay Rock Star', as if it defined my whole existence. They never seem to write 'Safe, Middle Of The Road, Heterosexual Rock Star, **** *******', for example.

In the same week we were booked to film another 'Top Of The Pops' for 'Two Tribes'. Michael Hurl, the regular producer, was off and had been replaced by another producer. He asked me to appear reading a copy of *The Sun* during the orchestral introduction of the song, then tear it up in disgust as the pumping bassline began. This I did with relish.

* * *

During the summer, however, discontent grew within the band. While I was hanging out at Sarm one day, Rikah, the girl in charge of Perfect Songs Ltd, asked me what the publishing splits were, as far as the writers of the songs were concerned. I said I did not know and would ring the Performance Right Society for advice, which I did. I explained to the PRS representative that I had written the melody and the lyrics of these songs to a harmony or piece of music that had been created by two other people. In the case of 'Relax', the words and the melody had come to me

185

quite independently. The PRS replied that the lyrics alone entitle
the author to 50% of the writer's share of the song. So as I had
also written the melody I was entitled to a further third of the
remaining 50% which is allotted to the composer/s of the music.
This made a total of 66.6% of the writer's share of the song for
little old me. Rikah also rang the PRS to check on what I had told
her, as we were both somewhat inexperienced in these matters.

This news did not go down very well with the other members of
the band, especially Mark O'Tool. Ped had no argument with the
situation, as someone who had just provided a rhythm would not
normally qualify as a composer. Mark refused to sign the
publishing-split forms initially, and Nasher was asked to mediate.
We went for a drink and he explained that Culture Club, for
example, split publishing income five ways. But, I thought, why
should people who did not do the work get paid for it? I had been
writing songs for many years and had put a lot of effort into it.
Paul and Nasher had not even been in the band when our first
two hits were written. I discussed the problem with Wolfgang,
who came up with an idea. On this first album (which was in the
process of being made) I would take slightly less than the PRS
recommended publishing split. I think I took 60% on some of the
singles and just 50% on the other songs on the album. The
division of the remaining percentage was left up to the others. In
the future, in an attempt to keep the band sweet, publishing
royalties would be split five ways while the band remained
together, after which the royalties would revert back to the
respective writers. I put this idea to Tony Pope to relay to the
others, and it was accepted, albeit grudgingly.

During this row there was a meeting involving the band and
the directors of ZTT. Trevor actually said that he thought I was
being 'greedy' in taking so large a split of the publishing royalties
– pretty rich coming from him, whose companies were getting
35% of the publishing royalties (for doing nothing) while he
personally, as producer, got 4% of recommended retail price on
each record from ZTT. Not to mention the profit ZTT were
making in their deal with Island Records, or the profits of Sarm
Studios (owned by Jill and Trevor and family), where we were

obliged to record. Trevor's accusation of greed did nothing for the harmony of the band. It is true that we did have Trevor's expertise as a producer, which was a valuable commodity: but he was certainly being remunerated for it, just as I felt I should be for my songwriting abilities.

Chasing the Dragon

Since I had moved out of the Columbia, the three younger musicians of our band – 'The Lads' as they became known – had moved in. They had impressed their personalities on Trevor by this time: he would ask them about their exploits with groupies and get off on the general vibe. They represented Teenage Wildlife, which Trevor perhaps found refreshing after working with two 'ferocious homosexuals'. Trevor began to think of the concept of 'The Lads' as a loud and hedonistic stadium rock band. The notion of the band having two separate factions soon spilled over into the media. And of course 'The Lads' were keen to let everyone know that *they* weren't Queer.

The social scene round the band also started to be invaded by heroin. The only time I ever 'Chased the Dragon' with this set was during one Saturday night out in 1983, when curiosity led me to think 'How does it feel?' It felt like mild nausea and a not-caring. I ended up in Jodie's with some of the group, where a rather ugly (and probably heterosexual) rent-boy pounced on me and led me to the toilet. He gave me a quick wank then frisked me to see if I had any money to pay him. I didn't have a penny. I was so depressed by all of this that I spent the next afternoon alone in Liverpool's Roman Catholic Cathedral making a pact with God. I'd always believed in the God who was a force for good in the Universe, but not the God of dogma and organised religion, the God who condemns people to Hell-fire. Gold crucifix in hand, I knelt down and wept over the level that I felt my life had sunk to. I prayed for the strength to keep away from that all-consuming drug.

* * *

The controversial 'Two Tribes' video was directed by two friends of Trevor's, Kevin Godley and Lol Creme. Their first idea that we discussed was to make a kind of 'Rollerball-in-the-mud' video, in which two teams of warriors would fight it out. Eventually this got distilled to the idea of Ronald Reagan and Konstantin Chernenko (the then Russian leader) slugging it out in a cock-fighting ring watched by a multi-racial audience symbolising the whole world. I was asked to play a news reporter, with the rest of the band playing my film crew. The idea that the actual leaders had to fight it out personally was very amusing. My intentions when I wrote the lyric, inspired by *Mad Max 2*, had been to depict the threat of Armageddon between the two most powerful nations on Earth at that time, the USSR and the USA, fighting over the last oil fields.

I was a bit disappointed when I saw the version of the video for the seven-inch as I thought it lacked colour and concentrated too much on the slapstick violence. They later did a scratch edit, twelve-inch version, with specially recorded sound effects, a ground-breaking pop video with a sense of humour. 'The Tube' had a special midnight showing of it, and we flew to Newcastle to be interviewed before transmission. Sadly the interview was a bit of a shambles. We had all been waiting round for what seemed like hours and were, I suppose, a bit the worse for drink. The BBC had refused to play the video of course, saying it was of a violent nature, although they plugged the record to death. Watching now, I see that the video was quite disturbing, hardly light entertainment – but then that's not what Frankie were about.

Most press interviews were done at Island Records. Regine Moylett (then assistant to Rob Partridge, Head of Press at Island) would usher endless journalists into a small room at the back of Island's offices. I would be left with a sore throat at the end of the day as I had answered so many questions. I preferred to do interviews on my own, as I didn't like doing them with other members of the band, having to deal with opinions that did not fit my vision. But ZTT determined to give the other members of the band a high profile, not wanting me to get the idea I was the most important Frankie. I was often accused of being a prima donna; and I would be the first to admit it. After all, I was twenty four years old and part of a meteoric success story.

I didn't become as abusive to other people as 'The Lads' did, though. They were now nineteen or twenty and for them it must have been even harder to handle. The frustrating thing for them must have been not really playing on the most successful tracks. Steve Lipson played most of the guitar parts, and the rest were usually sequenced synthesizers, samplers or drum machines. All this must have made them feel very insecure, something they covered up with their extremely boisterous and football-hooligan behaviour.

* * *

We had no real signed contract with Tony Pope, but we did sign a letter of intent, so Tony could prove to ZTT that he had an agreement with us. We all felt that Tony was an honest, hard working person and would not rip us off. He became inundated with requests from people who wanted to be our booking agent. One agency tried to engage us in a three-year contract which was ridiculous. I decided that I had signed enough contracts, and had started to realise some of the implications of our ZTT agreement in the light of our success. We were selling a lot of records – both 'Relax' and 'Two Tribes' had gone platinum by this stage which meant sales of one million units. And that was just in the UK – both tracks were big hits all over the world; our gruelling yet exciting promotional trips had seen to that. But our very success meant that the professional scavengers descended quickly on the new pop phenomenon.

The other members of the band did not seem interested in the business side of things and were not keen on discussing the contract. I started to talk over the problems the band had with Wolfgang. It was he who first looked at the contract for me and suggested I take further legal advice. Eaton and Burley, a firm of music business solicitors, took all the correspondence I had from ZTT and looked over it. They came to Wolfgang's flat and explained to us that ZTT had no contractual obligation to release any of our records. They also suggested that we should try and renegotiate the contract in the light of the band's current success. I even think it was as early as this that it was suggested that the contract may have been in 'restraint of trade'; that is, potentially stopping us from making a living. Over the next two and a half years, despite the subsequent success of the album and third and fourth singles, ZTT failed to offer any significant renegotiations of the contract.

*　*　*

Wolfgang now suggested that I move in with him officially. It was a big decision, as I had now only known him for about six months – we had met in April and I moved in properly in September. My flat-mates Tony and Richard advised me against living with a boyfriend, as they believed that gay relationships ceased to work when couples moved in together. But I threw caution to the wind and followed my heart.

As a treat for Sunday lunch, we used to go to McDonald's on North End Road. It was strange having two massive hit records and being paid only about £40 a week. Once we were sitting on a bench eating when a van went past. The driver shouted out 'Frankie Goes To Hollywood, you Puff!' At least I was famous, we laughed.

Any extra money that we could squeeze out of ZTT went straight to the then-fashionable shops of South Molton Street. Paul would be there first whenever something new came in to either the Yohji Yamamoto shop or Bizarre. I remember buying a waistcoat there that was part of John Galliano's degree collection when he was still at St Martin's. Paul and I looked like a pair of clothes-horses most of the time. We started visiting Katherine Hamnett's warehouse and buying things for the whole band at cost price. We were the first group of the Eighties to wear these designer labels. I was asked to do a fashion spread for *You Magazine* in *The Mail On Sunday*, then both Paul and I were asked to do a feature for *Vogue*, modelling the new winter collections. We had definitely arrived.

The Pope of Pop

The rehearsals for our American tour started in a rehearsal room (Easy Hire) in North London. Ged O'Tool our ex-guitarist was hired as a second guitarist. He played the more difficult guitar passages, the ones Nasher was not up to. No one was really consulted about this: Mark just gave Ged the job. I suppose Mark felt guilty.

I was not required for the first few weeks of rehearsals as the band needed time to get their act together. Paul and I started turning up for a few hours a day after about two weeks. I think The Style Council were rehearsing in the next studio. The morning was usually spent in the cafe eating fried egg on toast and drinking cups of tea. By this time, there was an entourage of girl fans everywhere the band went, who would hang around outside Sarm or wherever they knew the band would be. Most of 'The Lads' had girlfriends, but I don't think that stopped them from sampling the odd groupie. They had moved into a three-bedroomed flat in Maida Vale. I never visited it, but I heard rumours of its dishevelled and pungent state, cans of lager apparently strewn everywhere. There was an incident when a shotgun was fired causing some damage, but I can't remember the details. It was just the high spirits of straight teenage scallywags, I suppose.

I had bought a bicycle and I remember Wolfgang and I cycling to Easy Hire one day – a long, up-hill ride. Wolfgang got a flat tyre on the return journey and wobbled home. He told me he had argued with his boss, who had apparently refused to pay Wolfgang bonuses that had been promised to him, so he had left his job. This left us in quite a bad financial position. Before I went on tour, I ordered three boxes of the then not yet released 'Welcome To The Pleasuredome' album from Island Records's sales department. I signed all of the copies and gave them to Wolfgang to see if he could sell them – a good indication of how absolutely broke we were. Unfortunately, when he tried to flog them no one would believe that they had really been signed by me!

One of the things I looked forward to the most was getting a *per diem* payment on the North American tour of about $25. At the end of October we flew out to Canada a day or two before the first show, and I remember it was freezing cold there. I used to wander off on my own, as had been my habit during European promotional trips, and I met some students in Ottawa who went to Carlton University, our first venue. When we sound-checked, they invited me to their common room for mocha or hot apple juice with a cinnamon stick thrown in. They were nice, middle-class kids. As usual I was able to sniff out the local gay club, which I visited alone.

During our first week in Canada I made friends with one of the support acts. I think it was in Montreal that we were supported by The Great Imposters, a group of five fabulous drag queens who impersonated famous women. The leader was Rusty Ryan – a big man in every way – who shared a flat with a famous Canadian children's entertainer. His impression of Divine was wonderful. I also remember Danny, who did a great Bette Midler. There was a wonderful 'Tina Turner' too, and maybe a 'Cher'. We immediately hit it off. They were good people who drove me around in their van and let me into the local jargon and where to find pizza delicacies. Everyone liked them so much that we persuaded the powers-that-be that we should take them as a support act to as many dates on the tour as possible. A bit of drag was very much part of the Frankie vibe. Since becoming a successful 'rock' act we had lost The Leather Pets, Juicy Lucy and other glitterati on the way, so it was wonderful to have The Great Imposters on board.

I remember telling them how much I missed Wolfgang and by the time we reached New York I was really pining for him. I didn't really socialise a lot with the band by this point. We had to spend so much time together anyway that it seemed that a break was needed now and again.

After playing Washington DC we flew to New York to do the TV show *Saturday Night Live*. During this period we stayed at the Berkshire Place Hotel. I hung out with Diane Brill and a guy called Don who worked for Andy Warhol on video projects. Diane was trying to organise a 'Frankie' party at The Danceteria, something that Tony Pope was averse to as he thought they were trying to make money out of the situation. I just thought it was great that they wanted to throw a party for us.

Don took me to meet Andy Warhol for the first time at The New Factory, which they were in the process of moving into. We hung around the building for a while and Don set up a camera to film me for *Andy Warhol's Fifteen Minutes*, a planned TV show. I stood in front of the camera and didn't know what to say. Andy walked in wearing a black Steven Sprouse suit with a leather jacket over the top, a dark red scarf round his neck and that famous silver wig that showed his natural dark hair underneath. I was wearing an off-white pinstriped Yohji Yamamoto wool suit, since New York is cold in the winter.

Andy shook hands with me and said, 'Gee Holly, you're so famous.' 'Not as famous as you, Andy,' was my reply. I couldn't think of a nicer thing to say to Andy Warhol. I was so excited and nervous about meeting him but he was really normal and unpretentious. I had missed meeting him on my first trip to New York. I had however already met Marc Balet, the art director of *Interview Magazine*. Marc had given me a couple of autographed Polaroids of Andy that said 'To Frankie Hollywood . . . Andy Warhol.' One of the first things Andy did was shoot off a reel of film of my face with an automatic camera. He probably did this to everyone, I thought, hoping they would commission a $25,000 portrait, something I wish I had done. I was holding a Coke can and smoking a Silk Cut. I said on film that I was wearing them, which he liked. I realised that smoking was banned on TV and I threw the cigarette off camera, rather guiltily, on to the clean parquet floor. Andy gave me a funny look.

I gave Andy a copy of 'The Pleasuredome' album showing him my quote inside: 'I get buzzed off the fact that Andy Warhol has heard of us, because he gets buzzed off the fact that Picasso had

194

heard of him.' What he liked the most was the word BANG printed on the back. He thought it was the name of the record company, asking me whose idea that was. He then sent out for a cassette version of the album so he could listen to it on his Walkman as he wandered off down the New York streets. For some reason I was surprised that he walked – I had imagined that he would take limousines everywhere after his shooting.

*   *   *

I was really missing Wolfgang by this time; I had done enough shopping and I needed some company. So I arranged for him to fly out to New York on Virgin Airlines, and somehow he scraped the fare together. Wearing my black floor-length Matsuda robe that I had just paid $1000 for, and with my hair slicked back, I met a sedated Wolfgang (he hates flying) with a limousine I had hired for the occasion. He described the greeting as a bit like a Gothic nightmare, being led into New York by some kind of vampire. It was November the 11th, and that night I had to travel to Philadelphia for a show, so I left Wolfgang at The Berkshire Place to sleep off the effects of his jet lag. When I returned the next day The Great Imposters had arrived to support us at the Ritz, into which we were booked for three nights. They all wanted to go to the party Diane Brill had arranged at The Danceteria. Sadly, Wolfgang still felt a bit rough, so after dinner at the hotel he went to bed early. The party Diane arranged was judged the third best party of the year in New York. There were living chandeliers arranged in pillars on the ground floor of the club (like something from a Cocteau film), made up of very scantily-clad topless girls decked out in white pearls, some holding white lights in their hands. As we entered the club, the 'jungle-atmosphere' opening to 'Welcome To The Pleasuredome' boomed out, and there was a lot of photographers. John Sex was there with his hair that stood on end; so was a big muscular Mr America in just a posing pouch; Cherry Vanilla; and Kid Creole's wife and chief Coconut Alex. Diane herself was dressed as Miss American Superhero.

At our first show at the Ritz I was extra nervous. This was our first New York date and I wanted it to be great. I was so on edge that I sang my heart out until my throat was red raw. Patti Austin the soul singer came back stage after the show as did Billy Idol and his girlfriend Perry. The next afternoon to avoid rescheduling the shows I was given a shot of the steroid Cortisone to reduce the inflammation in my throat, and slept for a few hours while the drug did its thing. I didn't realise that Cortisone can have side effects, one of which was weight gain. My stage clothes fitted snugly enough but after the Cortisone some of them were positively tight. I ballooned, especially in the face. Hotel room service and club sandwiches were no help either.

Spencer Bright, a journalist then working for the *Evening Standard*, came over to do interviews. We set up another meeting with Andy Warhol so Spencer could take photos and record the meeting. This time Wolfgang came with me to the old factory. We stood in front of a large painting of rats for the photograph. I asked Andy how I could get on the cover of *Interview Magazine*. He replied, 'You could sleep with the publisher?' in a rather dry manner.

'Who's the publisher?'

'I am.'

I asked Andy about some of his friends including my namesake Holly Woodlawn, and also if he knew Quentin Crisp. Andy picked up the phone and dialled a number, then handed me the receiver. Quentin Crisp answered the phone. I didn't know what to say. I explained who I was and invited him to our concert that night, but Quentin said that he had prior arrangements. What a pity, I thought. It was wonderful to speak to two heroes in one day. Luckily Wolfgang had the presence of mind to ask Andy for autographs, and he gave us three signed copies of *Interview Magazine*. One had a Grace Jones cover, another showed Joan Rivers – two of my favourite showbiz divas. One of them contained our first Frankie Goes To Hollywood *Interview* photospread.

Welcome to the Pleasuredome

When we left New York to continue the tour I asked Wolfgang to stay on with me. He didn't have a job to go to back home and I realised I wanted his help and company; it would keep me from going out after the show when I should be resting my voice. I decided to pay for Wolfgang's travel expenses and I shared my *per diem*s with him. For some reason however this was not a popular decision with the rest of the band. After a few dates (Atlanta, Cleveland and Detroit) we arrived in Chicago. Tony Pope came to me in my hotel room with some stupid story. He alleged that Wolfgang had insulted the sound mixer one night by complaining about the sound, and said that he and the other members of the band wanted Wolfgang sent home. I said that if Wolfgang was sent home then I would be going with him. Who did they think they were, giving me orders? It wasn't as if it was costing them anything, and it was certainly none of their business. Just because they wanted to go out on the town every night taking advantage of groupies didn't mean I had to. This of course alienated me further from the rest of the band.

'The Lads' had special passes made with a picture of a topless girl in stockings and suspenders and the slogan 'Chicken For The Lads'. They were passed out by the roadies to the more attractive girls who fought their way to the front of the stage. There were lots of stories retold in dressing rooms of their sexual exploits. Thankfully I had to retire to the hotel after every show in order to preserve my over-strained voice. I often had to do three nights on the trot without a day off, and I soon learned that this was too much for my voice. With my singing style, it is very hard to hold back and fake it.

In Chicago we played a theatre called the Bismarck. This particular theatre had had its seating removed and the audience

197

stood downstairs. Half-way through the set the audience near the stage started to sink. They began to scream as the carpet under their feet gave way. Luckily the carpet, which had been nailed down, saved them from falling through the floor that was collapsing near the front of the stage. Not surprisingly the show had to be stopped. We could only continue to play if the crowd agreed to stand back fifty feet from the stage. We did another couple of songs which seemed to please the audience. Obvious headlines ran the next day in the local press: 'Frankie Sink The Bismarck!'

The next show on the tour was Minneapolis. We played at First Avenue, the nightclub used in Prince's film *Purple Rain*. The audience shouted out, 'This is Erotic City man, so stop wanking.' The crowd seemed to be under the impression that we were trying to claim that we were more erotic than Prince.

After Denver (I had never seen so many cowboy hats before) we went to San Francisco, the town I was looking forward to the most. Paul had given me a detailed description of it after a trip a few years before, and it *is* to my mind the most beautiful city in America. We played one of our best and most memorable shows ever at the Kabuki theatre and stayed in a Japanese hotel next door.

A group of thirteen-year-old girls presented me with what looked like a used dildo; rubbery and kind of dirty. Wolfgang got badly scratched by one of these vixens. The wound seemed to have a curse on it, because it took ages to heal.

Trevor came over to see us. A version of 'The Power Of Love' had to be recorded for the video without the orchestra because of Musicians' Union rules, so he asked me to do another vocal over the original backing track. This was done in Narada Michael Walden's studio The Automat. I also saw Godley and Creme's 'Nativity' video for 'The Power Of Love'. It was shot in Israel without our being present or even really being consulted, and I thought it looked like a cheap Christmas card. It was obvious that this video could only really be shown at Christmas time, so as a promotional tool it had limitations. I also felt the video put a restriction on the song's meaning. It did the trick in one sense, though: 'The Power Of Love' went to number one in England, matching Gerry and The Pacemakers' previous record for a band's first three singles reaching number one in Britain.

In LA we were also invited by director Brian De Palma – who was cuddly and friendly, like Yogi Bear – to appear in his film *Body Double*. The film had already been shot and he was looking for a song to insert into it as a promotional device. This is a good way to advertise a movie and a sure-fire way of tapping into the MTV audience.

For *Body Double* we stayed at the Chateau Marmont Hotel, scene of John Belushi's drug death. We had two days of filming, most of which I had to work, while the rest of the band just hung around our trailer dressing room. Brian De Palma had very high standards, going for take after take. It was the middle of the summer, yet I was wearing a Jean Paul Gaultier woollen evening suit with a John Galliano waistcoat underneath, as well as a white shirt. Was I hot! The scenes I did were with Craig Wasson, the film's male lead, who was very pleasant to work with. One involved my being picked up by a bunch of leather boys and being thrown down on to a bar where a Japanese girl walked over my back. This was rehearsed and shot what seemed to me like a thousand times. I was black and blue all around my hip-bones by the end of the day. When I returned, Wolfgang suspected I had had rough S and M sex with some pick up. 'If only,' I thought.

We were booked to play LA's The Palace for three nights. I was extra nervous about playing this town, even getting stage fright and throwing up before the show – something that had never happened to me before. Maybe it was to do with the fact that Trevor and Jill had flown out to see us perform. After the show Jill told me off for partying in her school-ma'amish way. 'You should be back at the hotel resting your voice,' she said. Jill and Trevor didn't really approve of me having Wolfgang on tour with me. They kept repeating that when Trevor was on tour with Yes there were no 'wives' allowed. Anyway the other band members seemed to like the freedom from their partners that touring afforded them.

In order to save money, Wolfgang would wash our underwear

in the hotel sinks so we didn't have to use expensive hotel laundries. He had a frugal streak which curbed my natural extravagance, which had not been helped by my having been told by my accountant that I would probably never need to work again. It was true that the 'Welcome To The Pleasuredome' album shipped out more than a million copies in England alone, reaching number one in the album charts. It eventually sold approximately three million copies world wide, which, for a double album *and* the band's first, was rather remarkable. For some reason ZTT/Island decided to TV advertise the album after the initial orders, and we all know what that meant for our royalty rate, don't we?

No Room at the Inn

When the US tour ended, we returned home to London, then travelled to Liverpool to do two special concerts. They were to be at The Royal Court Theatre, Liverpool's second-biggest theatrical venue. It was a kind of 'Thank You' homecoming for our Liverpool fans who had bought a high proportion of our records. It also proved a chance for families and friends to show off. Certain band-members' families swanned around as if they owned the joint. When my mother tried to sit in her allotted seat she was told by one of the group's relations that it was reserved for his family, as if he were God. I think she ignored them and sat in her seat anyway.

The shows went down very well with the home crowd. There were quite a few journalists there who wanted to see if we could pull it off live, as these were our first British dates since our hit records. We played well. We had become a good live band during the American tour.

Each night there was a kind of after-the-show party at the Holiday Inn, where all the families and friends sat around in cliques, clocking each other. On the second night Wolfgang and I went up to our room taking Jayne, Ra, her son, and her new boyfriend Biffa, so we could have a quiet chat. My elder brother John rang me up in my room saying, 'Get down 'ere and buy yer two brothers a crate of ale, you should be down 'ere holding our end up.' So I told him to get lost. He wormed my room number out of one of 'The Lads', then came storming up to my room. Pounding on my door, he shouted abusively. I should have known he was in a violent mood, as when I had seen him earlier he was claiming that he was a Viking. I opened the door of my room a crack after first putting on the security chain, and threw out a tenner. Then he started to kick the door down, while I barricaded it with a chair. Jayne and Biffa were giggling on the bed. I remember John screaming that I had broken my father's heart until eventually he was removed by hotel security. My younger brother Jimmy then rang up, saying how dare I get John chucked out from the hotel by security men. I told him to mind his own business and put the phone down. The next day I decided that the best thing I could do was to get out of town before a certain angry Viking caught up with me.

We did *Wogan* to promote 'The Power Of Love' and I was interviewed. As Paul had no backing vocals to do for this song, he decided not to stand around the stage doing nothing, so he didn't come. In Europe, however, he would pretend limply to play the acoustic guitar.

* * *

Production rehearsals for the next tour were done at The Brixton Academy. Backstage one day, when Wolfgang had not accompanied me, Tony and a few of the band members said there would be a coach to take us from town to town on the forthcoming UK and European leg of the tour. They also said they had counted up the seats and there would be no room for Wolfgang on the coach. 'Oh really?' I replied. 'Then there will be no room for me on the coach either.' I decided to do the UK tour by British Rail and the European tour by air. Who wanted to travel with a bunch of lager drinkers in a smelly coach anyway?

They had obviously been bitching about Wolfgang and me behind our backs. Paul feigned neutrality in the situation, but his silence meant he sided with 'The Lads'. However, I depended on no one's approval or friendship. There was no way they were going to dictate to me.

Paul and Joe, his boyfriend, shared a flat with Joe's now ex-boyfriend Paul Cook, just around the corner from where Wolfgang and I lived, near Fulham's North End Road. Paul and Joe invited us around for Christmas dinner that year, my first Christmas away from Liverpool. Indeed all band-related feuding was put to rest for the holiday period. 'The Lads' bought me an

At-At, which was a Star Wars Walker toy. I bought everyone in the band presents from Soho sex shops. Tony Pope got a wanking machine, Paul got a Dolly Dildo in the design of a Bimbo-girl. I bought Mark a Dr Johnson's erection kit including erection creams, and someone else some novelty condoms. Each gift reflected just what I felt about each person.

No sooner was Christmas over then we were flown out to New York again – MTV had an all-night New Year's Eve extravaganza planned. As each time zone over the USA hit midnight, another band would start a three- or four-song set. UB40 were the other English band on the bill. We bumped into Juicy Lucy and Mark Tyme at the party just before the show. Juicy was living in New York for a while.

For some reason I walked on the stage and said to the audience, 'Has anyone here ever made it with Ronnie? [Reagan] I have, it was easy!' I must have been high on something. I was wearing a big fur Davy Crocket hat that Jayne gave me, a brown velvet wrapover tailcoat by Jean Paul Gaultier and a pair of cream Matsuda pants with a black strip down the sides. I thought I was gorgeous! The sound on stage was very strange but we managed to do our few numbers. Duran Duran jumped up on stage with us for *Relax*. It was one of those mad shows where no one knew what was going on.

After the show I made my way to The Saint, a gay disco built inside a planetarium. I was alone that night, as Wolfgang didn't want me to pay his fare for just two nights in New York, a town he has never really liked. At The Saint I met Mark and Juicy as well as a few old acquaintances from England who shoved some substance or other up my nose. I could have danced all night, leaving early in the morning to catch the plane home. By the time I reached England I looked dreadfully green around the gills. I vowed that my reckless drug-taking and all night party days were over.

Paradise

Sitting alone in my hotel room at the start of the first North American tour, I had started to get a strange feeling of insecurity. I felt very alone. I could no longer carry on with the free-floating, anchorless life that I had been so hellbent on. I was involved in a very precarious business that I had almost begged to be exploited by. I was a lodger in someone else's flat, throwing every penny I earned down the drains of high fashion to dress up our act. I started to feel the fear that this time next year, it could all be over, and I would be just another casualty of pop. Maybe this was just my 'Drama Queen' streak coming out, but I started to feel the unfashionable need to do something sensible!

In short, I got the mortgage bug, like lots of other people who were making money in the Eighties.

Eventually a Sloaney friend of Merry's decided to play estate agent for a friend of her's and showed me a house in Parsons Green, just off the New Kings Road. It was nice enough and I was so bored with looking for a house that I went for it, even paying more than the original asking price; greed was in the air. 'Never mind,' the surveyor said, 'it will be worth more next year.' It was, about 25% more. One of 'The Lads' taunted me when he heard about the house. 'By next year we'll all be in such a better financial position that we'll all be able to buy a lot more than a four-bedroomed terraced house in Fulham, you'll be blown right off!' he assured me.

Meanwhile Wolfgang and I needed a holiday so off we went to Barbados. I had bought myself a camera and started to take hundreds of photographs on holiday, few of which were successful. I had also started to draw and paint again. I was determined not to let the work I had poured into the Art School foundation course presentation slide away. I took many photographs of Wolfgang who looked fantastic in swimming trunks. He had been a model in the Sixties and early Seventies and still had a great body, not to mention a great face (Harrison Ford meets Brad Davis). Wolfgang, however, claimed that I was a lousy photographer and took only ugly photos of him. He announced, 'I don't vant to be in your photos any more!' It became the catch-phrase of the holiday.

Anthony Price, whom we visited in his villa, did a drawing of a stage costume I'd asked him to design for the forthcoming tour. It was of a kind of Prussian army officer's uniform in white, with huge shoulders and a nipped-in waist, rather like a high-ranking Tom Of Finland officer's uniform. Anthony's method of building a perfectly fitting garment was to build a model of the torso of the client. I won't divulge exactly how he did it but it involved an uncomfortable and humiliating process. I was a bit large around the middle at the time (33 inch waist), and Anthony said there might be some corsetting required. He took a photograph of me wrapped in this contraption – he claimed that it would be a fond memory for the future. I thought, 'More like a perfect blackmail photo of the future'.

He took us in his hired car to see the magnificent Bathsheba Beach on the other side of the island. He drove us speedily up a hill road which was a tunnel of trees that ended dramatically with a wonderful view of the bay. From shaded darkness to bright Barbados sunlight. Huge rocks jutted out of the ocean where giant waves raged and crashed on to the shore, in sharp contrast to the calmer sea on the other coast. There are no hotels near Bathsheba Beach, just a few cafés and the lush sugarcane fields where huge native women work in the blistering sun. They looked on unemotionally as a car load of western pleasure-seekers passed them by.

Barbados is one of the most beautiful places on the earth that I have seen, and ever since I have dreamed of living there. Whenever I want to conjure up an image of Paradise, I imagine its turquoise water and lilac hibiscus flowers.

Sex over the Phone

Back in London, there were further fittings for the stage costumes that Anthony was making. I told Paul that I had commissioned designs from Anthony so he went along and arranged for trousers for the band in a similar style.

One of my costumes was an elaborate loose-fitting cotton 'astronaut' suit with what seemed like hundreds of zips and pockets. Two of these were made, one in white and the other in a sky-blue/mauve colour. I wore these with personalised 'Holly' boxing boots especially made for me by Nike. Nike had been supplying us with all the training shoes we could possibly wear. We were, after all, the most photographed band of the year.

I also met a fashion PR for Armani. In exchange for posing for an advertisement in Italian *Vogue* wearing a Butler and Wilson medal and an Armani suit, I was given a wardrobe of Armani clothes to wear during the American tour.

Many people seemed to want a piece of Frankie Goes To Hollywood, but the media had begun to try to put us down, belittling our involvement in the making of the records. The general claim was that it was Trevor's success, and that we were just five wild idiots from Liverpool. And there were other instances of a bad press. I met Boy George once in Sarm Studios. He ordered two bodyguards to hang around the studio, following me wherever I went. I just walked up to him and told him to call his dogs off. I shamed him into being friendly I suppose. This was after 'Relax' had been a hit and just before 'Two Tribes' had been released. He asked me what our next single was about. I told him it was an anti-war song. In his increasing desperation for column inches he claimed (or was misquoted) in the tabloids that we tried to beat him up and plagued him with obscene phone calls. 'They did try to beat me up but luckily I had security men with me,' ran the tabloid quote.

206

Somewhere along the line we were invited to the British Phonographic Industry Awards (now called 'The Brit Awards'). That year the ceremony was to be held at the Grosvenor House Hotel, in huge banqueting halls underneath the magnificent chandeliers. This was to be the first year that the awards were televised. Although not on the 9th of February, as it is inaccurately reported in Dave Rimmer's snide little book *Like Punk Never Happened*, edited by the then closet pop star, Neil Tennant (assistant editor of *Smash Hits*). I enjoyed the pop gossip tone of the book, but it is riddled with the schoolyard sarcasm of *Smash Hits*, the teeny pop magazine that rose in the Eighties, and is slowly going 'down the dumper' in the Nineties, to use one of *Smash Hits'* favourite phrases. At the BPI Awards ceremony there was a mix-up with the seating and there did not seem to be room for Wolfgang: 'How unusual,' I thought. As we stood about conspicuously, Janice Long invited us to sit at her table. Jill Sinclair saw this and eventually insisted that we squeeze on to the ZTT table, to show some kind of pretend unity. Morley was there as was Trevor and all the members of the band. I wore a Claude Montana leather jacket with an eagle embroidered on the back. It had cost a ridiculous two thousand pounds. I would never pay that much again for one item of clothing, but I had dreamed of owning a Montana leather jacket ever since Paul started taking me to expensive clothes shops. It was a glittering night for tabloid land. Prince arrived with a pink feather boa and two huge bodyguards. His record company Warner Brothers had requested that I award him his prize for best international artist. On the Warner Brothers table I spotted Bill Drummond – then working for the label in A and R – wearing the same kilt he used to wear for Big In Japan shows. He gagged when I reminded him of the forging of my signature on a Warner Brothers publishing contract within earshot of his boss. Bill was one of the 'old friends' who queued up to give their comments about the 'Holly They Had Known' to tabloid journalists. It is miraculous how old friends, when confronted with the irritating success of a contemporary, can couch their comments in such a well-meaning yet belittling way.

Frankie Goes To Hollywood won the 'Best Newcomer of 1984' award. We also won a special Radio One Listeners' Award for Best Single, for 'Relax'. Tina Turner and Bronski Beat performed their latest hits. Wham! won 'Best Band', Sade 'Best Album', Alison Moyet 'Best Female Singer' and Paul Young (who, at his own admittance, had not done much that year) won 'Best Male Vocalist'. The Police, who were conspicuously black-tied, won some sort of 'Lifetime Achievement' award.

When it came time to present Prince with his award I had to think of something to say. Recently, The Village People had released a single called 'Sex Over The Phone'. It had, of course, been banned by the BBC, so I decided to make a joke out of the title. Before I announced his name I said, 'I've never met this man but we've had "Sex Over The Phone" several times.' On the huge video screens Prince's face visibly dropped – he hadn't seen the funny side. I suppose someone who goes to such great lengths to advertise his heterosexuality does not want some English Queen making jokes that imply he might be homosexual. First one of his bodyguards walked towards the stage, then the tiny Prince followed. I couldn't believe how small he was despite the six-inch stilettoes. He took the award without looking at me then he mumbled his acceptance speech. 'Oh dear,' I thought, 'I didn't mean to upset him.'

Wolfgang and I left and went for something to eat at Trader Vic's in Mayfair. I took one of the awards with me (designed like a big red, white and blue Radio One logo). It was just as well. Mark O'Tool took with him the other award for best newcomer and said it was stolen at a discotheque later that night.

At another, more low-key awards ceremony, almost a year later – The Ivor Novello Awards – we won 'Best Contemporary Song' for 'Two Tribes'. George Michael, who sat at the next table, was obviously pissed off that he did not win everything, but Elton John surprised me by coming over to our table, getting down on his haunches and chatting to me as if we were old friends. I was a bit disappointed, though, that the string of pearls that he wore were only costume jewellery.

* * *

I think it was on my birthday, 9th February, that we were headlining at San Remo, playing the annual Italian music festival there. Wolfgang had remained at home, since again we didn't think it was worth paying his plane fare for a couple of nights. Chaka Khan was there, as were Duran Duran and Spandau Ballet. Culture Club were conspicuous by their absence. I complimented Simon Le Bon on his tie so he took it off, gave it to me and said sweetly, 'Happy Birthday'. We did 'The Power Of Love' to an evening-dressed crowd. According to Dave Rimmer's book, Nasher was walking around haranguing people with the phrase, 'You are scum! You are shite!' It was a very Eighties Pop Star night.

I met the Leather Man and the Red Indian from The Village People at San Remo. They were there promoting 'Sex Over The Phone', which was getting some airplay in Europe. The gruff-looking Leather Man turned out to be a sweet and gentle New Yorker. They told me the story of selling 60 million records and the performers themselves getting little reward – I talked to them on the subject of handling 'The Gay Issue' in interviews. They were as dismayed as I by the media's constant exploitation and negative reporting of this subject. 'We tried every angle, and nothing worked,' was the main consensus.

* * *

ZTT wanted the fourth single off the album to be an edited version of 'Welcome To The Pleasuredome'. What had started out as a three-and-a-half-minute demo done at a John Peel session turned into a twenty-minute opus courtesy of Trevor's magic wand. Steve Lipson and Andy Richards had programmed long sequenced sections based on the original musical motifs of the demo. Lipson had also visited the aviary in Regent's Park Zoo for the exotic sound effects at the beginning of the track. This conjured up a kind of Paradise or Garden Of Eden soundscape, where statues sing with flute-like voices as the perfumed breeze blows over them. Then came a keyboard section of arpeggios composed by Andy Richards. Steve Howe,

209

an old friend of Trevor's from his Yes days, also contributed an acoustic guitar solo.

So the next thing was to turn it back into a three-and-a-half-minute pop song! Vicious editing was needed, and of course a promotional video. No expense was spared as ZTT were assured of massive royalties. Bernard Rose was called in again to create another epic-looking video. The budget was something between sixty and eighty thousand pounds.

All this was an attempt to make the fourth single into another number one, which was not to be. When it was released, many people had already bought the track on the album and the single stalled at number two in the Gallup charts. The video was also banned by the BBC as it showed 'The Lads' stealing a car, drinking while driving and running down two pedestrians (Morley and wife – if only!).

I wore an Anthony Price suit for the video but felt I looked a bit tired. Also ZTT had briefed Bernard Rose to make more use of the rest of the band rather than focusing the video on me lip-syncing the track, another attempt to make sure that I did not become 'too indispensable'.

While we were filming this video, Jill Sinclair asked us to go to Paris to do a TV show the day before we started our world tour, a day we desperately needed for packing etc. She came down to the video shoot to try to persuade us, but I was in no mood. I told her to fuck off. I was not going to be bullied, even though she was claiming that we could sell another hundred thousand units in France if we did the show. I have never regretted that particular moment as she promised I would do one day. She left the building at my request, tail between her little legs.

This was not the first time I had not played ball with ZTT. I had recently refused them the opportunity of doing a live video of The Frankies at the Liverpool Royal Court, because of the contractual terms that such a film would come under. They were still not offering any substantial renegotiations of the contract, despite our great success.

Non-Payola

With all my worldly goods stuffed into about nine suitcases, I started a year-long adventure out of the country. We flew to Dublin for the first date of the long world tour. The audience was fantastic. This was the first time all the costumes were worn and all the pyrotechnics went off on cue. We were on the crest of a wave. But still there were tensions. Wolfgang and I were driven to the hall, but there was obviously room on the coach for us to get to the show.

The next date was Sheffield, and to get there, Wolfgang and I turned up at the station with all the suitcases. We couldn't really believe what we were doing. Here I was, the most photographed Queen in England at that time, doing a tour on British Rail without a bodyguard! I was open to attack from any Queerbashers that we might meet. The rest of the band were travelling in a tour bus with a bodyguard to protect them in their nightclub skirmishes and pub crawls. I had already witnessed one of these fights caused by the presence of the group in a Brixton pub. Wally, one of the band's bodyguards, ended up fighting drunks over some comment or other. I got out of the pub before it exploded.

When the tour-bus arrived, after us, at the Sheffield hotel, I saw that there had been plenty of room on it for everyone. Tony Pope made some excuse, to the effect that this wasn't the scheduled bus, and had more seats than the original one. It was the first time I really blew up at Tony Pope, as I thought he was handling things badly. He was mating up with the rest of the band, taking orders from 'The Lads', who felt all of a sudden that they were giant stars. Understandable to a degree, I suppose, as they were so young and not exactly university graduates.

My mother turned up in Glasgow. She had befriended an

ardent Frankie fan, who had decided to follow us around the country seeing different shows. She also came to the Birmingham Odeon, and was sitting backstage when George Michael appeared. He had come to see the show accompanied by his female PA Pat Fernandez and radio-plugger Gary Farrow whom we shared as our independent radio promoter. My mother demanded a kiss from him as soon as she laid eyes on him and he gracefully obliged. He even jumped on the stage to share a microphone with Paul for 'Relax'.

It was the same night that Tina Turner played the NEC near Birmingham, with guest spots from David Bowie and Bryan Adams. Apparently 'The Lads' and Paul went out drinking with George Michael after our show. They rang Bowie in his room in another hotel, saying that Frankie and Wham! were downstairs, but he refused to come and meet them. I was back in my hotel room resting my voice as usual and missing out on the party. 'The Lads'' verdict on George Michael the next day was that 'he couldn't take his ale!'

By the time the circus had arrived in London to play the Hammersmith Odeon, Wolfgang and I had caught a 'flu bug, but somehow I managed to go on. Gary Glitter turned up backstage in silver cape for one of the Hammersmith shows, very pleasant and sparkling. I can't remember whether or not he joined us on stage for 'Relax', but what a man!

There was a poolside party after one of the Hammersmith shows. Honey Heath and Anastasia, whom I hadn't really seen (except once in the street) since I was fifteen, turned up. They dropped the odd glamorous name like Grace Jones, who was a friend of theirs. Honey Heath was apparently working as a fashion designer. He now spoke in an exaggeratedly posh way. It was hard to match this new voice with the person I once knew, although as I wrote in the earlier section on our teenage years, I longed to be able to phone him and reminisce.

'The Lads' were in the swimming pool after a few drinks, acting the goat and jumping in from places they shouldn't jump from. Paul turned up with an entourage of his old cronies. One of them tactlessly tried to embarrass me in front of Wolfgang by saying they had just seen a Greek bodybuilder I had copped off with during a promotional trip to Greece in early 1984 – an ex-Mr Greece and physique model that I somehow talked into bed.

After the London shows it was off to Europe. This is where travel became a bit easier for Wolfgang and me. We went by air all the way, while the others had to travel, sometimes overnight, by smelly lager-lout coach on which the toilet was blocked.

I wrote regular postcards back to Liverpool from all the European cities, usually complaining about the on tour antics of the group. Touring does seem to bring out the worst in people. There is a kind of weird male camaraderie that makes gross behaviour acceptable. It's hard not to become part of a distorted reality when every night, thousands of people are paying for and applauding your appearance.

Whenever we got a few hours off, Wolfgang and I would try and visit local art galleries, and this way we saw many of the great paintings of Europe.

After the European part of the tour there was a break of about two weeks before the American leg. We were booked into Studio Mediterraneo on Ibiza to record some demos, new songs that we had managed to write amongst all of the madness. I didn't really want to stay at the residential facility with the rest of the band, so I hired Lulu's villa (Yes! the world-famous Scots chanteuse), just a taxi-ride outside Ibiza Old Town. 'The Lads' preferred to go to San Antonio for kicks. I went with them one night, without Wolfgang and, in fact, had a great laugh.

I realised that if Wolfgang wasn't with me the band would be a lot more friendly, but their attitude was due to their prejudice, and I was not going to bow down to it. Nevertheless, it all started to put a strain on our relationship and the two of us started to argue at Lulu's villa. There were serious rows, especially after the night I went out on my own. By now, Wolfgang and I had spent a lot of time stuck together in hotel rooms and I wasn't sure whether we could survive the next leg of the tour. As this was a crucial moment in our relationship, I got drunk and copped off with some Spaniard I had met on my last trip to Ibiza. I didn't stay the night with him, but something remotely sexual must have happened. There was a hell of a row.

We were off to a club called Metro in Boston for the first show of our second American tour. I had searched round for a barber shop so I could get a real American crew cut, but the haircut I got in the end was a disaster. Joining us as support act for the US was Belouis Some, or Neville as he was called – his song 'Imagination' was getting a lot of airplay. He was a good looking and personable ex-public school boy who hung out with 'The Lads' in hotel swimming pools. One of his backing singers was a girl called Robin who was the wife of Carlos Alomar, David Bowie's guitarist and a long-time hero of mine. I was thrilled when Carlos joined the tour for a few dates.

We went back to Canada, where we again met up with The Great Imposters, the drag troupe that had been a support act the year before. Rusty Ryan, their leader, took Wolfgang and me to Toronto Zoo for a day out. I found the Zoo very sad, so unlike my childhood memories of Chester Zoo with its rainbow-coloured pavements and cages. I suppose children don't see that the animals are depressed behind those bars.

The concerts we were playing on this tour were generally at bigger venues than the last time; we had, after all, had a lot more MTV exposure since our last outing. But the magical success that had come so easily in Europe did not seem to follow in America. Island Records was considered a small label in America at that time, not half as powerful as Warners or CBS. We were told that each single needed a promotion budget of at least $50,000 to get onto two thousand separate American radio stations. It was a different world.

The End of the Road

During the American leg of the 1984 and 1985 tours I received several phone calls from Bob Geldof, urging me and the band to fly to England to participate on the Band Aid single and, later, the Live Aid concert. There was no persuading the rest of the band but I did do a voice over for the B side of the single. Bob asked me to declaim 'Feed The World!', then laugh in my best 'Pleasuredome' laugh, which I didn't really feel was appropriate, but anything to oblige.

I could not believe that the rest of the band refused to do the Live Aid concert, though. No one liked the idea that it would cost at least twenty thousand pounds to play. Bob kept ringing me in various hotel rooms across America saying it was going to be great event and that we should get involved. I agreed with him, but whenever I put it to the band they had no interest whatsoever.

Then Tony Pope relayed a message that there would be a lot of money available if the band were to do one concert in South Africa, and that did raise some interest. I could not believe that they were contemplating two modes of career suicide in one day. The Florida heat must have gone to their heads.

One of the nicer people to work with on tour was Joanie the wardrobe mistress. She was a fast-talking Italian girl from New Jersey who had somehow got involved with the world of touring rock groups. She loved our costumes. I suppose she was used to Spandex trousers, the kind of thing I imagine bands like Motley Crue would wear. We were without doubt the most stylish pop group of the Eighties: even though Duran and Spandau tried, they never quite managed to outdo our look, while the Bowies and the Ferrys were too busy trying to become *L'Uomo Vogue* cover-stars to actually wear anything truly stylish.

*   *   *

On tour there would be daily interviews with the local radio stations or press. These things became more intense in the larger cities of New York or LA. Answers would become more and more abrupt as the tour continued and tiredness set in. By the end of the North American tour we all looked, felt, and sounded, pretty dreadful.

But we couldn't rest at the end of the North American tour: there was Japan to follow. When we reached Tokyo, the promotional grind started almost immediately; endless interviews and a couple of TV shows. We seemed to be sponsored by some kind of Japanese beer. It was explained to me by Tony Pope that we would not have been able to afford touring in Japan if it had not been for the sponsorship of this lager-producing company. Everything it seemed was a commercial exercise in Japan. Due to transport costs we had had to leave our set behind, so we did not have the full visual production of the show with us. This seemed ridiculous, as the Japanese would probably have appreciated this more than any other nation we had visited thus far.

During the last show in Tokyo the band played a prank on me. For the final encore, we always did 'Relax'. I started to sing as normal then I realised there was something strange about the way the song was being played. I looked at the audience and there was the band – Paul, Mark, Nasher and Ped – in the front row, dancing and laughing at me. I turned round and there, on the stage, were all the roadies playing the band's instruments. I thought 'Bugger this,' and jumped off the stage to dance with the rest of the band in the audience.

In Tokyo we had the company of Joanne, who had won a *Smash Hits* competition to meet Frankie Goes to Hollywood. She was only about fourteen, but she insisted on drinking sake. Then she would go out with 'The Lads' till past midnight, playing in the video-game arcades. Wolfgang told her off one night. He felt that she should not have been drinking and staying up so late at her age. She burst into tears and went crying back to the hotel.

I do remember one strange thing about these concerts. Outside the theatre, pubescent Japanese girls would all shout out in unison 'Horry! Horry!', which made me feel as if I was late for everything.

As we checked out of the hotel in Tokyo I felt a wave of nausea and ran to the lavatory where I threw up. Wolfgang followed me. He had some weird idea that I was cottaging; we argued. The strain of touring must have really got to him – here I was not feeling well, and he was accusing me of giving blow-jobs to Japanese men in the hotel toilet. We definitely needed a holiday.

Wolfgang and I limped into Hawaii airport looking rather dishevelled and worse for wear. We had air tickets that only took us as far as Hawaii, which set off some kind of alarm bell in the suspicious minds of the United States Immigration Department. They detained us for over an hour and questioned us. I explained to them that we planned to stay a couple of weeks in Hawaii then fly to LA before we returned to Europe. They were concerned that Wolfgang might ask his sister (a naturalised American citizen) who lives in Pittsburgh to claim him into the country. He explained that America was the last place he would want to be claimed into, but they didn't seem to be satisfied until they took away our credit cards to check whether we had the credit rating to buy air tickets home. They then let us in. I hadn't even realised that Hawaii was an American state.

We checked into The Kahala Hilton, deciding to go for an exorbitant room with a balcony overlooking the hotel's lagoon. We were pleased that we did – when we walked out on to our first-floor balcony, we were greeted by a pair of dolphins playing beneath our window. They were beautiful, I had never even seen a dolphin before. It was a precious, almost spiritual, experience that words cannot describe.

I thought I had seen someone who looked like Arnold Schwarzenegger in the hotel lobby. I had always been a bit of a muscle fan, finding the overdeveloped bodies of bodybuilders both compelling and repellant at the same time. I was almost sure it was him. This was confirmed when we went out to sunbathe on the hotel's beach; it was Arnold alright, holidaying with his

217

fiancée Maria Shriver. He didn't look as pumped up as he does in his movies though.

No sooner had Arnold Schwarzenegger checked out of the hotel, then Sylvester Stallone, that other doyen of the violently butch movie, checked in. He didn't have such a good vibe as Arnold. He looked all built up above the waist with skinny legs. Brigitte Nielson seemed to tower over him, as did their bodyguard. An old lady ran after Stallone with her camera, only to be told by the bodyguard that photographs were not allowed. Stallone was a much bigger star than Arnold at that time, but seemed to have much less grace. I took a photograph of his skinny ass in the distance, which I later threw away.

The only Hula girls we saw were employed by the hotel to put on some kind of rather expensive Hawaiian show, while spectators ate homogenised Hawaiian food. It all seemed a bit contrived. I had expected girls in Hula skirts with leis round their necks to be everywhere. But no, Hawaii was definitely a state of the US of A, as built-up and urban as any other I'd seen.

Maybe if one of us had held a driver's licence we could have explored the island more, and we could have found the beaches where all the surf boys go. It would have been nice to stumble on to the set of the Elvis movie, *Blue Hawaii*, back in the Sixties, through some kind of magical, Hawaiian timewarp.

* * *

When we got back to Paris we booked into The Hotel Lutetia in the Boulevard Raspail, where we had stayed before on promotional trips. For the first week we were in a constant daze and slept most of the time. I had forgotten how traumatic it was coming back from LA time to European time. It had always taken me a good two weeks to recover.

I decided to fly my mother out to Paris for a weekend treat and we went to the airport to meet her. She had never been out of England before in her life. She told me when the plane went above the clouds that she thought all the white fluffy stuff was the sea. We did a lot of touristy things like take a coach trip to

Versailles. Our tour guide was called Babette or something just as cute. I remember the wonderful paintings on the ceilings of the palace.

On the Monday morning we planned to take Pat to the airport. I had bought her an Eiffel Tower candle. We were already in the taxi on the way to the airport when she realised she'd left it in her room. She burst into tears and would just not stop. The taxi driver kept giving us filthy looks. He thought we must have done something terrible to this poor woman, who was crying her eyes out for the whole journey.

Money-Go-Round

After Paris, our next stop was Ireland. Tony Pope had found a huge old manor house, Borris House, for the band to stay in. Borris is a small village in County Carlow, not the most beautiful place in Ireland, I have since been told by several Dubliners. We were paying quite a price per week for this grand but drafty old place.

When 'The Lads' were there they would rehearse for a few hours a day until the pubs opened – then it was all down the pub. Sometimes they would come and rehearse after the pub as well, but not often. The local pub seemed to double as an all-purpose grocery and farming supplies shop, with Wellington boots and other items hanging from the ceiling. The natives were very friendly, as are most Irish people I've ever met. I would have the occasional pint of Guinness, which I thought was the appropriate drink to sup in Ireland. I would sometimes mix it with cider or blackcurrant for an extra-lethal brew.

It was strange for a city child to wake up in the morning, look out of the window and see a field of sheep and rolling emerald hillsides. I could never remember a time when I had woken up in countryside like this. The place was a bit cold and damp however, and I would suffer aches and pains in some of my joints. This must be what rheumatism feels like, I thought. I also started to worry secretly about AIDS, and I would inspect my arms for purple lesions every morning. It seemed that every gay person who had slept with more than one partner in the last few years was now at risk, although the propaganda at this time was that only one or two people in ten who had been exposed to the virus would develop the disease. I kept my fears to myself, so as not to alarm Wolfgang. Feeling ill and drained after all the touring made me worry more.

The words of my old friend Jake kept reverberating around my mind. We had been stoned at his flat in Stoke Newington, one night in the winter of 1983, and had been discussing Karl, whom we had visited earlier that day. Jake said that there were going to be lots of employment openings in this new field of AIDS and that he might try and get a job in counselling people. He also said that both of us must face up to the fact that we might have already contracted the disease. I was struck dumb with fear when he said this. My eyes widened and I said 'Oh no, it's unlikely. We haven't been to America like Karl has.' I was still living in cloud-cuckoo-land, listening to the gay world gossip. I made my way to the lavatory, then all of a sudden in a dark corridor leading to the bathroom my legs went weak, and my whole body felt paralysed. I called out to Jake and he came to see what was wrong. I was holding on to the wall for support. I couldn't move. He helped me into the bedroom and laid me down on the bed. After a couple of minutes of rest, the feeling passed. I had either had a mild heart attack or some kind of panic or anxiety attack, brought on by the hashish and the gloomy late-night conversation.

*　　*　　*

Ron Weisner, our American manager, and Tony Pope came to see us while we were in Borris. We all discussed the attempts at renegotiating our contract with ZTT. Everyone seemed to think that securing Trevor's involvement with our second album was the carrot that ZTT were dangling in front of us, and that if we rocked the boat too much, we would lose Trevor as producer. So we all decided to go ahead with the second album before attempting litigation, if any, over the recording contract.

A spell in the studios took place on Ibiza. Wolfgang and I spent most days hanging round the studio grounds waiting for the others to get up and to start work. The idea of the 'Rock-'n'-Roll Lifestyle' had become deeply ingrained into the band's behaviour. They were young and energetic and wanted to go out, partying all night and sleeping in the daytime. By contrast I was in a relationship with a man who was older and who had always been an early riser, and I suppose I felt that our relationship was more important than nightclubbing. I did still feel the call of the wild on occasion though.

For him, it must have been difficult to have a relationship with someone quite a few years his junior who was also now internationally famous. He knew that if we were out and about, I might succumb to the temptations of some handsome young thing. There are enough difficulties involved in maintaining gay relationships; not being accepted as a couple within society is just one of the pressures that has to be contended with. Also the natural tendency for males to be sexually promiscuous is doubled within a gay relationship. Many gay relationships that I came across in London were of the 'open' variety, where both halves of the couple had lots of different sexual relationships outside it. Eventually the core relationship would become completely non-sexual and sex would be sought elsewhere. However, because of the spread of AIDS, this lifestyle was becoming more and more untenable.

Tony Pope came out to Ibiza with the September accountings from ZTT. There was massive disappointment from everyone. Lubbock Fine had calculated *double* the amount that we actually received. Due to a few TV adverts in England, ZTT had halved our royalty rate on a worldwide basis, as per the Island/ZTT contract (unbeknown to Lubbock Fine). The validity of this we now questioned. Some members of the band, especially the ones not receiving much of the publishing royalties (Paul and Nasher), were disappointed with the spoils of all that hard work, promoting around Europe.

The two tours we had just done didn't seem to bring home the bacon either. We only appeared to make money on the merchandising, not on the actual concerts themselves; this sounded ridiculous – we were playing quite large venues. Someone, somewhere, was making money out of all of this, but not us. The lack of huge sums of money in the recording royalty accountings didn't do much to increase my popularity, since the others knew I was getting the lion's share of the publishing. It must have seemed to them that I had planned it, but I was hardly in a position to manipulate things all my own way. We had sold millions of records but were far from being the 'Mersey Millionaires' everyone thought we were. We were mere hobby-horses on Jill and Trevor's money-go-round.

A few days later Trevor turned up at the studio. All bitterness about the accountings was put aside by the group and he was welcomed. He always claimed to have nothing to do with the business aspect of his companies. It was during this visit that he sat with Wolfgang and me by the turquoise swimming pool. He assured me that he would be producing our second album. He did mention that he had also committed himself to further work with Yes, but it should not really affect our record too much. This conversation was to be the source of much of my future discontent with ZTT.

Sickhouse

The planned recording of our second album was to take place in Holland, just outside Amsterdam in a studio called Wisselord, near Hilversum. Wolfgang started complaining that he had an abscess in a delicate place. I wasn't sure what he meant by abscess, apparently he had had one before about fifteen years ago. I remember Karl had had one of these in a similar place the first time he got ill so I started to worry. We had got a doctor to come to the hotel room to see Wolfgang. He suggested a small operation which he did in a local hospital. It was an attempt to drain the abscess but it wasn't very successful, and now, after a few weeks, the abscess returned.

We were all installed in The Golden Tulip Jan Tabak Hotel in Bussum, a taxi-ride from Wisselord recording studios. Steve Lipson and an assistant, Heff Moraes, were there to start the album, but no Trevor. Lipson was a tall, skinny, sallow-faced character with stringy long hair and eyes that popped out at you, like a toad's. He spoke like an estate agent turned hippie. I noticed that he was very 'umble when Trevor was around. I was a bit confused by Trevor's absence, as he had said to me that he would be producing the album. Then, over the first couple of weeks, it all came out. Steve Lipson had been offered points on our second album. This had never been discussed with me. I told Steve Lipson that I was not very happy with the situation. He claimed that he had 'produced' the first album to a certain degree, but I did not trust his abilities as a producer.

The studio hours started off quite normally, but they soon ended up like Seventies rock-n-roll hours. The band and Lipson would get up about two o'clock in the afternoon, come into the studio about four, have breakfast for an hour, then finally start work about five or six. The first ciggie would be smoked about seven o'clock, and most of the band would be playing on the table football machine. By this time I would be really pissed off, having been up since eight or nine in the morning waiting for the rest of them to start work. I would go back to the hotel about seven or eight o'clock at night, just as they were starting. They told me that they worked into the night and would end up going back to the hotel at six or seven the next morning. I was not going to live like that. If they wanted my involvement in the record, then Lipson would have to get up early and record me in the afternoon, when I felt I could give my best vocal performances.

As well as the hours they kept, I couldn't believe *what* they were recording. All of a sudden the band had decided that they wanted to make a 'rock' album in the hope that they would sell in America. So these people, who had hardly played on the first – and very successful – electronic album, were all of a sudden calling the shots as if they knew what was best. I was at my wit's end. I liked electronic production and didn't have any desire to be in a Heavy Metal band. I would come into the studio and say things like, 'Yes, that's all well and good, but no one can *dance* to it.' The great thing about our earlier records had been the Universal Disco Beat with all this grandiose stuff on top. We had created a new kind of dance music, and now we were abandoning it.

*   *   *

Meanwhile Wolfgang became extremely ill. He needed a major operation that involved the surgeon cutting deep into the flesh to remove the abscess once and for all. This they did, but they made the mistake of sewing him up afterwards instead of leaving the wound open and packing it, so it would heal from the inside out. After Wolfgang roared with the pain, they finally opened the wound up and started to pack it every day.

I didn't explain to the others how ill Wolfgang was, because they were not the type of people to be sympathetic. I would spend a lot of the daytime at the hospital and eventually stopped going into the studio every day. I thought that Wolfgang might

225

die, he got so thin in the hospital, almost the way that Karl had looked a few years before.

Wolfgang started screaming at me during his hospital stay that I should dump the band and go solo. He said that the album was going to be rubbish without Trevor, and that I should get out now. I should have listened to him. The recording costs over the next few months were to be offset against the royalties from the 'Pleasuredome' album, therefore it would be years before we received further recording royalties. I was afraid to leave; I was afraid to continue. Finally I felt that now I had started the album I had better finish it, even though I was very unhappy with the musical direction it was taking.

Wolfgang also pointed out that the band had started to spend money again in recording studios, money that we probably would never be able to recoup. He felt the deal we had was like working in a Victorian sweatshop, as if ZTT intended to keep us as hungry as possible so we would keep producing new material.

As time went on I felt like I was going to have a nervous breakdown. I felt as if Trevor had betrayed me completely by not turning up for the recording. The band had run amok with their rock album, and our relationships were very strained. I thought Wolfgang was going to die just like Karl. I was a long way from home, trying to juggle seeing Wolfgang in hospital with trying to arrange afternoon sessions for vocals with Lipson. My belief in a power of good in the universe was really being put to the test. One afternoon when I was alone in the studio with Lipson, I just started unloading all the things I was thinking. I told him that I didn't know if I should leave the band; that I wasn't happy with the way the recording was going; that I didn't think that Tony Pope was a very good manager. I even said that I didn't think Lipson was a producer in the same league as Trevor.

It was about midnight the next day and I was in my hotel room alone, as Wolfgang was still in hospital, lying in bed about to go to sleep, when I got a knock on the door. I opened it and the whole band and Tony Pope walked in. They knew of course that Wolfgang wasn't there to give me any moral support. Tony Pope started saying that Lipson had told him that I had been slagging him off so he had flown over from England. They were all trying to intimidate me. Even Paul, usually rather cowardly, was giving me bad vibes, bolstered by the other members of the band. Things got pretty nasty, so I told them that I wasn't sure whether I wanted to be in this band with them any more. Then I kicked them out of my room. I felt very alone that night.

It was almost Christmas. A few week's break in recording had already been scheduled. The band and Lipson all left the hotel to do their various things. Meanwhile Wolfgang was getting impatient at the hospital and checked himself out early. We decided to fly to Hanau in Germany to visit his mother, then fly to Liverpool and visit my family over the New Year, an ambitious itinerary considering Wolfgang's health. He had to learn to dress his own wound every day with the aid of a mirror which he held between his legs. I couldn't bring myself to pack yards of lint into this gaping, vagina-like wound.

We spent Christmas in Hanau, although Wolfgang was rather depressed; so was I for that matter. Everyone speaking German around me made it worse and I felt a long way from home. Wolfgang was still rather ill and had difficulty in walking. His mother kept saying, 'What's wrong with you?' One night at the hotel room in Hanau he just burst into tears for about half an hour, and there was nothing I could do to make him feel better. After a few days we flew on to Liverpool. Wolfgang was in agony. I took him to the Liverpool Royal Hospital Casualty department. It was a grey, miserable place. There the doctors said that he would have to have a small operation to stretch the scar tissue. They kept him 'nil by mouth' for nearly twenty-four hours before they actually did the operation.

I visited Jayne and her boyfriend Biffa and told them all about the problems I was having with Wolfgang, the band, Tony Pope and ZTT. Jayne came to visit Wolfgang with me. He had turned a funny yellow colour and was really thin. He had got food poisoning and started to have painful diarrhoea. He had been asking the nurses for yoghurt and they kept saying there wasn't any, though there must have been some somewhere, as colostomy patients have to have it.

Grace's eighteen-year-old son Billy was suffering from a brain tumour and was in the same hospital for treatment, so he went to visit Wolfgang. His head was all bandaged up so he wore a hat to hide it. As Billy was sitting talking to Wolfgang, five doctors walked into his room and threw Billy out in a very rude and abrupt manner. Wolfgang said, 'That poor boy is a patient with a brain tumour; you had no right to just throw him out.' They stood around Wolfgang's bed and told him that the abscess was one of the symptoms associated with the new disease that gay people had, called AIDS. They said that he had lots of symptoms and that they had done a blood test (without his permission) which pointed to the fact. They offered him no sort of counselling whatsoever. Wolfgang was alone in the room and got very upset. After the doctors left, the sister, who had previously been a bit cold, gave him a stiff drink of brandy and they both cried. The sister said that Wolfgang should keep his AIDS diagnosis quiet as the nurses might refuse to dress his wound. As it was, they came in dressed as if they were going into a Radiation Zone with masks and gloves. There was a lot of ignorance about the disease at that time, especially amongst health workers.

An hour or so after this bombshell I turned up with Pat, my mother. As soon as I walked into the room Wolfgang started to cry. I knew there was something wrong and that I had to get rid of my mother, so we could talk alone. I said I would go into town to get him some food and return later. He made me promise that I wouldn't be long. Pat went back to work, I think, and I went back to the hospital. Wolfgang burst into tears again and told me what had happened. He presumed that I had the disease as well and said he felt terrible that I was so young and had so much to offer. We both had a good cry. An older doctor, a so-called AIDS specialist, came to see us both and gave us a leaflet about AIDS. He reiterated that they were sure that Wolfgang had the disease. He did look very ill. The doctor advised him not to have sex but to have 'lots of dirty thoughts' instead. Wolfgang didn't want to stay in that hospital a moment longer. He checked himself out and we both went to the Holiday Inn to spend New Year's Eve. It was one of the most miserable New Years we've ever had. I read the leaflet, which claimed that only one or two people in ten who were told they were HIV-positive actually developed the disease. I kept repeating this to Wolfgang and myself, even though I knew Wolfgang looked just like Karl had done when he started to degenerate. We watched *Seven Brides For Seven Brothers* on TV and tried to blot out what had happened. 'What else can possibly go wrong now?' I thought.

Ruby Slippers

After spending a nervous day at my parents' house we travelled back to London. Our new house was freezing and dusty. Bruce the architect had found us a bed and a duvet by this time, but every room still had dirty bare floorboards. Not the most hygienic place in which to look after Wolfgang and his wound. Wolfgang's GP arranged for a district nurse to come round and check on him. She provided him with extra dressings and advised him to get out of the unfurnished, cold and damp house.

Meanwhile, plans had been made for the band to go and stay in a hotel in Jersey to write more songs for the album. I rang Tony Pope to ask him where this place was exactly. He said that I should ring the band in Jersey. I did this and spoke to Nasher, but he was rather nasty – not that unusual for him at that time. Like a child trying to get back at me for what I'd said before Christmas, he told me that now they weren't sure whether they even wanted me to continue as their singer.

Later I heard a rumour that they had interviewed Pete Wiley, the singer from Wah Heat, as a possible replacement for me during this period. In retrospect I find this highly amusing, but I don't expect I did at the time. I couldn't blame Wiley for wanting to step into my ruby slippers, but in reality he would never have had the style to carry it off.

Wolfgang and I decided to go to Guernsey, booking into a pleasant hotel on the top of a hill, about fifteen minutes walk from the town. Guernsey was lovely and the hotel food was excellent, which was just as well, as we both came down with the most awful 'flu bug that lasted for weeks.

While we were there I received a solicitor's letter. It said that if I didn't finish the album and then promote it, I would cause the rest of the band to be in breach of contract, and it implied that I would be held responsible if this happened.

A few weeks later a big meeting in Jersey was planned. The intention was that the band would meet with Trevor and Tony Pope to try and sort out all the various problems. Wolfgang and I flew in from Guernsey, joining the band at a place called St Anne's in a tiny hotel which they had taken over. It was not a swish place by any means, but at least the people who ran it were friendly. Wolfgang decided to stay out of the meeting.

Trevor said to the band something on the lines of, 'You've got to understand that Holly and Wolfgang are like a married couple'. I didn't say much. I felt the other members of the band were being unreasonable. I wore my glasses, a suit and dickie bow. Everyone else looked like tramps. Spiritually I had already left the group.

I told Trevor that I was extremely disappointed that he had not come to the sessions in Holland as he had promised to do. He told me he was still working on the Yes album, but he would do some work on our record after the Lipson sessions.

I wrote the lyrics of 'Watching The Wildlife' while I was there. It was about the situation I was in. I felt surrounded by wild animals who were sly, out to get me, and full of hate. 'Get free from hate and get in love,' was the chorus line.

There were a few slight compensations for the unpleasant atmosphere. One was a great barmaid at the hotel who used to be a singer. She was nostalgic for the days when she had been with a band, and she had a good voice. She and the owners were the only people who seemed friendly towards us.

Whenever Wolfgang and I went to town we looked at the jewellery shops that were everywhere. Both our birthdays happened when we were there: I tried to keep it quiet but Wolfgang let it out. It was quite embarrassing, as no one in the band wanted to say 'Happy Birthday' or anything like that, and nothing festive happened, except I think the nice lady who owned the hotel made us a cake.

After a few weeks we all went back to Holland to record. Nothing had really changed. The band's working still started late and went through the night, so I hardly went to the studio. The consensus was 'Holly is being difficult', but it was *they* who were being difficult in my view.

Morley came out on one occasion. He kept giving me sideways glances as he made his little speech. It wasn't me being paranoid; his little jibes about handling things professionally were directed at me. By this stage, my attitude to Morley was less than positive. While we were out of the country it seemed to me that he had used the opportunity to do lots of interviews on the subject of his 'marketing expertise', claiming for ZTT all the plaudits, which of course the media swallowed whole, just like a rent-boy swallowing the come of a punter. I think it's amazing that he's never been able to apply this 'marketing expertise' to another artist since Frankie Goes To Hollywood. He did do the marketing for two albums by his wife, whose name I won't even bother to mention, because you won't have heard of her.

Meanwhile Wolfgang returned to a Dutch hospital to be examined, where a doctor told him to ignore what he had been told in Liverpool. The Dutch doctor said he had a more advanced AIDS test than the English and that he would have known if Wolfgang had AIDS. We didn't know what to believe. We had already presumed that if Wolfgang had it, then so did I. We just pretended that it wasn't happening.

Wolfgang and I decided to return to Venice, a place we had visited the year before in September. Then we had booked straight into the Excelsior Lido. Our room looked out on to the beach and the sea. Rows of beach tents seemed to stretch for miles. I had been transported by the beauty of it all, by the brown bodies on the beach in the brightest swimwear.

So in April we found ourselves in Venice again. This time we had an interest in jewellers shops. One, Ca D'oro, was very pleasant. The staff recognised me and we all became instant friends. Our rings were taken off us and were polished and returned to us as a friendly gesture. A ring Wolfgang bought was engraved on the inside with his name as well as mine. The master jeweller, Lauro, communicated that he liked my music, although he couldn't speak much English. We made friends with Lauro and with Angelo, a rather elegant, stylish and slightly camp young Italian who was the assistant in the jewellery shop. He took us to a special pizza restaurant that was off the tourist track

– the best pizza I had ever tasted. I wrote a poem back in the hotel room about my Venetian experiences, called 'On The Lido'.

Young Italians come and go
Sculpted by Michelangelo
The sun, it shines, their bodies glow
On the beach, while Venice sleeps
With temples and balconies.
The taxi-boat is still afloat
With gondola grandeur
Women knitting on the sand
In the shade, rows of Moorish tents for rent
Where beach-hut beauty changes from fashion to fashion
Brown skin covered in a briefest flash
The newest man-made colours slash, the naked perfection
Thank God for swimwear, lends erotic mystery
To bumps and crevices
The sea breathes in and out life's breath
I'll never understand that Death
In Venice playing tennis with the blue
Mediterranean
Living and loving in Italian,
Grazia mille,
Prego.

Montreux

A lot of this year was spent buying the trappings of domestic bliss. Things like pots and pans, curtains, TV and a video machine, things like that. I bought too much black furniture, though it was hard to get anything else in the Eighties.

In a diary entry for April 1986 I wrote that I was licking my plate at the dinner table after a delicious roast dinner (an uncouth habit I know). Outside my rather posh next door neighbour was parking her car, watching me through the window and laughing her head off. I was embarrassed but covered it up by giving her a two-fingered salute through the window. The poor woman, she must have thought that some kind of yob pop star had moved in next door.

We did an appearance at the Montreux Music Festival, which used to be a big media event for the most current pop acts with product to promote. Morley and Jill Sinclair came along with us – for what reason I'm not sure. It was beautiful spring weather, I remember.

I remember, too, Paul Morley haranguing me nastily before the show, saying he hoped my performance would be different from the last round of TV shows we did. He seemed to me to be drunk again.

Shortly before the show, Rudderpuff called me a cunt, probably because I would not comply with his styling suggestions. He wanted us all to dress in black and white, with leather jackets if possible. This was his 'new' idea. He had progressed slightly from the moustachioed gay clone look to the trendy-in-a-black-polo-neck look. Paul had become the darling of a new scene of stylists, models, hairdressers and lesser-known pop journalists, the kind of people who only wear black (still).

I had suggested to Ped after the rehearsals that he should kick over his drum kit for dramatic effect at the end of 'Rage Hard' and 'Warriors Of The Wasteland', but during the show this escalated into the whole band smashing up the equipment. I was hit on the ankle by Mark's bass guitar and had to go for an X-ray after the show. The media lapped the whole thing up and we made headlines back in England. The band seemed to enjoy this new wave of 'bad-boy' publicity, but I wasn't so sure that acting like football hooligans was the wisest way of getting coverage.

'HOLLY THREATENS TO QUIT AS FRANKIE GO BERSERK! £100,000 HAVOC,' screamed *The Sun* on Monday May 12th 1986. An exaggerated and partly fictitious article continued in the same vein, using bold print for words like DESTROYED, ABUSED, GROPED and WRECKED. The article quoted me as saying 'I want nothing to do with a group that takes part in cheap and nasty stunts', a comment that I absolutely did not make.

When it was time to release 'Rage Hard', the first single from the album, our first promotional trip was to Holland to do 'The Countdown' TV programme. During the long wait between rehearsals Wolfgang suggested that we do a 'Rocky Horror Show' look for our forthcoming 'Top Of The Pops' appearance. This got watered down to a kind of 'Street-Life-with-money' look. The only stockings that were worn were those over the heads of Nasher and Paul, distorting their features. Mark wore his Gold Amex card glued to his forehead, a witty statement I thought. I wore ruched cycling shorts and fishnets rolled down to motorcycle boots, with my Claude Montana jacket on top. We threw a lot of fake money around the stage, and silver coins shone in our ears. It was a classic 'Top Of The Pops' performance. Chris Blackwell even bought the videotape from the BBC for use as a promotional tool in America. This was, I remember, the last performance where there was any kind of unity within the band. It was almost like the old days when we had fun with the bondage-wear. Back home in Liverpool it was rumoured that Eric, believing the money to be real, shouted at the TV screen, 'The bastard never throws any of his pfuckking money at me!' The general consensus after this 'Top Of The

235

Pops' was, 'Frankie has pulled it off again' – which indeed we had. The media myth that the 'Liverpool' album was a commercial disaster spread a few years later, but this was not the case. How many albums that cost nearly a million pounds to make actually recoup out of a meagre band royalty rate of 8%, which the 'Liverpool' album eventually did? (in 1991.)

* * *

Not long before this I had started a course of singing lessons with Helena Shanel, one of the most fashionable teachers of the time. I had hoped that she could teach me ways of preserving my voice on tour, as I knew a tour to promote the new album would be inevitable. I remember she was so popular that I could never get a morning appointment with her; I had to take a four-thirty slot. This was inconvenient: if I got a taxi to the Edgware Road, I would be stuck in traffic for over an hour, and if I got the tube, it would be full of schoolboys shouting 'Queerboy' at me.

On another occasion, a group of schoolgirls hustled me for my autograph. I got tired of signing eventually and waltzed off. One disappointed teenage girl called out after me, 'I hope yer get AIDS.'

Over My Dead Body

When Trevor finally stopped fiddling with the album, a meeting was called at ZTT where its title was discussed. There was an almost unanimous decision that it should be called 'Liverpool' following an initial suggestion from Morley. I thought this was a ridiculous and hypocritical title as none of us lived there any longer, and none of the songs on the album was about Liverpool.

My suggestion was 'From The Diamond Mine To The Factory', the opening line of 'Warriors Of The Wasteland'. This was rejected by everyone. Their forcing the album title 'Liverpool' on me meant I felt betrayed once more. I believed it was my job as lyricist to choose the title of the album, not the job of some corporate committee. This just added to the embarrassment I felt over the musical direction taken by this record. During this same meeting, I also found out that Paul had sung 'Do You Think I'm Sexy' in the studio and Trevor wanted to put it on the B side of 'Warriors Of The Wasteland'. I said something like 'Over my dead body', and threatened to leave the band then and there if such a tacky song went out with the name Frankie Goes To Hollywood on it. Not only had they recorded it behind my back, but they intended to play it live as a showcase for Paul, perhaps all part of his attempt to replace me when I left the group. I'd already had a major row with Lipson (in the studio) who had put on some Winston Churchill diatribe on the 'threat of Hitler' over the introduction of 'Warriors Of The Wasteland'. I despise Churchill. He was someone who only came alive when there was a war, sending many to unnecessary deaths. I also felt dredging up a reference to Adolf Hitler was in extremely bad taste, and, what's more, a veiled dig at Wolfgang.

ZTT decided to take over the press and advertising from Island Records, who had just won an award for the press campaign for

237

the previous album. I think ZTT wanted to change the nature of their agreement with Island Records so they could retain even more of the profits. All of a sudden, quarter and eighth-of-a-page advertising for the album and singles started to appear. Lorraine Reid, who had been Jill's secretary/PA for two years, was put in charge of press. Although she was an efficient and pleasant employee, she hardly had the experience of Regine Moylett, who had just won an award for the Frankie Goes To Hollywood press compaign. This whole exercise was leading up to a court case that ZTT brought against Island – not exactly the right thing to do when we were depending on Island to distribute the album successfully. I heard a rumour that Island Records were deliberately not going to promote the album in the USA because of ZTT fighting them in court.

*　*　*

I found out that Tony Pope had been paid a large amount by Tight Box Ltd, the company set up to regulate the band's business, without my consultation or knowledge. He was also paid on a basis that I would never have agreed to. This was, that he was paid not only on the income of the band but on a percentage of the gross, including recording costs that the band still had to recoup. This happened behind my back as only three signatures were needed on the company cheques. The rest of the band had decided to pay their 'mate' Tony.

We called a meeting of the band and their representatives to try and sort the problems out. An argument occurred that I remember most vividly. I complained that money was being spent from the Tight Box account without my knowledge, so I requested that I become a compulsory signatory for all company cheques. The response was that because I didn't hang around the band's office [ordering taxis and using the phone all day] I was not around when cheques were signed, so if I wanted to sign cheques I would have to come to the office more often, like the rest of them. This was not totally convincing: cheques could always be presented by post for me to sign. I told them there and then that if I did not become a compulsory signatory to the cheques, I would leave the band, but I was aware of their previous threat that if I did not promote the album, they would hold *me* responsible for any related 'breach-of-contract' action that might be brought against the band. I was furious that these, in my opinion, irresponsible directors had the company's cheque book in their sweaty little hands. They seemed not to be bothered by my threat to leave, being under some illusion that they could survive successfully in the industry as Frankie Goes To Hollywood without me. A concept that was to be proved wholly wrong.

The question of entering into litigation over the ZTT contract was also raised. However, I knew that the band was no longer a united force, and so this was no time to embark on litigation that would probably keep the band in the wilderness for anything up to two years. I discouraged any suggestion of litigation to the band. It seemed a bit like a U turn on my behalf, as I had always championed the idea, but I had my reasons. I would never again involve myself in a situation where I could be outvoted by these people if I could possibly avoid it. To me they were just fools who believed fame to be a passport to getting away with all kinds of bad behaviour. In turn, they believed that I was a greedy prima donna.

Americanos

After a period of denial, Wolfgang decided to have an official HIV test. A few nervous weeks passed before the result came through. Wolfgang's doctor telephoned with the result which was 'negative'. We were very relieved with the result, but also very angry about what we had been put through by the doctors at The Royal Liverpool Hospital. We chose not to pursue it further as we would, no doubt, have had to suffer much publicity over the matter. I can't begin to explain how distressing this experience was for both of us. Many people have committed suicide in reaction to false diagnoses.

I knew that it did not necessarily mean that I would test negative for HIV. I convinced myself that it was likely that I would be negative also, but I was too afraid to take the test. I realise that this was rather selfish and adolescent of me. We had, however, been practising Safe Sex with each other since 1985. The good news of Wolfgang's HIV-negative status came on the day that we filmed a promotional video for 'Rage Hard' with photographer David Bailey as director. Wolfgang and I went to the filming in a marvellous mood.

ZTT found David Bailey's edit of the video to be 'too boring'. Morley took it upon himself to do a scratch edit to liven things up a bit, but the result was a mish-mash of images that jarred aesthetically with Bailey's monochrome, slow-moving film. The Morley version was voted worst video of the year by readers of a popular magazine and viewers of a TV chart show. So much for marketing genius. Nevertheless 'Rage Hard' reached number four in the British Charts and number one in Germany, our most successful market. It was a good song based on the Dylan Thomas poem 'Do not go gentle into that good night'.

* * *

Every Saturday, Wolfgang and I used to walk up the Kings Road, shopping and meeting friends in the Chenil Gallery garden restaurant. We would pass Vivienne Westwood's old shop, World's End, then an empty shell. I used to wonder what had happened to my heroine, and why the shop was now closed down. Then, sometime during 1986-87, I noticed strange goings on in the premises. I dragged Wolfgang into the shop one day to find that there was no lighting or electricity by which you could look at the rails of printed denim clothes. An old woman sat in the corner sewing buttons on things in the dim light, while another middle-aged red-headed woman rummaged about, apologising for the lack of lighting or electricity.

Over the next few months Vivienne repaired her damaged business, and got the lights back on. With the help of her two sons and some of the original staff from the days of SEX, she rebuilt her emporium. I bought one of the first men's Savile Row suits that she designed. I became a regular customer in fact.

It was arranged that Vivienne and I would do a photo session for a glossy fashion magazine together. She gave me a silk tie to wear with it that bore the legend BIG SKY and her trademark orb that she had adapted from the Harris Tweed logo. Unfortunately the make-up artist for the session seemed to be rather inexperienced, covering Vivienne in foundation which made her look a hundred years old. Vivienne told her off, saying, 'I looked better without the make up', which was true. I posed with a bunch of red roses behind my back, lips pursed ready to kiss Vivienne, symbolically welcoming her back to England. Vivienne decided that she would interview me after the photo shoot, but she could not for the life of her think of any questions to ask me, so I started to ask my own questions, then giving the stock answers into her tape recorder. She kept complaining in her strong Northern accent, 'We 'avent got anythin' crunchie yet thou' 'ave we?' So I tried to make it a bit more 'crunchie' by asking her if she'd ever had a lesbian experience. But this talk of homosexuality did not seem to provide the 'crunch' that she required. I remember discussing *The Sun* and its ilk with her. She could not understand why I would not allow an interview of mine to appear in it, believing that these people were just there to be exploited when artists had ideas to sell. Unfortunately, the negatives of this photo session, according to the photographer, were lost by the magazine who had commissioned them. Only one print survived.

I became an avid collector of Vivienne's creations and applauded loudly when she took her place again in the starry firmament of fashion design. She was later, twice concurrently, voted British Fashion Designer of The Year. I hope this happens a third time.

* * *

I commissioned Katherine Hamnett to make some lightweight stage suits for me. She said that she would make amendments to an already existing suit design of hers, using raw silk and shortening the jacket and sleeve lengths etc.

One day, during rehearsals for the forthcoming tour, I took Paul aside and asked if he would approach the rest of the band about producing a 'Frankie Says . . . Use A Condom' T-shirt. I felt that if they knew it was my idea, it would get a negative response. He eventually told me they were in agreement, so I asked Katherine Hamnett if she would produce some for us, which she kindly did. The idea proved quite popular in America I believe. People had got tired of the bootleg 'Who gives a Fuck what Frankie Says' T-shirts.

While at Katherine's office I made friends with Nancy – Katherine Hamnett's PA – who told me that she lived with the son of Paul Roche. Paul had been companion to Duncan Grant, the Bloomsbury artist, for the last years of his life, and had inherited a large part of the estate when Duncan Grant died. Nancy told us Paul had just bought a house on Mallorca and that he needed money. She suggested that we should holiday with him and pay him rent to help him out; then, of course, we could see his collection. Wolfgang, an avid collector of Grant's work, was especially interested in the idea.

For the Christmas of 1986 I suggested to Wolfgang that we visit his sister Brigitte Rossi and her family in Pittsburgh, Pennsylvania. He had not seen her for many years, nor met any of his five nieces, who in turn had produced their own children. He rang her and asked her if she could recommend a suitable hotel nearby, and she replied that we could stay with her. We had a wonderful time experiencing a real American Christmas. Everything in the shopping-mall at Monroeville seemed inexpensive compared to London. Most of the time we were entertained by Heidi, one of Brigitte's daughters who drove us round in an old car – you could see the road speed past through its floor. I loved going to the supermarket with her: such an array of unusual groceries – peanut butter and blackcurrant jelly in the same squeezable bottle, Oreo Cookies and Wonderwhip. Mike, fiancé of another daughter, Patty, is a successful photographer with his own studio. He specialised in high-school yearbooks and wedding albums, drenched in American suburban kitsch. The last page of his award-winning wedding album depicted the happy couple superimposed on a cloudy sky: 'A Marriage Made In Heaven'.

These Americans made cups of tea in a microwave oven and chatted endlessly on the phone to other members of the family. In America local calls are free, which amazed me. We watched Home Box Office on cable, where recent movies played all day, and of course MTV. I bought the whole series of 'Pee Wee's Playhouse' on video – it was unavailable in England; I also bought Pee Wee Watches and talking dolls.

All of the Rossi family were most hospitable to their estranged Uncle Wolfgang and his English friend. When we arrived we were told that we could share a 'queen-size bed' in the spare room. I burst out laughing at this, the only accidental reference to our sexuality.

While we were there, a damning review of the 'Liverpool' album appeared in *People* magazine (America's most popular). With it was a photo of the band which included a shot of Wolfgang in the audience, which was passed around the family providing a bit of excitement.

We had Christmas dinner at Barbara and Mike's house.

Barbara had decorated the house in a traditional American way reminiscent of 'The Waltons' or 'Little House On The Prairie', and there we had turkey and yellow corn bread, which was delicious. All in all we were treated to the utmost hospitality and had a great Christmas, which we really needed after all the stresses of the previous year.

Bordel de Merde

We flew back to England with a few days to go before the
Frankie Goes To Hollywood 1987 European tour, which was to
be the last. I had already made up my mind that the next musical
venture I got involved with would be a solo project, so I would
have more control over the finished product. Already the idea for
a new song had germinated in my mind after my American
Christmas. Americanos! was a word I kept repeating to myself
after hearing a news report on Radio Pittsburgh concerning
Spanish speaking immigrants, who were multiplying so fast that
Spanish had become the second language of the USA. I needed
to get away from the pompous, designer-rock sound that Frankie
Goes To Hollywood had just put out, wanting instead to make
pop music with a definite dance influence that street people
would appreciate.

The first half of the set we were to play on tour was mostly the
new rock songs from the 'Liverpool' album. Some of them were
hard work to put across to the audience (they were all written in a
hurry and under stress – you couldn't really dance to them), and
the songs from the first album always got the best reception. I
noticed, too, that the photographs used in the programme and
the merchandising were not all good, and the T-shirt designs
lacklustre – everything seemed geared to cheapness and
maximum profits.

We drove to Wembley Arena through the snow to do our
second night there. It was freezing backstage. Someone told me
that the night before Capital Radio had taped the concert for
transmission at a later date, in return for advertising the two
concerts on the air. I had a huge temper tantrum when I heard
this, screaming at Tony Pope. I couldn't believe that he would
arrange something like this without first informing me. As I was

laying into Tony, Mark O'Tool tried to intervene. I told him to 'Fuck off' – this argument was nothing to do with him, but his huge ego just couldn't take *that*, and he started to kick me and lash out with his hands. Luckily Ron Weisner and Tony Pope pulled him away and restrained him. I was still furious and screamed at Tony that he was 'history' as far as I was concerned. And this all happened two minutes before we were to go onstage! It was one of our best concerts, because of the adrenalin caused by the backstage argument.

After the concert Ron Weisner said to me, 'Don't let them ruin you're life, H'. Things certainly had come to a desperate level. Mark seemed pretty pleased with himself, and I don't think any of the other members of the band reproached him in any way; they all went out partying together afterwards. Lemmy from Motorhead took me aside after the show and warned me that, if I left the band, things would not be the same for me in the music business again. It seemed that he had been asked to give me this advice by someone in the band.

People who have to resort to physical fights had always been low in my estimation. I had spent years avoiding them in Liverpool. Now here I was stuck in a situation where I had to work with just that kind. Wolfgang was extremely angry, demanding I have a personal bodyguard and that I should travel separately from the rest of the band – a request we had already made in writing before the tour.

The rest of the tour was absolute hell. There was no way I was going to socialise with the rest of the band, as they all seemed to be patting Mark on the back. The atmosphere was like ice. We would stand backstage before going on, not speaking or even looking at each other. It was like being back at secondary school, in the line for lessons.

The behaviour of the band seemed to get worse and worse as the tour progressed – hotel carpets were ruined and rooms trashed. It was all such a cliché. Perhaps they knew it would be the last time that they would be able to get away with it. Even Paul, who I thought was supposed to be a bit more grown up, claimed that he smashed the mirrors in one of the hotel rooms.

He seemed almost proud of the fact when he related the story, as if this made him big or heroic in some way.

We played Brussels on my birthday and the whole audience sang 'Happy Birthday', which was rather embarrassing as not one person on the tour had acknowledged the fact. Most of the time Wolfgang and I travelled separately with a so-called bodyguard who was always unwashed and bleary eyed in the morning after spending the night in some nightclub protecting the rest of the band. We knew that anything we said about them would get right back to the band the same evening. So we. slagged them off whenever he was in earshot.

There was a brief respite when we had a few days off during the French leg of the tour. Wolfgang and I took the TGV (a fast train) to Paris where we met up with Catherine Remy, our French record company's promotion person, booking into the Hotel Warwick, just off the Champs-Elysées. At this time there were demonstrations in the streets over the closing down of Channel 6, a kind of Pop Music TV channel. The French are very political and are always demonstrating about something.

We were doing an interview in Pub Renault, a large glass-fronted showroom on the Champs-Elysées – it had been taken over for the week by Radio NRG. We were sitting at a table in the window, where there were special flower arrangements to decorate the scene, while a hundred or so onlookers pressed their faces up against the glass. The next day, one of the radio station employees (who had been kind and given me a Le Clip watch) noticed, when she tried to move a flower arrangement, that it was unusually heavy. Further inspection revealed high explosives and a detonation device. She called security, who immediately started to move the arrangement down into the basement car-park of the building. While they were doing this, the device exploded, killing one of the security guards. If the device had exploded in the window hundreds of glass splinters would have shattered into the face of the children who were watching the transmission. It was a narrow escape for me too, sitting right next to the bomb making Liverpudlian wisecracks over the airways.

While in Paris Wolfgang and I were taken by Catherine Remy

to the final show of Channel 6. Catherine Remy was unlike most record company employees. She looked like Annie Lennox shrunken in a washing machine and had boundless energy. She made us do five TV shows in one day, but in such a way that it was a pleasure. The first time I met her was in a limousine at Charles de Gaulle airport. We had just flown in and didn't realise that there would be a film crew. I ran away from the cameras as I wasn't in the mood. I think I might have even told the interviewer and director of the film (Pierre Banain) to 'Get lost', so he was hopping mad as we swept off in the limousine. Catherine was determined to smooth things over and charmed the boots off me, and by the time we got to the hotel we were old friends. She taught me wonderful French swear words like 'Bordel de merde de caca prout' (I'm not sure of the exact spelling!)

After the Channel 6 episode, Catherine drove with us to Lille in her usual limousine. She helped me write a satirical French pop song called 'Fromage d'Amour', which, to me, describes most French pop music. I wonder why the French get almost everything right except pop?

Things reached a sort of fever pitch when we played Lille. 'The Lads' went on a rampage which started off with someone throwing the manager of the hotel into the swimming pool. Eyeholes were burned into pillowcases to create Ku-Klux-Klan-like masks, which were worn up and down the corridors of the hotel. I am a heavy sleeper so I didn't hear the banging on our hotel room door and the shouts of 'Come out you fucking Nazi bastards!' but Wolfgang, who is a light sleeper, told me about it in the morning. He remembers Paul hissing hyena-laughter as 'The Lads' hurled abuse through our hotel room door.

We decided from that day on that it would be best if we stayed in a separate hotel. It wasn't always easy to find a satisfactory alternative, and we would often check out one or two before deciding which one to stay in, much to the annoyance of our Medallion Man bodyguard. He was the type of person who would brag about his knowledge of 'seven different ways to kill a man with his bare hands' which, he informed us, he had learned in the army. He needn't have bothered: just one whiff of his BO would have done the trick.

Towards the end of the tour the dates started to get closer together and at one point I had to do three or four concerts on the trot, something I had warned Tony Pope about as my voice couldn't take it. Predictably, he had ignored my warning. As a result I contracted laryngitis, and some of the dates had to be rescheduled. This caused a lengthening of the tour and of our agony.

The band had delusions of grandeur and chartered a private jet to fly themselves back to England after the last show. The bodyguard handed Wolfgang our scheduled air tickets and said he had been invited on to the private jet with the rest of the band.

At the end of the tour a live appearance on Ben Elton's Saturday night show had been scheduled to promote 'Watching The Wildlife', Frankie's last single. I gave ZTT's Karen Goodman a whole week's warning that I might not be able to do the show as my voice was shot and I didn't want to sing live on TV in that state. ZTT, however, didn't inform the show's producers until the last minute, which resulted in Ben Elton slagging me off to the nation who had tuned in. This was the last straw. As far as I was concerned, Frankie Goes To Hollywood were History. I had fulfilled my obligation to promote the album, and I was now free. Or so I hoped.

Years later Nasher, in an attempt to promote his own ill-fated rock group, claimed in an interview for the *Daily Star* that the rest of the band had planned to humiliate me publicly by sacking me from the band live on 'Saturday Night Live'. He also claimed that I had got wind of this and had beaten them to it by leaving the band before they had the chance. I cannot comment on what their actual plans were, but I had not got wind of any scheme of theirs. In reality I had left the group over a year before this event, and was only fulfilling my contractual obligations by completing the tour.

What had started as a creative and exciting adventure had deteriorated into a cliché-ridden rock-'n'-roll nightmare. It would take years, and huge legal fees, to extricate myself from that unhappy situation.

Sunbeam Rapier

The previous September I had taken lots of driving lessons with an ex-army Scotsman called Jimmy. He didn't hesitate to shout at me like a sergeant major every time I made an error, which, I suppose, made him a good teacher. I applied for my test after about twenty or so lessons.

Just before I took my driving test I bought a Sunbeam Rapier Mark Three – John Gaillard, the band's roadie, found it for me. It was in good condition, and still had the original two-tone paint job: pearl grey and pippin red. I liked the little fins on the back and the sparkling chrome work. I bought it from a young couple somewhere in the East End of London. She told me that they used to drive it down the Kings Road on a Saturday. John let me drive the car home along the Embankment. It wasn't an easy car to drive for a learner used to a Metro – the hand-brake was on the right hand side for a start. It was night time and I had never driven in the dark. All I could see were endless dazzling headlights heading straight for me. Somehow we managed to get home in one piece.

Wolfgang didn't believe I would pass my driving test, and secretly I feared that he might be right. On the day I was petrified, sweating visibly even before the examiner gave the direction to drive off. Jimmy, the instructor, waited for me on the pavement, confident he would get at least another ten lessons out of me.

When I told Wolfgang I had passed he accused me of bribing the examiner!

About two months after passing my test we were driving in the West End. It was raining and the traffic was heavy. I turned on to Park Lane and proceeded to the Hyde Park roundabout, where I changed lanes a few times, thinking that I had to be on the inside

250

lane in order to turn right at the end. Wolfgang was going crazy at my lane changing. Suddenly I noticed a car move off from the kerb, signalling that it was going to position itself in the lane I was in. The driver quickly moved in front of me, giving me no time to slow down in the fast-moving traffic. I slammed on my brakes which locked, and the car started swerving this way and that. I couldn't get things under control. We crashed into the back of another car and finally came to a stop. Traffic moved around us on the wet road; it was a miracle other cars didn't smash into the back of us causing a pile up. This was right outside the Dorchester Hotel, so we went inside its lobby to telephone the RAC. The lobby was snooing with journalists, because Princess Michael of Kent was having her book launched in the hotel. We had to wait for hours before a pick-up truck came and hoisted my poor smashed car on to its trailer. While we were waiting, some arsehole rang *The Sun*, to inform them that I had been involved in a car accident outside the hotel. 'Outrageous Gay Rock Star In Pile Up With Princess'. When contacted by the tabloids we denied that there had been an incident, and no story appeared.

Wolfgang vowed he would never get in a car with me again; this was the excuse he had been waiting for. He had been against the idea of me driving all along, and now kept repeating that he would not wheel me around in a wheelchair if I was crippled in an accident. 'You're not the driving type,' he would go on. Quite true really, I suppose, I'm too busy eyeing up the world. I've always been the same, visually devouring passers-by or shop windows, or undressing construction workers.

* * *

After the tour I heaved a huge sigh of relief. We had all made some money out of this tour, so at least it had been worth it financially, unlike our other tours.

Now at last I was free to make an album of my own work. I threw myself full time into songwriting, realising that I would need new material to perform as a solo artist. I also felt I had to become more acquainted with studio technology. I had a meeting with Trevor and Jill to talk about it. We talked about the kind of album I wanted to make. I told them I would like to work with an American producer possibly, and make a slick Dance/Pop record. They seemed to be interested in this idea, and I even got the impression that Trevor would have liked to produce it, but I hoped that with another producer the record would cost substantially less than Trevor's efforts.

The provisions in the recording contract that the group had signed with ZTT were a bit vague when dealing with a member leaving the group. It stated that the leaving member was obliged to enter into an identical agreement to the one signed by the whole group, but it was not made clear whether that person had to go back to the beginning of the contract and start all over again with the option periods, or carry on from the point that had already been reached. In fact it was a badly written document on the whole, according to subsequent expert opinions.

I asked David Lowman and Wolfgang to try and negotiate new terms for me as a solo performer. The current terms of the contract were still very restrictive creatively, and rather measly from a financial viewpoint; according to the agreement I might have been expected to make a solo single for ZTT for an advance of £250 if the contract were taken literally. Also, if the terms of the contract were implemented, then ZTT would have no obligation to release the record or any subsequent record that I was allowed to make – in their studio, and with their choice of producer and material.

Wolfgang and David Lowman arranged a meeting with Jill Sinclair. David Lowman criticised the contract, I believe, and asked for a renegotiation of the terms, to which Jill reportedly replied, 'I have nothing to put on the table . . . and I would like you to leave now.' David and Wolfgang told me that Jill had been particularly unreasonable in the meeting; they were both shaking with anger after it and had to go to a pub to have a stiff drink. She was obviously of the opinion that her contract with me was watertight.

In the light of this meeting I was extremely surprised to read in a press interview given by Jill Sinclair a few years later the quote, 'A meeting was called by me with his manager and financial advisor . . . They said, "We can renegotiate, we can sue you or you can let us go for a negotiated settlement." I said, "Fine, we should talk about it." And they never came back. What Holly is saying is not true at all. We were always prepared to discuss it.'

The upshot of David and Wolfgang's meeting with Jill then was that I must somehow endeavour to get out of the contract. ZTT were obviously not interested in creating goodwill in our relationship. I must admit I was afraid of entering into a long legal wrangle with them. I was not financially secure enough to be able to afford a lengthy law suit, and I might find by the time it was all over that I was a forgotten artist. Wolfgang, however, kept pushing me into the idea of taking legal action. He always seemed confident the contract was unenforceable.

David Lowman, my financial adviser, introduced me to a firm of solicitors called Joynson Hicks who applied for the opinion of council. The council taken was from a barrister called Robert Engelhart.

Meanwhile the tabloids were running stories that Wolfgang had been responsible for the break up of the band and that I was a prima donna. These stories were obviously coming from some of the other band members or ZTT, who were taking the opportunity to slag me and Wolfgang off publicly whenever possible. This just illustrated to me how right I was to leave. 'Holly's fella blamed for Frankie split,' sang *The Sun*, 16th March 1987. The article also claimed that 'the rest of the band hate Holly' and 'there is no way any of them want to work with Holly again'. They weren't given any choice.

The Party

In early 1987 I met a TV producer called Veronica Bodnarec who was involved in a number of projects concerning AIDS awareness. I participated in a documentary that Veronica produced for Central Television called 'Coming Soon To A Bed Near You'. I did a 'How to put a condom on a banana' sketch, wearing a 'Frankie Says . . . Use A Condom' T-shirt. This kind of early consciousness-raising has been much criticised by so-called experts, who now cue up to say 'cock', 'fuck' and 'arse' to camera in an orgy of 'communicating in a common language'. Their argument was that celebrities putting condoms on bananas was not a great help. I disagree. Teenagers are more likely to listen to pop stars than to doctors.

Through Veronica I met the late George Cant, who was involved in setting up a concert at Wembley Arena for an International Aids Day in aid of the Terence Higgins Trust. George's partner, Tony Whitehead, was a director of the Trust and had helped set up the organisation. The event was to be called 'The Party' in an attempt to keep the atmosphere up-beat. Lots of people I knew offered their services: the art-work was done by the same people who did the Frankie Goes To Hollywood graphics, for example.

As I no longer had a band at my disposal I chose to sing with the excellent house band, put together by John Entwistle, the bass player from The Who. On the night John Entwistle was on bass guitar, Herbie Hancock and Steve Naive on keyboards, Andy Summers and Robin Le Mesurier on guitars, Zach Starkey (Ringo Starr's son) on drums and Jodie on percussion. There was also a vocal group called the Soultanas who did backing vocals. I performed two songs: 'The Power Of Love' and Bruce Springsteen's 'Born To Run'. Having recently come off tour, I gave a fairly polished performance. The thing I enjoyed most though was wearing a Gold Hairpin Levi jacket made especially for me by Leigh Bowery. Backstage at Wembley Arena, Boy George and George Michael were trying to sing harmonies in the exact spot where Mark O'Tool had attacked me. Boy George was still getting over his heroin addiction at the time and looked rather sedated to say the least, though not too sedated however to come out with one of his famous schoolyard retorts. I asked him if he had a comb before I went on stage and he replied, 'Oh, you Comb-O-Sexual'.

Notable performances that evening came from Jimmy Sommerville and George Michael, who both brought their own bands with them. Even Andrew Ridgeley put in an appearance. Elton John appeared in his 'Peroxide Friar Tuck' stage. I went to shake his hand and he kissed me instead. He was always a disarming and pleasant person to bump into, unpretentious and down to earth.

After the show Gary Farrow, Frankie's ex-record plugger, introduced me to David Simone who was scouting round for acts to sign to MCA records in the UK and the reincarnated UNI label in America. He had just left Phonogram for this new job which was important as he was to coordinate the UK label and restart the UNI label in the USA. This was a fortuitous meeting for me, although it was also the start of a stormy relationship.

At this time Veronica introduced me to a friend of hers called Lisa, one of the first women in the UK to be diagnosed as having AIDS. She had appeared on the TV news (in a wig) to appeal to the drug company Wellcome to give her the anti-AIDS drug AZT. AZT was already available in the USA but, I believe, had not been licensed in the UK at that time. Lisa had lived in a small community in the countryside, where her parents ran a grocery shop. When it was discovered that Lisa had AIDS, people stopped buying food there. In a wonderful gesture of support, Lisa's parents sold up and moved to Fulham in London so Lisa could be near to the Kobler Centre at St Stephen's Hospital, the first clinic set up in the UK to help PWAs (people with Aids). Lisa was a beautiful young girl who had been infected by a boyfriend, probably her first. I must admit that I was nervous meeting PWAs because it dredged up my own fears of having the disease. The irrational fear of catching the disease from ordinary human contact was hiding somewhere in my subconscious. I had not been at all nervous when visiting Karl years earlier at home or in hospital for some reason, but by this time we all knew a little bit more about the spread of HIV. It was an example of that 'little bit of knowledge' that is so dangerous.

We sometimes went out to The Blue Elephant, our favourite new Thai restaurant where Lisa would eat vegetarian food and drink no wine. She seemed to glow with health, it was hard to believe she was ill. She would say she would not let the disease beat her.

It got more and more depressing seeing Veronica, however, as the subject of conversation always turned to AIDS. For me, a dope-smoking, paranoid Queen, it became too much and we saw less of her as time went by. The last time I saw her she wore an amulet around her neck. She said it was filled with the ashes of George Cant who had died saying, 'You'll have to learn to roll a joint some day, you stupid cow!' According to Veronica.

She told us that she had been to fifteen funerals that year. It was a good job her wardrobe consisted entirely of black.

Death in Fun City

Wolfgang was now convinced that the only way forward was to extricate myself from my contractual obligations to ZTT and Perfect Songs. Millions of records had been sold yet the band were still in an unrecouped position. It did not seem possible at this time that we would ever recoup the £790,000 that ZTT claimed that 'Liverpool' had cost.

I had no idea how much litigation would cost but I did know that I might end up paying the other side's costs as well as my own, and possibly further damages. I also had the Inland Revenue breathing down my neck for a large sum of money that I wasn't sure that I still had. And there were large mortgage repayments to be met. I was worried and very unsure of the future. I knew that it would take a good deal of work to dig myself out of this hole, so I threw myself into songwriting, something I had not done on my own for about four years.

During the summer I employed an old friend, David Martin, to play bass and a colleague of his called Christian to play keyboards. They helped with arrangement ideas on demos that I had written over a simple one- or two-chord backing track – usually a bass line and a drum pattern. Some of the songs we worked on I decided to abandon and some I knew needed to be developed further.

During that summer we took a holiday to Majorca. We stayed as paying guests with Paul Roche (Duncan Grant's old companion) in his house in a village over the mountains from Palma. We were interested in his collection of paintings by Duncan Grant. I had read that Duncan had met Paul Roche wandering round wearing a sort of sailor suit in Piccadilly one afternoon. Duncan asked Paul if he would like to see some pictures. Paul apparently thought that Duncan meant the cinema

257

and went off with him. The relationship continued until Duncan Grant's death in the late Seventies, following which Paul inherited some of Grant's estate.

During our stay Paul lavished water on his rather beautiful garden with its wonderful views of the mountains. This resulted in the water supply to the bathroom drying up on several occasions, which was a bit inconvenient. Paul, at seventy something years old, sunbathed in the garden or wandered around the house completely naked, unless ladies were present when he would put on a pair of M&S briefs. He sunbathed so much that his skin had turned a vibrant orange, and he covered himself in an oily substance of his own concoction that he called his Unguent. To protect his eyes from the sun he wore a visor which was a piece of corrugated, manilla cardboard attached to a piece of elastic. His hair was a patchwork of beige and pink. It seemed that he believed himself to be as handsome and virile as he may once have been when he posed for nude studies by Duncan Grant, many of which were on display in his house.

In the hot summer sun Paul would read to us excerpts from his poetry. 'Death in Fun City' was one I particularly remember. He also kindly gave us signed copies of two books of poetry he had written. He deluged us with anecdotes of his friendship with 'Duncan' and we admired his collection of paintings, then sadly depleted due to a settlement with his ex-wife.

We spent about three weeks staying in Paul's house with its home-made chandeliers made of broken blue glass precariously wired together. I declined his daily Bloody Mary cocktails after sampling one which seemed to contain nine parts vodka to one part tomato juice. I assumed that these were responsible for Paul's advanced state of preservation.

Wolfgang managed to persuade Paul to part with one or two paintings from his collection, works that Paul was not overly fond of. One was a painting that Duncan Grant had painted two versions of circa 1916, showing the sitter, probably Vanessa Bell, in a tub. It is an extremely good example of British avant garde art of that period. The other painting was by Vanessa Bell, a study for her famous 'Tents' screen. The money paid for these two paintings I believe was invested in much-needed improvements to Paul's bathroom and water supply.

* * *

The tactics chosen by Russells, my solicitors, was that they would send letters out to ZTT and Perfect Songs outlining the belief that the recording contract I had signed was in restraint of trade and therefore unenforceable. The letter also suggested that as the signing of the Perfect Songs agreement was a condition of the recording agreement, then it too would be deemed unenforceable. The agreement was attacked as being only relevant to compositions that were jointly written with the other members of the group. These letters were sent out in late July 1987. The intention behind firing the first shot was to draw ZTT into either capitulating, or taking immediate action and thereby putting me in the position of defendant in any legal action that might be instigated by them. In the same letter ZTT were notified officially that I was a leaving member of Frankie Goes To Hollywood. The clause concerning a leaving member we claimed to be void due to uncertainty. There also followed a whole list of other criticisms concerning the unfairness of the agreement.

The plan was that I would come up with some ideas. We could then possibly approach other record companies in an attempt to get them to underwrite the case on my behalf, by putting up the money, which was estimated roughly at about £150,000. I might have had something in the region of this amount in the bank but I knew that it would be a risk to pay out savings earmarked for tax payments.

A reply to the Russells letter was made on behalf of ZTT and Perfect Songs Ltd by Halliwell Rodwell, a firm of solicitors. ZTT defended themselves against all our allegations, and threatened legal action if I did not, in the next forty eight hours, assure them that I would comply with their contract.

So a court date for the full hearing was set for January or February of the next year, 1988, and a fax was sent by ZTT to all major record companies, suggesting that I should not be signed up by any of them.

* * *

The same summer I received a telephone call from Steve Lovell, my old flat mate from Liverpool. He had been working as a minor record producer for the last few years. He was not entirely happy with his situation, but he enjoyed the security of the regular salary. He had recently produced a hit with a Samantha Fox song – 'musical road sweeping' in his own words. He offered to help me in setting up a studio in the hope of securing some work in the future. I also think he felt some sympathy with my situation after bumping into some of the ex-members of Frankie Goes To Hollywood, who were still slagging me off according to Steve all over town whenever they got the opportunity.

Steve refused to accept any payment for his services setting up the studio that we did together over the next three months. We both put in a lot of hard work on the project which was done secretly in the studio that I put together in my house.

After much hard work with Steve and also with Steve Howell, the studio was completed. We also got more technical advice from Guy Chambers, the keyboard player from World Party. The result was quite polished.

Tony Russell, my new solicitor, alerted some key A and R departments to the situation. The idea was that representatives could come to my home and talk over my ideas, the concept of which they would not disclose. If they were then interested in the ideas, they would have to advance us £150,000 to fight ZTT in court, on condition that if I won, I would sign to their particular label. If I lost, then they would have to wait until my contract with ZTT expired, which might be a very long time. I did not hold great hopes for the plan, knowing the lack of foresight in many record companies. Virgin Records sent a representative and Muff Winwood and Paul Russell came from CBS, Tracy Bennet from London Records and Rob Dickens from Warner

Brothers. They all showed interest, but none had the nerve to make the investment. But then David Simone, on behalf of MCA Records (UK), whom I'd met at The Party, said that he was about to take over as label coordinator as well as restarting MCA's UNI label in America. We, of course, didn't let David know that he was the only party prepared to put his money where his mouth was. It would after all set a legal precedent; no artist had previously managed to get out of a recording agreement. There had been only one instance where a songwriter had managed to get out of a publishing agreement, the famous Schroeder *v*. Macauley case.

A letter of intent was drawn up between me and MCA agreeing that I would sign to them if I won the case. Basic deal points were outlined, such as advances and percentages. All seemed a huge improvement on the advances and percentages I could ever hope to get from ZTT.

Wolfgang had offered to sell his collection of paintings to underwrite the court case, but I didn't really want the loss of that, his pride and joy, on my conscience. After the signing of the letter of intent, which was for a five or six album contract, I did feel a little depressed at the thought that I was contracted so far into the future, even though the combined advances I might receive under the agreement added up to several million pounds. That was only money, not happiness or creative fulfilment.

I was not the only person involved in litigation and misery with ZTT. There had been several unhappy artists contractually bound in a similar way to me. The German group Propaganda had the year before sought freedom from their contract. Some of the members were granted legal aid and were eventually let go by ZTT. The grievances of some of the members of Propaganda were not unlike my own. Another group, Das Psycho Rangers, were also mooning about the offices of ZTT, unhappy with their situation and intent on legal proceedings.

* * *

I saw a lot of Jayne and Biffa from Liverpool at this time. They would come and stay with us for the odd weekend bringing groovy vintage clothes and gifts that could only be bought in Liverpool. Jayne was now working as promotions director for the Bluecoat Chambers Arts Centre. She organised musical and theatrical events, and with Biffa's help on set designing and general presentation ideas the once stuffy and exclusively middle-class venue was transformed into a genuine centre of the arts, where anyone would feel comfortable. She had at last got the court where she could play Queen Bee that she had craved for so long.

On one of our weekend house parties Biffa made an amateur pop video using the demo of my song 'Boyfriend 65' as a soundtrack. It shows Jayne, Wolfgang and me in our garden. I am seen ignoring Jayne and her advances and chatting up Wolfgang. She storms out and I follow reluctantly. We drive off into the sunset in my Sunbeam Rapier.

During the long winter waiting for the court case to come up we lunched almost daily in the sadly missed Chenil Galleries Garden Restaurant in the Kings Road, a social centre for local antique and art dealers. It was run by Giorgio, now an old friend, who made great pasta and vegetarian dishes. I started to collect the occasional twentieth-century design classic – a sculpture by Martell or a Lalique clock, for example – but not antiques, which have never interested me. We learned a whole new language and a dictionary of names that the dealers rolled off their silver tongues.

We also organised a photo session with Alistair Thane so we would have some photos to accompany our press release. Alistair's studio was in London EC1 and run by his business partner Gill Woods, who also managed Alistair's career. She had helped to catapult him from obscure surrealist student photographer to well known advertising campaign photographer in the space of ten years.

Gill introduced me to David Robilliard and his partner Andrew Heard who had a studio just around the corner from Gill's. I had been a fan of David's unique Ortonesque poetry since I bought his book *Inevitable* in 1984, published by the artists

Gilbert and George. They seemed to preside parentally over this small group of young artists, and proclaimed that David was their favourite living writer. He also provided them with introductions to the many boys that they photographed for their artwork. I got on well with David immediately; we shared an interest in pop music, especially David Bowie's earlier career. At that time I didn't appreciate the originality of David Robilliard's paintings which were simple rainbow-coloured line drawings on a white ground. Years later I saw an exhibition of his work at the Festival Hall and was astounded by them. The title of the exhibition was 'Life Isn't Good It's Excellent'; the name of a painting David executed shortly after being diagnosed with AIDS, and it is even more poignant in the light of that knowledge. I was also amazed by Andrew Heard's paintings: large canvases influenced by Gilbert and George, yet with their own particular, very English vision. Wolfgang had taken over my easel and paints for a few months. Seeing Andrew's work made me want to take up the brush again.

The same year Andy Warhol died, and Sotheby's auctioned his collection of objects, art and furniture. A few of these were on show at Sotheby's in Bond Street to publicise the sale to be held in New York. I dragged Wolfgang along to see the remnants of my favourite artist. I was a bit disappointed by the rather dull Picasso and the meagre display of Art Deco jewellery – I suppose the best things were kept in New York. As I was leaving the showroom I heard a commotion across the road. Walking straight towards me dressed all in black with black sunglasses, supported by a woman also dressed in black and flanked by two bodyguards, was David Bowie. I had an LSD flashback in which he appeared to me as wizened, unshaven and old, as if he had spent the last fifteen years constantly harassed by the world. I had a fleeting vision that this man might have once sold his soul to the devil. It was an illusion and he was probably just suffering from a late night. He swept passed me looking straight ahead. I was dumbstruck. I had seen the hero of my teenage years close up and in the flesh. I wrote a letter to David Robilliard telling him about this momentous sighting, and we gossiped about it on the phone. He asked me to come and visit him again. He said, 'Don't be afraid that I've got AIDS – I don't look like a leper or anything like that.'

I said, 'Don't worry, I've known people who have died before,' then bit my tongue, knowing I had said absolutely the wrong thing. He replied that life had been a living hell since his diagnosis, and I did not know what else to say. I never saw David again as he died of pneumonia shortly afterwards, but not before he sent me a box of poems printed on cards with a cassette of his voice reciting his work. Something to cherish forever.

Cinderella Goes to Court

The court hearing was set for 18th January 1988. Wolfgang was under an extra strain, having discovered that his sister Heidi was undergoing chemotherapy for leukaemia. He wanted to go and visit her in Germany, but he did not want to leave me to face the court case alone. Heidi in turn urged him to stay in England, insisting that she only wanted Wolfgang to see her when she was looking and feeling better.

During the next three weeks we had to get up early and dress smartly. On a few occasions Wolfgang freaked at the amount of pomade I used to slick my hair back – he can be so fussy. We would then take a taxi to the High Court Of Justice in the Strand. We were driven through the cold morning air by a cheery-faced African called Charles, who played calypso music on cassette, while Wolfgang and I smoked as many cigarettes as we could in the back seat. Invariably we would be a few minutes early and would have a cup of tea in the Lite Bite Café opposite the court. After dodging the press photographers, we were searched at the door by a security guard then directed downstairs to the courtroom. As the defendant I had to sit on the opposite end of the same hard wooden bench as the plaintiffs. Wolfgang sat directly behind me at the suggestion of Brian Howard, our litigation solicitor.

On the first day of court Jill Sinclair, Trevor Horn and their familiars, Steve Lipson and his wife, all arrived. In my nervous, nightmare state they appeared as reptiles, repulsive with ugly souls. I felt like Cinderella with a surfeit of ugly sisters. It seemed to me that whenever I had to pass Steve Lipson in the corridor, he would snigger loudly and leer in my direction in an attempt to unnerve me, like a middle-aged schoolboy. His bulbous eyes, yellow teeth, pallid complexion and thin strands of long hair put me in mind of Klaus Kinski's Nosferatu.

For the first week or so, while ZTT were giving their evidence, the gentlemen of the press were there feverishly writing down ZTT's accusations and slurs on my character. The plaintiffs' tactics seemed to consist of trying to persuade the court that I was lacking in singing ability and was an awkward person. This attempted character assassination was to continue for the next two weeks. The press made much of ZTT's statement that on our first two number one hit records 'Relax' and 'Two Tribes' there was no actual playing done by any member of the band but me. Parallels were drawn with The Bay City Rollers, The Monkees etc., and the words 'manufactured pop group' were bandied about a lot. Most of these articles failed to point out that the band had written the songs, unlike any of the aforementioned manufactured pop groups. At least Trevor had the decency to testify, 'I could never have done these records in isolation. There was no actual playing by the band on either record but all the music was by the band and the whole feeling came from the band.' There was the fact that I had sung on all these records, but ZTT plotted to bring even that into question, with further claims about my 'inept' singing.

The only writers to see right through these allegations were David Sinclair and Andrew Billen in an article that appeared in *The Times* on 6th February 1988: 'But if Holly Johnson's singing was nothing more than a convenient tonal source from which Horn was able to build perfect pop songs, why is he so keen to keep the singer on his label? ... Practically all the instrumentation on Stevie Wonder's last album was generated by Synclavier, and other prominent users of the computer synthesizer include Sting and Peter Gabriel. Yet nobody accuses those artists of sitting back and letting machines produce their music.' Furthermore, no one had ever asked for their money back after seeing me sing live during the hundred plus concerts that I had performed in the last few years.

* * *

The benches we had to sit on were rock-hard and uncomfortable, the courtroom overheated. Sessions lasted from nine o'clock until twelve, then from one until four. The barrister for the other side was called Mr Andrew Bateson QC. He had locked horns with my barrister Mark Cran in an earlier music business court case, over the Wham!/Innervision contract.

After the first day at court we were called to Mark Cran's chambers where lots of questions were asked. It lasted until eight o'clock and was completely exhausting. Wolfgang seemed to enjoy the whole process, as he had a positive vision of the proceedings, believing that we would win. I on the other hand was full of trepidation.

The judge, Mr Justice Whitford, seemed bored and angry with the case from the word go. In fact, as the case progressed the judge became more and more angry that the case was not settled out of court. On a number of occasions he suggested that the drawing out of the proceedings smacked of a battle of the bank balances rather than a real attempt to settle a dispute.

Jill Sinclair was the first witness to take the stand, requesting that she should be questioned sitting down due to some medical complaint, the poor thing. She dripped some kind of brown liquid into a glass of water from an eye dropper. After about half an hour her eyes took on a glazed appearance. She gave evidence over several days, often not answering the questions properly and wandering off into her own little agenda. She claimed that this was the first record contract that she had negotiated and that she depended wholly on her solicitor's advice.

The judge commented disapprovingly on the way Jill Sinclair gave evidence, not answering the questions properly and succinctly, if I remember rightly. Trevor sat on the bench prompting her constantly with hand signals and mouthing words in her direction.

On the third day ZTT claimed that in order that their evidence should be clear to him, the judge should visit Sarm Studios. The evidence in question was the reason behind the claim that the 'Liverpool' album had cost £800,000 to record.

Lola the studio manager greeted the judge and barristers and showed them round the complex. They were then taken to studio two where Lipson demonstrated the 'wonders' of the Synclavier. He played samples of the all girl vocal group The Mint Juleps (whose album Trevor and Lipson were working on – another relationship to end acrimoniously in the wake of huge costs and failed singles).

In an attempt to show the judge how much Trevor's expertise had contributed to the success of the band, the demo of 'Relax' recorded in a few hours at the BBC studios in Maida Vale was played to him. Then the polished, seven-inch version of 'Relax' was played, the recording of which had taken three months. After about a minute of this version the judge said, 'That's enough, we've just heard that'. Trevor's mouth fell open quite visibly at this comment. Trevor and his bug-eyed accomplice Lipson had lost that round.

Courtroom Karma

By the end of the first week in court the judge said some sort of settlement should be made by both parties. However, in the event, the weekend negotiations came to nothing because ZTT's demands were too high.

Trevor took the stand on the Monday morning, looking very nervous. Jill rushed over to the stand to administer her brown potion to Trevor's drinking water and about a half hour later he too had that glazed look in his eyes. Mr Bateson made a big show of how many awards Trevor had received for his work as a producer. Trevor burst out laughing at one point with what seemed like smug self satisfaction, but was possibly nerves. His eyes seemed rather wide as if he was in a state of permanent shock, and this effect, heightened by the magnification of his rather Seventies spectacles, gave him the look of a rather terrified owl.

Trevor denied that he had told me that he was going to produce our second album. There was more talk of how difficult I was, especially over the question of the band's publishing splits. Trevor had to admit that the publishing splits were technically correct.

Sometime during this particular day Paul Rutherford, Ped and Mark turned up at the courtroom. Later on I bumped into Paul who said that he had come to offer moral support, but I really felt no warmth in his presence. I made an attempt to chat to him like a old friend but there was nothing left. Years later he told me that they had all turned up at the court in an attempt to intimidate Trevor while he gave evidence, and indeed this may have been their intention, who knows. In the afternoon Steve Lipson and his sidekick Heff Moraes gave their evidence. They both claimed they did not remember my telling Lipson that I was unhappy with him producing the 'Liverpool' album. 'I don't remember' was a much-used line during the giving of ZTT's evidence.

At the end of the second week the judge announced that it was unlikely that the injunction would stand. Although this was no guarantee that I would get off scot free, it did seem to indicate that I would be allowed to record for MCA.

During all of this, Wolfgang was suffering from terrible stomach cramps and back pains. He was worried about his sister, still ill in Germany. My nerves were completely shot, especially as it was nearing the time I would have to go into the witness stand to be cross examined. I asked my doctor to prescribe something that would keep me calm yet alert. He came up with Pranalol, which is commonly used by snooker players to stop their hands shaking on television.

When I took the stand, Mr Bateson came out with a string of quick-fire questions designed to make me look ungrateful towards ZTT. His main argument was that I had been a complete unknown collecting Social Security before I met Trevor Horn. He suggested that I had gone from poverty to earning hundreds of thousands of pounds solely due to the efforts of Trevor. Much was made of the million pounds in payments that had been made to me or were about to be made to me, mainly from Perfect Songs. All I could answer to his questions was 'Yes' or 'No', mostly 'Yes'. I could not deny that partly through the efforts of ZTT I had become a well-known recording artist, and had earned a substantial amount of money. I did not believe, however, that I should be forever grateful and allow them my soul for eternity.

Luckily this first cross examination only lasted about fifteen minutes. I was not on winning form. For a start I had Jill Sinclair, Trevor Horn and friends grimacing and pulling faces at me in an attempt to put me off my stride. To me they looked like little goblins sitting behind their barrister, gesticulating for all they were worth, looking at each other in mock horror as I came out with a certain phrase, the next minute mouthing telling curses in my direction.

The next morning was a different story. I seemed to have an

answer for all of Mr Bateson's questions. He no longer intimidated me. In fact he seemed to me rather desperate when he tried to drag my sexuality into it. He asked me whether Trevor had suggested to the rest of the band at a meeting on Jersey that 'Holly and Wolfgang should be thought of as a married couple'. I answered 'Yes, Trevor did say that,' neither confirming nor denying my sexuality. My answer to this question was widely reported in the press the next day: GAY STAR AND HIS 'WIFE' appeared in *The Sun*, as if homosexuality was a crime one admits to!

Mr Bateson then produced a folder of photographs for both me and the judge to peruse. All the shots of the band in bondage wear taken by John Stoddard in the folder were labelled BEFORE ZTT, and the photographs of the band in expensive designer suits were labelled AFTER ZTT. This was a truly desperate action, attempting to imply that we were creatures of degradation before coming into contact with the moralising influence of a caring, benevolent record company. ZTT had absolutely no say in what we wore at any time. They had obviously forgotten to put that clause in the contract, thank heavens.

After my second cross examination by Mr Bateson, the score was nil to him and ten to me. I managed to confuse him by telling him the story of the other band members banging on my hotel door late at night in Ku-Klux-Klan masks shouting, 'Come out you Nazi bastards!' He feverishly looked through his notes, not remembering whether or not the event had been mentioned before. Mark Cran gestured to me to continue talking. His accusations against Wolfgang I swept aside effortlessly, saying that Wolfgang was used by everyone as a scapegoat and had not been responsible for the break up of the band as had been suggested.

Fleet Street of course lapped up the 'Klan' anecdote, a story I had not intended to tell; it just came out. KU KLUX KLAN RAID ON HOLLY'S GAY PAL screamed *Today*. HOLLY'S KU KLUX ORDEAL echoed *The Daily Mirror*.

That night as we rode home along the Embankment a rainbow

glowed like a bridge over the Thames. It seemed like a sign that things were going our way.

Mark Cran began his summing up on Wednesday morning. It consisted of a detailed analysis of the contract. Some time during the case I remember the judge saying that according to the contract, 'Mr Johnson could be seventy years old and still be bound to this contract, then I suspect even the Synclavier could not enhance his performance'.

Brian Howard told me that a ZTT solicitor had come round to Russells' office with another settlement offer. I would have to reimburse all of ZTT's costs and also allow them the publishing rights to my next three albums. We calculated that their costs were in the region of £200,000. I couldn't possibly have got that amount together and furthermore I didn't like the idea of them having the copyright of the fruits of my future labours.

Over the next couple of days Mr Bateson gave his summing up. He claimed that there had been an equality of bargaining position when the contract had been signed. The judge knew by now whether that was true or not.

Friday the 5th of February was the last day of the hearing. Another settlement offer was put on the table by ZTT. This time the terms were that each side should pay its own costs, but I had to pay them a percentage of the profits on an unspecified number of albums and give them the publishing rights on my next album. I thought about it all morning. A few people urged me to accept the offer, including Mark Cran, who said a settlement would buy me certainty, especially from an appeal, if I won this hearing. I tried to persuade myself to settle, but couldn't help thinking that after all the effort and the expense there would be no judgement to show for it. If I won, the judgement would help future artists. I had read legal notes on other cases including one by Wham! and another that involved The Tourists (Annie Lennox and Dave Stewart). As these cases had been settled out of court there had been no progress involving these types of agreement. Wolfgang believed we would win and urged me not to settle. So on the last day of the hearing we turned down ZTT's offer of settlement.

Victory and Vitriol

My absolute favourite tabloid story appeared that February in *The Daily Mirror*. 'FRANKIE STOLE MY BOYFRIEND – "losing a bloke to another girl was one thing but to lose him to Holly was just too much," says dancing girl Julie Muscatelli.' Julie was one of the Muscatelli sisters who were, for a short time only, The Leather Pets. Maybe next time she will remember not to take her boyfriend to a gay club, which was where I met this particular gentleman on the night in question. I believe that he asked me if he could stay at my flat that night. I do hope that she got paid well for that particular little gem. It was one of the few wholly true stories that have ever been printed about me.

After a few days we received a date on which the judgement would be read, the day between my birthday and Wolfgang's, the 10th of February 1988. On the evening of the ninth, we celebrated our combined birthdays at a dinner party at The Blue Elephant, a local Thai restaurant. Sue Cunningham, a friend, gave Wolfgang a book, *The Divine Marlene*, about his favourite movie star Dietrich. When Marlene died a few years later, Wolfgang was heard saying, 'Now I have the best legs in the world.'

Just before we left for the dinner party, I got a call from Brian Howard; ZTT had attempted some further settlement negotiations. Our last word on the matter was that I should be set free from the contract and each party would pay their own costs. ZTT's sense of greed or pride could not accept that, and they asked for the publishing rights to my next album for five years on an eighty/twenty split in my favour. I was urged to settle by both Tony Russell and Brian Howard, who kept repeating that I would be ensured certainty.

I finally decided we might as well take the risk and hear the judgement, as otherwise all this effort would have been wasted as

273

far as any change in the law was concerned. If we won, it would be the first time an artist was to be released from a recording agreement on the basis that it was in restraint of trade. Besides, if I were to settle now, I would always be left wondering what the outcome would have been.

The next day the court room was full. There were reporters from press, television and radio. Many music business lawyers and record company business affairs department heads had turned up to hear the verdict, as this judgement would have a direct influence on the kind of recording agreements they were allowed to draw up. I was on tenterhooks as the judge began to read his lengthy judgement. I must admit that after hearing it I still wasn't sure whether we had won or lost. I had to ask Tony Russell who was sitting next to me. I remember Simon Garfield the journalist congratulating me, then we left the court. Mariella Frostrup, my publicist, suggested that she should guide me out of the court where TV news people were waiting, probably so she could get in on the pictures. I was a bit dazed but I'm sure I had a huge grin on my face. I couldn't bring myself to look at Jill and Trevor. I didn't want appear as smug as I felt. I remember saying dramatically something like, 'It's a great day for all artists everywhere, future generations will never be under such extreme restraints again'.

It was arranged for me to do an interview on TVam the next morning. Anne Diamond was currently in a dispute with her manager over a contract and hoped that my case would have a bearing on hers. I had expected not to like Ms Diamond, but it was hard not to like her in such an ebullient mood. There was also an appearance on the BBC's 'Breakfast Time'. I could have made several more TV appearances – 'Wogan' etc. – but I felt that I didn't want to become famous only for court cases. I did do an interview for the *NME*, one of the few times they weren't completely critical of me. All of a sudden I had become a media event, after a year of being in the wilderness.

Not all the press was favourable of course. While we were in the news one journalist chose her moment to write her extremely racist and homophobic article 'How Gay Wolfman Got His Claws Into Holly'.

Sometime around September 1987 I had done an interview with a tabloid journalist. I asked for copy approval, and we had a signed agreement. She came to our house and we chatted in the garden and had tea and cakes. It was all very pleasant. Possibly in an attempt to ingratiate herself, she told me that she was a lesbian, probably after her tape recorder was switched off. She also said that her girlfriend had died and because there was no last will and testament, she did not inherit her girlfriend's estate, including the home they shared. We discussed the unfairness of this situation. For those who don't know, partners in a homosexual or lesbian couple are not recognised by English Law as being each other's next of kin. In fact, some families have gone so far as not allowing the remaining partner to attend the funeral of their deceased partner.

I made a few amendments to her article, probably cutting unnecessary and sensational references to my sexuality. It was published and I thought that was the end of it all, until a few weeks later when she contacted me and asked for my permission to sell the article to *The Sun*. I was peeved, as she knew that I would not have agreed to the interview in the first place if it had been for *The Sun*. She tried to make me feel guilty about the fact that she would lose money if I did not allow her to sell the article. Still I said no.

A while later she turned up at a rehearsal session to interview Mark O'Tool. Wolfgang said to Mark that he shouldn't really do an interview with 'that cow!' as she had tried to sell my interview to *The Sun*, or something to that effect – a comment which she overheard.

Almost eighteen months later, just after the court case, Wolfgang and I were photographed by a woman sitting in a car outside our house. She had obviously been lying in wait. When Wolfgang asked what she was doing, she lied, saying she was just a fan who wanted a photo. She quickly rolled up her window and sped off. The following Sunday the article appeared in *The News Of The World*. The article claimed to be the story of the 'Sinister German who has taken over rock idol's life'. It was a most ridiculous yet malicious article. It described Wolfgang as a

'Domineering Hun' who was 'virtually Holly's MASTER'. The word 'Hun' I have always found just as repellent as the words 'Kike' and 'Nigger'. I was apparently forced to do the housework by him and had become a willing servant, she claimed. Not only is it a racist article but it also depicts a stereotypical image of a gay relationship, Master and Servant, Butch and Bitch, in a crude and vindictive manner.

* * *

We had about ten days of business meetings and a few parties. Margit Riette, English correspondent for German-based *Bravo* magazine (the biggest selling pop magazine in the world), had a fancy-dress birthday party in her home outside London. She was a vibrant and interesting woman from East Germany who worked in film production and music journalism. Ever since I had met her in 1984 I knew that she was suffering from some form of cancer, but she just went on living it up regardless. That night she was dressed all in silver. She said she had come as 'Space 1999', a Seventies sci-fi TV series. Kim Wilde was also at the party dressed as a cossack with two American Policemen as armed guards; she looked stunning. The idea was for the party to be a genuine Bal Masqué where guests removed their masks at midnight to reveal their true identity.

I spend most of the evening talking to Andy Pandy and Oscar Wilde, a quarrelsome couple. Andy Pandy had just written a play called 'Screamers' about the loss of innocence of a fifteen-year-old boy hairdresser. He accused me of talking to Oscar only because he was rich. I told him not to be so stupid. He attempted a literary witticism as Wolfgang ushered me out of the door. I shut him up with a pointed look in Oscar Wilde's direction. 'OOOER!' was all Andy Pandy could manage.

Our sense of victory and celebration did not last long. Only ten days after the judgement, Wolfgang chatted to his sister Heidi on the phone in her intensive care hospital room. She had just eaten two large slices of strawberry gâteau and was feeling fine. An hour or so later he received another call, this time from his sister

Crystal, who broke the news to him that Heidi had died. Wolfgang cried and cried. We spent the rest of the afternoon organising flights to Germany, so we could attend Heidi's funeral. I felt powerless to help Wolfgang in his loss. I found it difficult to talk to him about it. I had not known Heidi very well and I didn't realise that Wolfgang needed to talk about her in order to come to terms with it. I thought that I should try and distract him from thinking too much about her, which was a mistake. So like a rollercoaster ride we were down in the valleys again after being so very up in the clouds.

Blast

A few days after returning from the funeral of Wolfgang's sister in Germany, we heard the news that we had been granted all court costs. This meant that, as well as paying their own costs, ZTT had to pay all of mine as well.

We now found ourselves up to our necks in new contractual negotiations, as we only had signed a preliminary agreement with MCA. A proper contract had to be negotiated. For this exercise an experienced music business solicitor was required. The cost of negotiating a major record deal can cost (and in fact did cost us) sixty thousand pounds. The artist has to pay this out of his/her advance, as well as management commission – anything up to 20% on the gross.

* * *

In an attempt to escape from it all, I persuaded Wolfgang to take a holiday in Barbados. We booked two rooms in a small private hotel called The Palace – in fact, it only had two rooms. In one room I could write songs and record them on a portable four track. In the other we could both sleep. The hotel was run by a native Bajan, an ageing ex-dancer/model called Carl. We were told about it by friends – Anthony Price had stayed there the year before.

Things were pretty idyllic for the first week until the owner told us he had let the room that I was using to work in to two Americans. The house was small and we didn't want, all of a sudden, to have to share the space that we felt that we had rented. So we moved out to The Paradise Beach Hotel near Bridgetown. We had fun there with the British Airways staff, who had been given holidays and a discount at the hotel. The two air hostesses we ended up spending the most of our time with were Melody and Rhapsody. I was surprised to discover that they were also on the hunt for some grass. We gave some money to a beach bum Rasta called Nicholas Parsons, who came back eventually with the precious leaves, and we all got stoned in Melody's room. When we spotted a huge insect on her bedside lamp, paranoia ensued, and we laughed hysterically as she started to bang and shake her glossy black mane of tight curls. We gave the insect a name: Charlene – The Bajan Queen.

The next day on the beach we were approached by some Dutch sailors (and a sailoress, Yolande, the radio operator). They recognised me from Dutch TV. We were invited to their warship which was bound for Curaçao. Wolfgang stayed on deck talking to a blonde, blue-eyed 'Querelle', while I braved the galley down below. I couldn't believe the cramped conditions down there. I suppose they get used to all that close proximity. It put me in mind of a story told by Jean Cocteau, of how he and a friend smoked opium below decks with somnambulist sailors, their naked bodies entwined. This was much less of an orgy. I was only allowed to take photographs of certain parts of the ship in case I was some kind of spy. I was amazed and pleased to see a hundred bicycles in the hold where the weapons of war would usually be kept. The Dutch really are a nation of cyclists.

I listened to Radio Liberty playing Calypso music at six am, as the sound of the sea would wake me early in the morning. Wolfgang looked out of our window and saw a beach kid climb effortlessly up a coconut tree, grab a large fruit and slide elegantly down again. Breakfast in Barbados. Before we left I spotted Oliver Reed at a beachside café, Giggles Bar. His cornflower-blue eyes stood out against the turquoise of the sea. It was easy to see why he was a movie star with those pale sapphire pupils. He was drinking with a young blonde woman. I said hello as we were leaving and he gave me a big wink.

After a few more days of Bajan sunshine, we flew home on the same plane as our air hostess friends. They kindly upgraded our tickets which made for a more comfortable ride.

The beauty of Barbados inspired me to write the music to two songs while I was there – 'Love Will Come' and 'Got It Made' – which both made it on to the 'BLAST' album that I was soon to record. I had already written both lyrics back in England and the melodies seemed to float in on the sea breeze.

* * *

My vision for the new album was to dress it up in the graphics and typography of Vorticism. Early this century Wyndham Lewis, the artist and writer, broke away from the Bloomsbury set and Omega workshop created by Roger Fry. In doing so he formed an opposing movement that was partly a reaction to the romanticism and decorative aspects of Bloomsbury. He called this movement Vorticism and with the help of Ezra Pound, published a puce-coloured iconoclastic magazine called *BLAST*. There was even a manifesto signed by the artists of the day: William Roberts, Frederick Etchells and so on. Mostly inspired by the Italian Futurist movement and Cubism, it was the only organised British art movement this century. Never really successful in wide terms of popularity, it soon fizzled out, but it was the product of an incredibly forceful personality. I had started to collect reprints of the *BLAST* publications (Black Sparrow Press) and decided to use the visual language in a pop context. I took my ideas to Roysten and David at the design company called Accident, as they had both been involved with the designs for the Frankie Goes To Hollywood products. Some of these record sleeves now reside in the Victoria and Albert Museum's permanent collection of packaging design.

S.U.C.C.E.S.S.?

When I got home I realised that my honeymoon period with MCA was over. It seems that once they believe they 'own' you, record company staff start trying to impose their will on you. I was convinced I could make a good record with the help of Steve Lovell, and Andy Richards, who had done a lot of the programming on the Frankie records. MCA were extremely doubtful as these two weren't big international names in the field of production. After much argument though, MCA allowed me to record two tracks with these two co-producing. I felt that I owed it to Steve especially, as he had helped me so diligently with the demos.

Steve and Andy plumped for the best two songs, 'Americanos' and 'Love Train'. They both wanted to work on songs they thought were the potential hits. Things went swimmingly with 'Love Train', which came alive as Andy programmed away. 'Americanos' was more difficult as the demo had been so good. We couldn't somehow recreate the magic. Wolfgang and I decided that it needed a new approach. The slow-moving R and B bassline seemed inappropriate and plodding all of a sudden, to us anyway. This caused a bit of a stink in the studio as Steve and Andy didn't want to present the record company with something radically different from what was expected. To make matters worse, Andy played the half-finished tracks to Jill Steen, the A and R person. This had a terrible effect on our in-the-studio relationships. Steve and I also felt that Andy spent too much time on the instrumentation and not enough on the vocals, the single most important thing in any recording.

A stroke of luck and an act of genuine kindness during the recording helped the final product a lot. I was walking back to the studio when I bumped into Brian May from Queen. Brian shook

my hand and said something like, 'Anyone who can stick it to
**** ******** is alright by me'. I was amazed as I gazed up at
this giant in clogs. I thanked him and told him how much I liked
the soundtrack for the film *Highlander* that Queen had
composed, especially 'Who Wants To Live Forever'. Later I got
Andy to ask Brian if he would contribute a guitar solo to 'Love
Train' which he did in just a few takes, leaving several of his
sixpence pieces, which he used as plectrums, behind in the
studio.

In an attempt to bring the album in on budget, things were
hurried along at the mixing stage. When I finally played the two
tracks to David Simone, he hit the roof. He didn't think they
were good enough. He exploded, screaming something like 'I've
spent £300,000 on you so far and I don't even have a signed
contract'. He demanded I sack Steve and Andy from the song
project. I felt rather guilty. I knew the recordings were good, but
I also knew that they lacked some 'X' factor. I told David Simone
that I was unhappy with Jill Steen as an A and R person, refusing
to work with her any longer. Simone didn't know what to do
about that side of things as he didn't have any other A and R
people except for Tim Bullymint. He was wheeled into a
subsequent meeting and started to slag off the two tracks that I
had presented. I was getting my first lessons in record company
politics.

In desperation, I contacted producer Stephen Hague myself. I
loved the work he had done with Malcolm McLaren and The Pet
Shop Boys, and had heard that he had played all the keyboards
on their first hit, 'West End Girls'. I got an agreement from him
that he would do additional production on 'Love Train' and
would produce two other tracks, 'S.U.C.C.E.S.S.' and 'Heaven's
Here'. I had to wait several months for him though, as he was
booked up. During this time I demo'ed more material at home
with Nick Bagnall, a keyboard/bass player from Newcastle who
Bullymint had introduced me to.

I enjoyed working with Nick; a trained musician, he helped a
lot in terms of arrangement ideas. He had narrowly escaped
signing to ZTT as part of a group called the V Corporation. He

had met Jill Sinclair for the first time in the reception area of Sarm Studios in the late Eighties. One of the first things she said to him according to Nick, a complete stranger to her, was, 'We are having trouble with Holly Johnson at the moment.' More trouble than she then knew. I think this event made Nick immediately wary of getting involved with a record company whose owners complain about their artists to people they have never met before.

In the end the Hague sessions took up one third of our whole album budget for two tracks and a remix. One track ('S.U.C.C.E.S.S.') we ended up scrapping because it was so overdone. What Stephen did achieve however was a marked improvement on 'Love Train' and a very polished version of 'Heaven's Here'. We worked hard on the vocals of 'Love Train' and Stephen also reprogrammed some of the drums. I had enjoyed working with him and his engineer Spike. I might have continued to work with him but he had a Père Ubu album project all of a sudden and wouldn't be free till the following year. It was now the end of September 1988.

A stroke of luck then occurred: Bullymint introduced me to Dan Hartman – another American producer and someone I got on with really well. I was worried that Dan might be a bit middle-of-the-road or R and B at first, thinking that he wouldn't understand the kind of electronic album I wanted to make, although I loved the work he had done with James Brown. Luckily Dan seemed to pull the rest of the album together for me. He had some great brass samples and, like Stephen Hague, he used the same Sequencer Programme 'Performer' that I used on my Apple Macintosh computer. Dan taught me things that I would never have learned on the machine. He also co-wrote 'Atomic City' with me. 'Atomic City' was a 'concept' and a string of disconnected musical ideas that I already had composed. Dan helped me to put them all together and created the funky backdrop that was needed.

Meanwhile Stock, Aitken and Waterman mixers Ian Curnow and Phil Harding had done a very commercial remix of 'Americanos'. I found it too commercial really, just a bit too

Kylie and Jason. Dan eventually helped me to combine the better elements from the two versions of 'Americanos' to form the final version that satisfied my snobbery.

Wolfgang and I visited Wolfgang's relatives in Pittsburgh at Christmas time, the idea being that we would spend Christmas there then go to West Port, Connecticut to spend New Year with Dan, since he had agreed to rerecord 'S.U.C.C.E.S.S.' in his own studio; studio time which he did not charge for. He also planned to mix a mammoth 48-track version of 'Atomic City' at The Hit Factory in New York.

We flew direct to Pittsburgh on the same day and time as the plane (bound for New York) involved in the tragic Lockerbie disaster. Meanwhile back in London at the rather drunken, journalist-filled MCA Christmas party, the rumour started to spread that I was on the ill-fated flight. In Pittsburgh, Wolfgang's sister heard an announcement on the TV news that we had been on the plane and it was even printed in *USA Today*. I had to ring home fast to let everyone know that I was still alive. I think some people in MCA might have been a little disappointed, as a dead singer in a famous air disaster would have done wonders for record sales.

The singles 'Love Train', 'Americanos' and 'Atomic City' did extremely well in Europe and the rest of the world, selling over a million singles between them, and 'Love Train' and 'Americanos' were both Top Five in the UK. They were helped along by a few rather expert and expensive videos. Maybe this was not as impressive as the five million plus that 'Relax' had sold on its own, but times were changing. People just weren't buying records in the same quantities any more. 'BLAST' went into the British charts at number one in April 1989 and got some extremely good reviews, even in the music press. MCA had not had a number one album for over ten years and I doubt they have had one since. 'BLAST' eventually went platinum. The 'Liverpool' album had only got to number four with Trevor Horn's name on it.

I'd proved I could sing and write songs without the help of Trevor Horn, but I didn't want to harp on about my success, because I knew how transient pop success can be. In America, I felt that it was going to be very difficult to get MCA to promote the 'BLAST' album. They were having huge success with Bobby Brown and Fine Young Cannibals, both acts that were signed direct to the American label. MCA UK, under a host of managing directors, have never really managed to persuade MCA America to promote one of their acts over there. All profits would have to show up on the UK company books, so no US employee was going to stick their neck out on their behalf. I also believed that no American record company was prepared to promote an artist who had been open about his homosexuality before he'd had much success over there. Erasure had not fulfilled their potential in America either. Boy George's US career seemed to take a dive when he came out of the closet, as did Elton John's, although a later marriage seemed to mend things a little. America has proved itself time and again to be the most homophobic nation. America's decision to ban the entry of any human being carrying the HIV virus is just an extension of that homophobia and bigotry. We employed Vicky Whickham, manager of Nona Hendryx and Dusty Springfield, to represent us and investigate the whole MCA America situation. She told us that David Simone, the English 'maverick', was not without his critics within the company and that his efforts for the UNI label were being blocked. He had managed to get 'Americanos' on to the soundtrack of the Susan Seidelman film *Cookie*, but MCA just would not cough up the $70,000 to promote 'Love Train'. We are told in the music business that this is the approximate amount of money required to get a single off the ground in the USA. One of the reasons for this we heard was that MCA had been recently involved in a government action involving some kind of radio payola scandal, so they were being very conservative with their independent promotion budgets. But for whatever reason, it did not happen for us in America in the way it was happening in Europe. We even foolishly turned down several European promotion trips to do an American promotion trip that kept getting rescheduled on us.

A and Rrseholes

Just before 'BLAST' was released, Wolfgang and I were invited to dinner by Elton John through our mutual record plugger Gary Farrow. George Michael was also invited, along with some other people including Elton's substantial entourage. I really couldn't miss the opportunity to have dinner with the Queen Mother of English Pop Music.

Elton had his rather good-looking friend, Gary, with him; the one whose support, I later discovered, had brought Elton back from the depths of drug and alcohol addiction (in a tabloid newspaper, at least). He was a kind of male Southern Belle in his prime, tall and tanned, looking like he had just stepped out of a glossy magazine fashion spread.

A crate of Cristal champagne was consumed. Elton informed me jokingly that I was much more 'common' than he thought I would be. I had to laugh at that one. I quizzed him about some of my heroes. He didn't have much to say about David Bowie, only some story about Bowie telling *Rolling Stone* magazine that he had taken Elton to a gay club at a time when Elton was far from public or comfortable about his sexuality. Elton said his marriage a few years previously was a serious thing, especially for his wife, Renata. My mouth dropped open visibly after he told me this.

George asked me if I was pleased with the album I had just finished; I told him I was. He and Elton then started talking about how many millions of albums 'so and so' had just sold and my mind just switched off. George and Elton disappeared from the table for a few minutes, when George asked Elton if he would like to see his new Coca Cola advertisement on the video screen in the back of his gold Mercedes limousine. A moment of true glamour.

* * *

Later in 1989, Wolfgang organised a tour, but I chickened out of it. I had unhappy memories of the Frankie tours and didn't feel like it. MCA were also not prepared to pay tour support for some reason, which made me more nervous, even though the guarantees from the promoter were substantial. I am prepared to admit this was probably a big mistake. It would have helped promote the album in a way that TV appearances just cannot do. Touring seems to give an artist a certain cachet, and during the tour the levels of publicity surrounding the artist seem to escalate.

I had been working extremely hard promoting 'BLAST' into being a hit all over Europe but by Winter 1989 my health had started to suffer, and I had to cancel an important German TV show due to a very bad bout of 'flu I could not shake off. During a previous promotion trip to Germany for a televised *Bravo* magazine party, the glands in the right side of my neck had swollen up to the size of a golf ball. I knew that this was one of the symptoms of ARC (Aids Related Complex) and all my old fears came back to haunt me. I still could not pluck up the courage to have a HIV test. 'Everyone has got this very bad 'flu', I kept telling myself. These health fears were another reason why I did not want to tour, as I knew how physically wearing tours could be. Over the next year I had lots of strange infections, one particular ear infection seeming to go on for ever, making singing difficult. I was not also feeling pressure to write songs for my next album. I knew how disastrous second albums could be from the Frankie days, and was starting to suffer from stress.

*   *   *

I was approached by Tony Pope concerning the name Frankie Goes To Hollywood. Mark O'Tool, Brian Nash and Peter Gill had, with the aid of a new singer, managed to raise some interest at an independent record company called Siren. I was informed by Tony Pope that the only way that Siren would sign this band was if I allowed them to use the name Frankie Goes To Hollywood. He also claimed that if I did not, they would have to disband and go home to Liverpool. 'After all,' he went on, 'You have had so much success as a solo artist, what difference would it make to you if they used the name?' This little attempt at emotional blackmail did have me thinking for a while. Most of my friends (particularly Biffa) advised me, 'Don't let them have the name, you owe them nothing. It was they who treated you badly.' MCA also asked me not under any circumstances to allow them the use of the name. My solicitor advised me to get them to pay for the name, in terms of override points on future product and he started to negotiate with them. I eventually decided, though, that I did not want them to bring the name I had created into further disrepute. I was pretty sure that the songs they had written were not great: otherwise, why would the record company only want them if they could use the name? They obviously just wanted to sell the product on the name and had no real confidence in it. So, after much deliberation, I told my solicitor to inform them that they could not use it. I still had the document that we had all signed years before, the one that was drawn up to stop me from running off with the name and dumping them. It also stated that if a member left the group, then the others had to come to me for permission to use the name.

* * *

More and more I began to associate music and the making of it with the stressful business dealings surrounding it. I started to escape into painting, as a way of expressing myself uncompromised and unaided.

Over the next few years I started to hear about the deaths of other old friends. Tweela, Tim and Richard, all ex-flatmates of mine, died of AIDS-related illnesses. I was also told that Juicy Lucy, the fabulous drag queen who danced with the Frankies on our first promotional tour, had been diagnosed as having AIDS. During the filming of a video for 'Heaven's Here' from the 'BLAST' album I got to work with the legendary make up artist Pierre La Roche, the man who painted the original two-tone flash of lightning on David Bowie's face for the album cover of 'Aladdin Sane'. He too was struck down by the disease. The dreaded virus seemed to get closer and closer as I heard of each new diagnosis or death of an old friend or acquaintance, most of whom I had lost contact with in the frenzy of working like a madman on my 'career' and contractual obligations. These were starting to weight me down, like the stones in the pockets of Virginia Woolf.

For some reason MCA did not release the 'BLAST' video compilation at Christmas time. Considering those videos were some of the most-shown clips of 1989, it was extremely dumb of them. They were rather busy concentrating on a terrible group called Transvision Vamp. Around this time David Simone left in another of MCA's famous shake ups. I was now left high and dry at a record company without the man who had believed in me. I thought the remaining staff unspectacular in their abilities, especially the overextended A and R department. I was inspired to create a new title for the Artists and Repertoire department: to me they acted liked 'A and Rseholes'. Tony Powell, who had inherited the job of Managing Director, did not seem to have a grasp on what I wanted to achieve. My relationship with MCA started to go downhill very quickly.

During the spring of 1990 we finally forced MCA to release the 'BLAST' videos, although it was much too late by then. They also released a budget-priced album containing remixes of the 'BLAST' singles. There was a wonderful remix of 'Love Train' by the Godfather of house-music, Frankie Knuckles. It was the last creative thing that David Simone had done for me before his departure from MCA. The remix was not released in the UK and fans who wanted to buy it had to pay about ten pounds for the American import. We thought that it would be appreciated by fans if we created a remix album with unreleased remixes as well as some already released mixes at a low price. I also hoped that the album would be perceived as a contribution to the blooming dance music culture of the time. But 'Hollelujah', the resulting album, was hammered by the press who saw it as some kind of cash-in attempt. Only about three thousand albums were pressed by a reluctant MCA, so it was hardly that.

Taxi to the Pleasuredome

While still promoting the 'BLAST' album I did a photo session for the German *Bravo* magazine with my friend Margit. The day before I had visited Covent Garden to attend a dancers' casting session for the 'Atomic City' video shoot. I had noticed a small white dog in the window of a pet shop, looking almost like a spring lamb, and trying desperately to get out of the window. The next day I passed the shop again and insisted that we hire the dog for the photo session. Wolfgang fell in love with this wonderful puppy who was just twelve weeks old. We could not return him to the pet shop so we bought him. We named him Funky so we could say 'Get Down Funky!' whenever he sat on the table. In many ways he became our surrogate child.

Animals do not judge you by the way you look, the clothes you wear, how much money you have in the bank, or what your sexuality, colour or creed is. If you are kind to them they are kind to you. In fact he became more of a friend to me than many of the other fair-weather friends I had picked up then lost on the way. If I did not appear in the newspaper for a while then I would not hear from some of my so-called friends. It is something that you get used to after being in the public eye. People often judge or value one in terms of outward success.

Over the past few years I would say that my values have changed somewhat. I no longer seemed to crave worldly success in the same way as I had only a few years before. Most of the creative work that I have done in the past came out of an inner motivation.

* * *

Just before Christmas 1990, I bumped into Paul Rutherford in the

290

street, when I was taking Funky to the vet. He told me that while he was visiting Juicy Lucy in hospital he met Jake who was in another bed on the same ward. Jake too had been sick with an AIDS-related illness. This was quite a shock. I hadn't seen Jake for a few years and didn't even have his phone number. A few months later, Angela, the female dancer and star of the first 'Relax' video, phoned to say that Jake had died on Christmas Eve. I felt really bad that I had not made more of an attempt to contact him when I knew he was ill.

The last time I had spoken to Jake was on the phone. Tweela had just died and Jake was feeling guilty about the fact that they had fallen out over some stupid thing or other and had not been speaking. And now here I was feeling guilty for the same thing. Jake has appeared to me quite a few time in dreams, always smiling, healthy and happy. He gives me a hug in the same way as he did when he was alive and says, 'Everything is alright'. Maybe it's just my wishful thinking and maybe not.

*　*　*

MCA urged me to use their inhouse promotions department instead of Gary Farrow. And I certainly felt misunderstood by 1990. An album's worth of rather overproduced material was finished by September and MCA wanted to rush-release it for Christmas without time to formulate a proper marketing campaign. They knew that there was a feeling of recession in the air and believed Christmas was the last chance to sell substantial amounts of anything. We did not allow this to happen. In December they requested a period in which they could consider picking up the option of another album: they even offered us a substantial amount of money to grant the extension. But we felt that we had no real allies within the company at that time. The head of marketing had told Wolfgang over the phone that the marketing budget for my album was *ZERO*, quite remarkable considering the success of my previous album. So we waited until one week before the option deadline to turn down their application for an extension. They had no choice but to release us from the contract. We knew that this would result in MCA not promoting the album that I had made, and 'Dreams That Money Can't Buy' lay shelved at MCA for eight months after it was recorded. We believe that they would not have promoted it either way, as we had so few friends left at that company. Only a few thousand copies ever made it to the shops and only one advertisement was placed in this country.

In many ways it was a relief to have a debt of £600,000 wiped away in one fell swoop and freedom from all contractual obligations, but it was depressing that another relationship with another record company had gone sour. A few weeks after we parted company, MCA finally employed a Head of A and R who was unaware that I was no longer on the roster when he started his job. He spent a lot of time trying to get remixes done of some of the album tracks, but no marketing revenue was allotted to the fruits of his labour. It seemed that no one at MCA wanted a hit record out of an artist that they no longer owned.

I started to paint more and became quite withdrawn. 1990/91 was a period when record companies were savagely trimming their rosters rather than increasing them. I was rather reluctant to join in the scrabble, though I did record and write songs that summer.

* * *

Due to the multitude of minor ailments that I had been suffering from, I started to adapt a healthier lifestyle. I read books on nutrition and did daily exercise. In fact I became rather obsessive about it all, grasping at health but suffering from a frozen shoulder, eczema, fungal infections and a chest infection. I finally gave up smoking after ten years with the help of Louise Hays book *You Can Heal Your Life*, but even that didn't seem to have much of a positive effect on my health. I visited homeopaths and osteopaths and tried to embrace alternative therapies. Nothing seemed to work. I believed the stress of the Music Industry had taken its toll.

A couple of strange bumps started to appear on my skin in od places around the summer of 1991. I had a biopsy done on one on my stomach by a skin specialist at the Lister Hospital. I didn't hear from the doctor for a few weeks and when I finally did hear from him by phone, he wouldn't give me any information. Instead he referred me to another doctor at the same hospital, making an appointment for the same evening. I put the phone down and knew that there was something very wrong. Wolfgang wanted to go with me to the hospital but I wouldn't let him. It would have meant that our secretary would have had to stay behind to look after Funky and I didn't want her to see us come back from the hospital in an emotional state.

I took a black cab along the Embankment. It was October and the nights were drawing in. A pink-uniformed nurse asked me to wait while she took a tea tray to the doctor who was just about to start his evening clinic.

The doctor told me in a gentle way that the biopsy results showed that the lumps on my skin were Kaposi's Sarcoma, a rare cancer of the arteries. This disease, he told me, is associated with old Jewish men, people with syphilis and, more commonly, gay men with AIDS, which of course I knew. He urged me to have an HIV test and other tests, a T cell count for example. He talked about the drugs I could take, and also the safe sex measures that I had been practising for years anyway. After about half an hour of this I told him I wanted to leave, asking him how often he had to break this kind of news. 'Two or three times a week', he replied. I felt sorry for him. That can't be easy. I remember thinking, 'How is Wolfgang going to cope?' The fears of the last seven or eight years had all come true at once.

I rang for a taxi from the hospital lobby and waited numbly. I looked out of the window at the Chelsea Bridge, thinking I should just throw myself off it right now into the cold and murky Thames and have done with it. No, I wouldn't and couldn't. A big, strong-looking black man came through the electric doors and said 'Taxi for Pleasuredome?' I followed him and got in the back. He started talking about 'WAR', the Edwin Starr song that I had once sung, and also said he loved 'Welcome To The Pleasuredome'. He asked me if Frankie Goes To Hollywood

293

would ever reform. I tried to explain to him some of the perils of the music industry. We talked about money and how health was so important. He told me he was forty-five years old and did two hours of physical training per day. He looked fantastic!

Epilogue

Well I suppose I might have wandered the streets of Liverpool at fourteen, at two in the morning entertaining friends with a rendition of 'We're off to see the wizard . . . The Wonderful Wizard Of Oz' (dance steps included). I do however reserve the right to tell the story myself.

Readers of the manuscript have all questioned me why I chose this moment to end this particular story. I told myself that I did not want to end the book on such a black note; a note of despair. Perhaps I did not want to give the voyeur the full monte. 'What's it like to know you're going to die . . . sooner than later?' That is the question that I see on people's lips when they start to interview me on the subject of AIDS, etc. Nearer the truth perhaps is the fact that it is too soon for me to examine and analyse the process of coping with this particular piece of news. AIDS is THE modern day horror story, full of vampires – one of our biggest fears. Perhaps it was the way that the news crushed my *joie de vivre*, and perhaps my way of coping – a kind of gracelessness took over for a while – does not sit well with my vanity.

The truth is I felt very BAD, very sorry for myself . . . DIRTY, worthless, ANGRY, upset. I mourned my life, and apologised to Wolfgang that he had to experience this. I took it out on him. I am not proud about the way I coped immediately with the news. I was also not happy with some of the receptions that I received in the world of AIDS healthcare. But other such encounters were the most touching kindnesses that I have ever experienced . . . from the lower paid ends of the health service mostly.

I had to get over my own prejudices first. I do not pretend that I had not experienced feelings of discomfort when I was in the presence of PWAs (people with AIDS). Would a kiss from Lisa's

295

red painted lips somehow infect me? I went cold with fear. Would one tiny drop of Pierre's spittle which accidentally flew in my eye infect me? These feelings were perhaps symptoms of FEAR and DENIAL. I had a panic attack when I was told about the mysterious rash that was supposed to signify the onset of HIV infection. Perhaps it is still too BIG in my mind to examine the syndrome objectively.

The first time AIDS affected my creative work was a song called 'Is Anybody Out There?' from the 'Liverpool' album: 'If I could change the things I've done . . . Would I be the only one?' But no, I would have done all those things much more often.

One man on a phone-in television talk show expressed the opinion that PWA's deserved what they got as they had broken God's laws. This vile opinion lurks at the back of much judgmental diatribe on the subject of gays, those minorities whose sense of self-worth has been pummelled into submission from early childhood by a so-called Christian, heterosexual majority. Even one well-known, well-meaning AIDS-issue writer committed the ultimate insensitivity by telling me '. . . people with AIDS will endure a slow and painful death . . .' I was devastated by this remark, written in a trendy magazine, and lay in my hospital bed with it echoing round my brain.

I tolerate closet Queens less and less as I get older. They collude with the Roman Catholic church and others in promoting the belief that homosexuality is intrinsically evil. Be outed and be damned. Be found drunk in a gutter singing to the stars in a lime green tutu and turquoise stilettoes, waving a pink wand. 'But ye are in that wheelchair Blanche,' the world keeps reminding us. Well, this is one story of an ugly duckling who sprouted wings, wore ruby slippers, waved a magic wand, had three number-one records and learnt to fly right out of that wheelchair. And I'll be damned if I get back into it, unless it's designed by Vivienne Westwood!

Acknowledgements

Special thanks to: Manager; Wolfgang Kuhle.
Literary agent; Barbara Levy
EDITOR; MARK BOOTH
Assistants to the editor; Katrina Johnson, Lindsay Symons
Cover photo artists; Pierre et Gilles
Styling; Tomah, Hair; Tony Allen
Art director; Dennis Barker
Jacket design; The Senate, David Eldridge
Photo page design; Roger Walker
Conception; Holly Johnson, Wolfgang Kuhle, Mark Booth
Photo session co-ordinator; Yannick Morisot, Chris Billon
PR consultant; RMP, Regine Moylett
Century publicity; Liz Sich, Nicky Stonehill
Rights; Georgina Capell
Memory joggers; Wolfgang Kuhle, Clare Jones, Jayne Casey, Bob Johnson
All the staff at Random House
And all the nurses who worked on the Prince of Wales Ward in 1993.

Extracts from 'The Power of Love' (p.viii) and 'Relax' (p.151) reproduced by kind permission of Perfect Songs Ltd. Extracts from 'Suicide A Go-Go' (p.92), 'Nothing Special' (p.92-3) and 'S.C.U.M.' (p.93) reproduced by kind permission of Warner Chappell Music Ltd and International Music Publications Ltd.

Discography

Release Order

FRANKIE GOES TO HOLLYWOOD

Singles   *Albums*

Relax   Welcome To The Pleasuredome
Two Tribes   Liverpool
Power Of Love   Bang! The Greatest Hits Of F.G.T.H.
Welcome To The Pleasuredome
Rage Hard
Warriors Of The Wasteland
Watching the Wildlife
*Relax (Remixed)
Welcome To The Pleasuredome
(Remixed)
The Power Of Love (Remixed)

HOLLY JOHNSON

Singles   *Albums*

Love Train   Blast
Americanos   Hollelujah – Remix Album
Atomic City   Dreams That Money Can't Buy
Heaven's Here
Where Has Love Gone
Across The Universe
People Want To Dance

* Re-released 1993

FRANKIE GOES TO HOLLYWOOD
Official UK Discography

Singles

RELAX

7″	ZTAS	1	Relax/One September Monday (P) (Ltd Edition With Badge)
7″	PZTAS	1	Relax/One September Monday Picture Disc (Ltd Edition)
12″	12ZTAS	1	Relax (Original 16 Minute Mix)/Ferry/Instrumental (P) (33rpm)(1A 1U)
12″	12ZTAS	1	Relax (Sex Mix)/Ferry/Instrumental (P) (1A 1U)
12″	12ZTAS	1	Relax (7:20 US Remix)/Ferry/Instrumental (P) (1A 2U)
12″	12ZTAS	1	Relax (Sex Mix)/7″/Instrumental (P) (1A 4U)
12″	12ZTAS	1	Relax (Sex Mix)/Ferry/Instrumental (P) (1A 5U)
12″	12PZTAS	1	Relax (Sex Mix)/Ferry/Instrumental Picture Disc (Ltd Edition)
12″	12ZTAS	1	Relax (Sex Mix)/Ferry/Instrumental Re-Issue (ZTT Sleeve) (1A 5U)
12″	12ZTAS	1	Relax (Original 16 Minute Mix)/Ferry/Instrumental Re-Issue (ZTT Sleeve)(45rpm)
CASS	CTIS10	2	Relax "Greatest Bits" Cassingle (P) (Ltd Edition)

TWO TRIBES

7″	ZTAS	3	Two Tribes/One February Friday (P)
7″	PZTAS	3	Two Tribes (Diff Mix)/One February Friday Picture Disc (Ltd Edition)
12″	12ZTAS	3	Two Tribes (Annihilation)/War (Hide)/One February Friday/Surrender (P) (With Poster)
12″	XZTAS	3	Two Tribes (Carnage)/War (Hide)/One February Friday/Surrender (P)
12″	WARTZ	3	War (Hidden)/Two Tribes (Carnage)(P)
12″	WARTZ	3	War (Hidden)/Two Tribes (Carnage) Picture Disc (Ltd Edition)
12″	XZIP	1	Two Tribes (Hibakusha)/War (Hide)/One February Friday/Surrender (ZTT Sleeve)(Ltd Edition Remix)
CASS	CTIS10	3	Two Tribes "Keep The Peace" Cassingle (P) (Ltd Edition)

POWER OF LOVE

7″	ZTAS	5	Power Of Love/The World Is My Oyster (P) (In Ltd Edition Pink Envelope)
7″	PZTAS	5	Power Of Love/The World Is My Oyster Picture Disc (Ltd Edition)
12″	12ZTAS	5	Power Of Love (Extended)/The World Is My Oyster/Scrapped/Holier Than Thou (P) (In Ltd Edition Pink Envelope)

300

12″	12PZTAS	5	Power Of Love (Extended)/The World Is My Oyster/Scrapped/Holier Than Thou Picture Disc (Ltd Edition)
12″	XZTAS	5	Power Of Love/Pleasurefix/Starfix/The World Is My Oyster (P) (G/F) (With 5 B/W Prints)(Ltd Edition)
CASS	CTIS10	5	Power Of Love Cassingle (P) (In Ltd Edition Pink Envelope)

WELCOME TO THE PLEASUREDOME

7″	ZTAS	7	Pleasuredome/Get It On/Happy Hi (P) (ZTT Label)
7″	ZTAS	7	Pleasuredome (5:05 Video Remix)/Get It On/Happy Hi (P) (Black Label)(7A 7U)
10″	PZTAS	7	Pleasuredome (5:05 Video Remix)/Get It On/Happy Hi Apple Shaped Picture Disc (Ltd Edition)
12″	12ZTAS	7	Pleasuredome (Alternative To Real)/Get It On/Happy Hi/Relax (International)(P)
12″	12XZTAS	7	Pleasuredome (Alternative 8:30 Remix)/Get It On/Happy Hi/Born To Run (Live)(P)
CASS	CTIS10	7	Pleasuredome "All In The Mind, All In The Body" Cassingle (P) (Ltd Edition)

RAGE HARD

7″	ZTAS	22	Rage Hard/Don't Lose What's Left . . . (P)
7″	ZTD	22	Rage Hard/Don't Lose What's Left . . . (P) (G/F)(Pop-Up Sleeve)(Ltd Edition)
7″	ZTAX	22	Rage Hard (Stamped Remix)/Don't Lose What's Left . . . (P)
12″	12ZTAS	22	Rage Hard (+ Mix)/Suffragette City/Don't Lose What's Left . . . (P)
12″	12ZTAQ	22	Rage Hard (+ Mix)/Suffragette City/Don't Lose What's Left . . . (P) (With B/W Poster)(Ltd Edition)
12″	12ZTAX	22	Rage Hard (++ Remix)/Broadhouse Blues/Don't Lose What's Left . . . (P) (Ltd Edition)
12″	12ZTAX	22	Rage Hard (++ Remix)/Broadhouse Blues/Don't Lose What's Left . . . In Special Box (P) (Ltd Edition)
12″	ZTAB	22	Rage Hard Box Set Inc. 7″, G/F 7″, 12″, 12″ Remix, 12″ With Poster And CD (P) (Ltd Edition)
CD	ZCID	2	Rage Hard CD Single (P) (Ltd Edition)

WARRIORS OF THE WASTELAND

7″	ZTAS	25	Warriors Of The Wasteland (P) (Double 'A' Side)
12″	12ZTAS	25	Warriors Of The Wasteland (12 Wild Disciples)/Return/End (P)
12″	12ZTAX	25	Warriors Of The Wasteland (Turn Of The Knife)/Return/End (P) (Ltd Edition)
12″	12ZTAK	25	Warriors Of The Wasteland (Attack)/Return/End (P) (W/L) (Ltd Edition Remix)

CASS	CTIS	25	Warriors Of The Wasteland "Cassetted" Cassingle (P) (Ltd Edition)
CD	ZCID	25	Warriors Of The Wasteland "Compacted" CD Single (P) (Ltd Edition)

WATCHING THE WILDLIFE

7″	ZTAS	26	Watching The Wildlife/Waves (P) (Ltd Edition With Condoms)
12″	12ZTAS	26	Watching The Wildlife (Hotter 9:09)/Vocaless/Waves (P)
12″	12ZTAX	26	Watching The Wildlife (Movement 2 7:14)/Bit 3 (6:26)/Bit 4 (4:26)/Waves (3:02)(P)
12″	12ZTE	26	Watching The Wildlife (Die Letzen Tag Der Menscheit)/Vocaless/Waves (P) (Ltd Edition Remix)
CASS	CTIS	26	Watching The Wildlife "Cassetted" Cassingle (P) (Ltd Edition)

Re-releases

RELAX

7″	FGTH	1	4509-93382-7	Relax (3:55)/MCMXCIII 3:42)(P)
12″	FGTH	1T	4509-93383-0	Relax (Ollie J Remix 6:38)/(Trip Ship Edit 6:12)/(MCMXCIII 3:42)/(Jam & Spoon Hi N-R-G Mix 7:55)/(Jam & Spoon Trip-o-Matic Fairy Tale Mix 7:52)(P)
CD	FGTH	1CD	4509-93384-2	Relax (3:55)/(MCMXCIII 3:42)/(Ollie J Remix 6:38)/(Jam & Spoon Trip-o-Matic Fairy Tale Mix 7:52)/(Jam & Spoon Hi N-R-G Mix 7:55)/(New York Mix – The Original 12″ 7:22)(P)
CASS	FGTH	1C	4509-93382-4	Relax (3:55)/(MCMXCIII 3:42)Cassingle (P)

WELCOME TO THE PLEASUREDOME
7″
12″
CASS
CD

THE POWER OF LOVE
7″
12″
CASS
CD

Albums

WELCOME TO THE PLEASUREDOME

2LP	ZTT	1Q1	Welcome To The Pleasuredome (P) (G/F)(With Inner Bags)(13 Tracks)
2LP	NEAT	1	Welcome To The Pleasuredome Picture Disc (In G/F PVC Sleeve)
CASS	ZCIQ	1	Welcome To The Pleasuredome (P) (With Extended Inlay)
CD	CID	101	Welcome To The Pleasuredome (P) (Tracks As Cassette)
CD	CID	101	Welcome To The Pleasuredome (P) Re-Issue Containing "Two Tribes" (Annihilation) instead of LP version, The "Last Voice" and "Happy Hi". Deletes "San Jose" (The Way) and "Ferry" (Go)

LIVERPOOL

LP	ZTT	1Q8	Liverpool (P) (With Inner Bag)(8 Tracks)
CASS	ZCIQ	8	Liverpool (P) (With Extended Inlay)
CASS	ZCIQ	8	Liverpool (P) (Re-Issue In Diff Pink Sleeve With New Mix Of "Wildlife")
CD	ZCIDQ	8	Liverpool (P)
CD	IMCD	13	Liverpool (P) (Re-Issue)

Compilations

BANG! . . . THE GREATEST HITS OF F.G.T.H.

LP		Bang!
CASS		Bang!
CD	4509-93912-2	Bang!

Other Miscellaneous Releases

*7″	FGTH	–	Smash Hits Interview Flexi Disc
*7″	PRT	1	Two Tribes/Relax – London Symphony Orchestra (P)
7″	FEED		Do They Know It's Christmas/Feed The World – Band Aid (P)
*7″	FIRE	4	Atmosphere/Thoughts Of A Child – Russ Abott (P) ("Relax" Clip)
*12″	FG10	17B	Tell Tales Interview Picture Disc
*12″	BAK	2009	Interview Picture Disc
*12″	WEA	1	Relax – Captain Sensible (P)
12″	FEED	112	Do They Know It's Christmas (Extended)/Feed The World – Band Aid (P)
*12″	FIRET	4	Atmosphere (Extended)/Thoughts Of A Child – Russ Abott (P) ("Relax" Clip)
*12″	SOHOT	71	P4F – Propaganda For Frankie (P) ("Relax" Medley)
LP	ZULU	6	Zulu Compilation – Various Artists (P) (G/F)("Love Has Got A Gun" Demo/"Stand Alone" – Pink Industry)

LP	IQ	6	Zang Tumb Tuum Sampled – Various Artists (P) ("Disneyland"/"Born to Run" Live)
*LP	PRT	10049	Power Of Classic Rock – London Symphony Orchestra (P) ("Two Tribes"/"Relax")
LP	RL	137	Rock Over London – Various Artists (P) ("Two Tribes")
LP	DDTV	1	Dance Decade – Various Artists (P) ("Relax")
2LP	NOW	1	Now That's What I Call Music 1 – Various Artists (P) (G/F)("Relax")
2LP	NOW	3	Now That's What I Call Music 3 – Various Artists (P) (G/F)("Two Tribes")
2LP	HITS	5	Hits 5 – Various Artists (P) (G/F)("Rage Hard")
CASS	IQC	6	Zang Tumb Tuum Sampled – Various Artists (P) (Tracks as LP)
CASS	ISLC	252	Island Story – Various Artists (P) (Double)("Rage Hard")
CASS	DDTVC	1	Dance Decade – Various Artists (P) ("Relax")
CASS	COMM	64	"Pleasuregame" Inc. 5 Minute Cassette Featuring "Relax" (International)
CD		840621-2	Dance Decade – Various Artists (P) ("Relax")

Videos

VID	WARNER	–	Police Academy 1 (P) ("Relax")
VID	CVT	30582	Body Double (P) ("Relax")
VID	VIDAID	102	Video Aid – Various Artists (P) ("Relax")
VID	CFV	07202	Island Story – Various Artists (P) ("Rage Hard")
VID	GRA	16798	Rock Around The Dock – Various Artists (P) ("Rage Hard"/"Warriors Of The Wasteland") Shoot! Compilation Video of F.G.T.H. Promos

HOLLY JOHNSON
Official UK Discography

Singles

LOVE TRAIN

7"	MCA	1306	Love Train/Murder In Paradise (P)(MCA Label)
7"	MCA	1306	Love Train/Murder In Paradise (P)(Red 'H' Label)
12"	MCAT	1306	Love Train (A Train)/7"/Murder In Paradise (P)(MCA Label)
12"	MCAT	1306	Love Train (A Train)/7"/Murder in Paradise (P)(Red 'H' Label)
CASS	MCAC	1306	Love Train Cassingle (P)(In Special Box)
CD	DMCAT	1306	Love Train (A Train)/7"/Murder In Paradise CD Single (P)

AMERICANOS

7"	MCA	1323	Americanos/Americanos (Mambo Dub) (P)
12"	MCAT	1323	Americanos (Liberty)/7"/(Mambo Dub) (P)
12"	MCAX	1323	Americanos (Mag-Imix)/(Magimix Dub) (P)
CASS	MCAC	1323	Americanos Cassingle (P)(In Special Box)
CD	DMCAT	1323	Americanos (7")/(Liberty)/(Mambo Dub) CD Single (P)(With Special Inner Bag)

ATOMIC CITY

7"	MCA	1342	Atomic City/Beat The System (P)
12"	MCAT	1342	Atomic City (Extended)/Beat The System (P)
12"	MCAX	1342	Atomic City (Bona Biodegradable)/Beat The System/ (Environmental Instrumental) (P)
CASS	MCAC	1342	Atomic City Cassingle (P)
CD	DMCAT	1342	Atomic City (7")/Beat The System/(Extended) CD Single (P)

HEAVEN'S HERE

7"	MCA	1365	Heaven's Here/Hollelujah (P)
7"	MCA	1365	Heaven's Here/Hollelujah Box Set (P) (With Poster)(Ltd Edition)
12"	MCAT	1365	Heaven's Here/Hollelujah/Heaven's Here (P)
CASS	MCAC	1365	Heaven's Here Cassingle (P)
CD	DMCAT	1365	Heaven's Here (7")/Remix/Hollelujah CD Single (P)

WHERE HAS LOVE GONE

7"	MCA	1460	Where Has Love Gone/Perfume (P)
12"	MCAT	1460	Where Has Love Gone (Search For Love)/ Perfume (Aromatherapy) (P)

305

12″	MCAX	1460	Where Has Love Gone (GTO)/(Dreaming) (P)
CASS	MCAC	1460	Where Has Love Gone Cassingle (P)
CD	DMCAT	1460	Where Has Love Gone/Perfume (Aromatherapy)/(Search For Love) CD Single (P)

ACROSS THE UNIVERSE

7″	MCS	1513	Across The Universe/Funky Paradise (P)
12″	MCST	1513	Across The Universe (Space-A-Go-Go)/7″/Funky Paradise (P)
CASS	MCSC	1513	Across The Universe Cassingle (P)
CD	MCSTD	1513	Across The Universe (7″)/(Space-A-Go-Go)/Funky Paradise CD Single (P)

PEOPLE WANT TO DANCE

7″	MCS	1563	People Want To Dance (Rave Hard!) (P)
12″	MCST	1563	People Want To Dance (Raving Harder!)/(Apollo 440)/Love Train (Americanos Big Beat) (P)
CD	MCSTD	1563	People Want To Dance (Rave Hard!)/Love Train (Americanos Big Beat)/(Raving Harder!) CD Single (P)

Albums

BLAST

LP	MCG	6042	Blast (P)(With Inner Bag)(10 Tracks)
CASS	MCGC	6042	Blast (P)(With Inlay)
CD	DMCG	6042	Blast (P)
VID	MCV	9005	Blast (P)

HOLLELUJAH – REMIX ALBUM

LP	MCL	1902	Hollelujah – Remix Album (P)(6 Tracks)
CASS	MCLC	1902	Hollelujah – Remix Album (P)
CD	DMCL	1902	Hollelujah – Remix Album (P)

DREAMS THAT MONEY CAN'T BUY

LP	MCA	10278	Dreams That Money Can't Buy (P)(10 Tracks)
CASS	MCAC	10278	Dreams That Money Can't Buy (P)
CD	MCAD	10278	Dreams That Money Can't Buy (P)

Other Miscellaneous Releases

7″	ERICS	0001	Big In Japan/Chuddy Nuddies – Big In Japan (P)
7″	ZOOCAGE	001	From Y to Z and Never Again – Big In Japan (P)(G/F)(4 Track EP)
7″	ERICS	003	Yankee Rose/Treasure Island/Desperate Dan – Holly (P)
7″	ERICS	007	Hobo Joe/Stars Of The Bars – Holly (P)(G/F)

306

7"	AHP	1	Live-In World – Anti Heroin Project (P)
7"	PWL	41	Ferry 'Cross The Mersey – Various Artists (P)(Hillsborough)
12"	SP	-011	Atomic City (Megamix) (P)(2 Disc Set)
12"	RSI	-2	Rhythm Stick (P)("Love Train" 7:53)
LP	ZOO	FOUR	To The Shores Of Lake Placid – Various Artists (P)(G/F) "S.C.U.M."/"Suicide-A-Go-Go" – Big In Japan
2LP	AHP	LP1	Live-In World – Anti Heroin Project (P)(G/F)("Live-In World" – Various/"Slay The Dragon" – Holly)
2LP	NMELP	38/39	Last Temptation Of Elvis – Various Artists (P)(G/F)("Love Me Tender" – Holly)
LP	STAR	2389	Greatest Hits '89 – Various Artists (P)("Americanos")
CASS	TCAHP	LP1	Live-In World – Anti Heroin Project (P)(Double)(Tracks As LP)
CASS	NMECAS	38/39	Last Temptation Of Elvis – Various Artists (P)(Double)(Tracks as LP)
CASS	STAC	2389	Greatest Hits '89 – Various Artists (P)(Tracks as LP)
CD	PWCD	41	Ferry 'Cross The Mersey – Various Artists CD Single (P)(Hillsborough)
CD	TCD	2389	Greatest Hits '89 – Various Artists (P)(Double)(Tracks as LP)
CD	CCD	8	Smash Hits Party '89 – Various Artists (P)(Double)("Love Train")

Videos

VID	GUILD	8552	Cookie (P)("Americanos")

The Following Abbreviations Denote:

G/F – Gatefold Sleeve
B/W – Black And White
W/L – White Label
(P) – Original Picture Bag/Sleeve/Inlay
* – Cover Songs/Clips/Other

All items listed where available/detained through normal retail outlets at time of release

Discography compiled by D. King

307

Plate Section Captions

1 The Happy Family: (*Back row Eric William Francis Johnson. Front row L to R Clare Patricia Johnson nee Mcglouchlin, John Joseph Johnson and Clare Johnson*) before they gave birth to a monster ego (yours truly). Photographer unknown.

2 *L to R Clare, James, William or Billy Johnson (me) and Bugs Bunny.* I 'created' until I was included in this photo session. Bugs had a ring at the back, which, when pulled, caused him to utter 'What's Up Doc' etc. Photographer unknown.

3 Happy days, in Butlins Dining Hall, 1964.

4 Me in whitewashed back yard of 206 Rathbone Road. For me scuffed shoes, shirttail out, was the usual thing. Later, due to my habit of falling over, holes in the knees of brand new pants drove my poor mother to distraction. Photographer unknown.

5 Big In Japan, circa 1977. *L to R Kevin Ward, Ian Broudie, Jayne Casey, William Butterworth, Holly Johnson.* The eye of the 'Illuminatus' is missing from the apex of the black pyramid. Photographer Kevin Cummins.

6 'Holly Johnson Leatherboy.' In Lindens' Huskisson Street flat circa 1978. Photographer Peter Asprey.

7 *L to R my sister Clare Jones, mother Pat Johnson and me.* February 9th 1981. My twenty-first birthday outside the Faulkner Street flat. Friends arrived early that morning and got me completely stoned – when Clare and Pat turned up on a surprise visit. This exact spot is where the coaches full of policemen were parked during the Toxteth riots, which passed me almost unnoticed. Photographer Ron Boocock.

8 Appearing on Granada TV's 'Celebration' programme in 1980. Performing 'Yankee Rose' astride a rocking horse, with my favourite guitar. Photographer Marco Cecere.

9 On The Waterfront or Fairy Across the Mersey. Looking unemployed at the Pier Head. Too poor even for a bottle of Nestle Light. Photographer Marco Cecere.

10 Fellatio with a knife 1982: wearing SEX 'Venus' T shirt designed by Vivienne Westwood and Malcolm McLaren. Our first FGTH photo session designed to attract record company attention. Later sold as a postcard that caused quite a rumpus in the mid eighties. Photographer John Stoddart.

11 Larks in the Park 1982. Open air concert where I exposed my arse (not pictured) to the world. Photographer John Stoddart.

12 This portrait was used in the first press advert for "Relax" shot in 1982/3. I was trying to regain my 1977 look. Photographer John Stoddart.

13 The bondage and water sports scene from the first 'Relax' video, directed by Bernard Rose. This video was banned by almost every TV station in the world. Note the person wearing the Katherine Hamnett slogan jacket LIFE that was to 'inspire' the typographical style of the famous FGTH T shirts. Photographer Chris Garnham.

14 A still from the 'Two Tribes' video directed by Godley and Creme 1984. Photographer unknown.

15 Welcome to the Pleasuredome. Posing for the album cover. *L to R Mark O'Toole, Paul Rutherford – the potted Andrew Ridgley, Holly Johnson, Peter Gill (Ped) and Brian Nash (Nasher).* Photographer Peter Ashworth. Courtesy of ZTT.

16 Pop Art statement No. 536. Meeting Andy Warhol for the second time. Photographed here in front of the Andy Warhol/Jean Michell Basquiat collaboration painting. HJ: 'How do I get on the cover of "Interview", Andy?' AW: 'Sleep with the publisher, Holly'. Photographer Spencer Bright.

17 On the set of the 'Love Train' video shoot late 1988. *L to R Pinkie Braithwaite, Holly Johnson.* Pinkie arrived looking like this – in her everyday clothing. Photographer Claire Muller. Courtesy of Pleasuredome Productions.

18 'Americanos' video shoot. I showed a video of John Waters' 'Hairspray' to the director and this was the result. *L to R Tracy Clarke, Holly Johnson.* Photographer AJ Barrett. Courtesy of Pleasuredome Productions.

19 DREAMS THAT MONEY CAN'T BUY cover design by ME Company. Using a photo by Richard Houghton. Courtesy of MCA.

20 HOLLELUJAH (the remix album) cover design by Accident. Detail from a portrait of Holly Johnson by Peter Maclaren. Oil on board. Courtesy of MCA.

21 BLAST cover design by Accident (Royston Edwards) now part of the V&A permanent collection. Courtesy of MCA.

22 LIVERPOOL cover design by Accident, incorporating photos by Anton Corbijn. Courtesy of ZTT.

23 WELCOME TO THE PLEASUREDOME cover design by XL, incorporating paintings by artist Lo Cole. Courtesy of ZTT.

24 BANG! THE GREATEST HITS OF FRANKIE GOES TO HOLLYWOOD cover design by ME Company, using logo designed by XL. Courtesy of ZTT/WEA.

25 RELAX seven inch single cover design by XL, using illustration by Yvonne Gilbert. Courtesy of ZTT.
26 TWO TRIBES twelve inch single cover designed by XL, incorporating a photo by Anton Corbijn. Courtesy of ZTT.
27 Wolfgang Kuhle, swimming in the surf at the Kahala Hilton Hotel on Oahu, Hawaii 1985. Photographer Holly Johnson.
28 Frankie Goes To Hollywood with Gene Kelly holding up the Frankie T shirt. I asked him to teach me a dance step but he said that he was past that sort of thing. Photograph © Rex Features.
29 My favourite photo. *L to R Divine, Holly Johnson and a German bodybuilder*. My ideal threesome. © Network, photographer Homer Sykes.
30 SAILOR (oil on canvass) © Holly Johnson 1990.
31 On the set of the 'Atomic City' video shoot with a 12 week old Funky the dog. The suit is from a design by Giacamo Balla the Italian Futurist painter. Styling Judy Blame, makeup Sarah Gregory. Photographer Clare Muller. Courtesy of Pleasuredome Productions.
32 Holly Johnson circa 1988. Photographer Alistair Thane.

Every effort has been made to trace photographers for permission to use the above photographs. Please send all queries on this matter to Wolfgang Kuhle c/o Mangowork Ltd, PO Box 425, London SW6 3TX, UK.